THE SPECIAL ONE

THE SECRET WORLD OF JOSÉ MOURINHO

DIEGO TORRES   TRANSLATED BY PETE JENSON

HarperSport

An Imprint of HarperCollins*Publishers*

HarperSport
An imprint of HarperCollins*Publishers*
77–85 Fulham Palace Road,
Hammersmith, London W6 8JB

www.harpercollins.co.uk

First published as *Prepárense para perder* by Ediciones B 2013
This edition published by HarperSport 2014

1 3 5 7 9 10 8 6 4 2

© Diego Torres 2014
English translation © HarperCollins*Publishers* 2014

Diego Torres asserts the moral right to be
identified as the author of this work

A catalogue record of this book is
available from the British Library

ISBN 978-0-00-755303-7

Printed and bound in Great Britain by
Clays Ltd, St Ives plc

MIX
Paper from
responsible sources
FSC
www.fsc.org **FSC™ C007454**

FSC™ is a non-profit international organisation established to promote
the responsible management of the world's forests. Products carrying the
FSC label are independently certified to assure customers that they come
from forests that are managed to meet the social, economic and
ecological needs of present and future generations,
and other controlled sources.

Find out more about HarperCollins and the environment at
www.harpercollins.co.uk/green

CONTENTS

CHAPTER 1

CRYING

'Think of this: When they present you with a watch they are giving you a tiny flowering hell, a wreath of roses, a dungeon of air.'

JULIO CORTÁZAR, 'Preamble to the Instructions for Winding a Watch'

'He was crying! He was crying …!'

GESTIFUTE EMPLOYEE

On 8 May 2013, the employees of Gestão de Carreiras de Profissionais Desportivos S.A., Gestifute, the most important agency in the football industry, were to be found in a state of unusual excitement. José Mourinho kept calling employees. They had heard him sobbing loudly down the line and word quickly spread. The man most feared by many in the company had been crushed.

The news that Sir Alex Ferguson had named David Moyes as his successor as manager of Manchester United had caused an earthquake. United, the most valuable club in the world according to the stock market, were the equivalent of the great imperial crown of football marketing, and the position of manager, occupied for almost 27 years by a magnificent patriarch, had mythical connotations.

1

The terms of Ferguson's abdication were the 'scoop' most coveted by the traffickers of the Premier League's secrets. There were those who had toiled for years preparing a web of privileged connections to enable them to guess before anyone else when the vacancy would occur. Jorge Mendes, president and owner of Gestifute, had more ties with Old Trafford than any other agent. No agent had done as many deals, nor such strange ones, with Ferguson. No one had more painstakingly prepared an heir to the throne or succeeded in conveying the idea to the media that there was a predestined successor. If this propaganda had seeped into the consciousness of one man, that man was the aspiring applicant himself. Mourinho, encouraged by his devoted agent, believed that Ferguson was also an ally, a friend and protector. He became convinced that they were united by a relationship of genuine trust. He thought his own fabulous collection of trophies – two European Champion Leagues, one UEFA Cup, seven league titles and four domestic cups in four different countries – constituted a portfolio far outstripping those of the other suitors. When he learned that Ferguson had chosen David Moyes, the Everton manager, he was struck by an awful sense of disbelief. Moyes had never won anything!

These were the most miserable hours of Mourinho's time as manager of Real Madrid. He endured them half asleep, half awake, glued to his mobile phone in search of clarification during the night of 7 to 8 May in the Sheraton Madrid Mirasierra hotel. He had arrived in his silver Audi in the afternoon along with his 12-year-old son, José Mario, with no suspicion of what was coming. On his left wrist he wore his €20,000 deLaCour 'Mourinho City Ego' watch, with the words 'I am not afraid of the consequences of my decisions' inscribed on the casing of sapphire crystal.

Mourinho was fascinated by luxury watches. He not only wore his sponsor's brand – he collected watches compulsively. He maintained that you could not wear just any object on your wrist, stressing the need for something unique and distinguished intimately touching your skin.

That afternoon he was preparing to meet up with his team before playing the 36th league game of the season against Málaga at the Bernabéu. He was more than a little upset. He knew that his reputation as a charismatic leader was damaged, something he attributed to his stay in Chamartín. The behaviour of the Spanish seemed suffocating: the organisation of the club had never come up to his expectations and he was sick of his players. He had told the president, Florentino Pérez, that they had been disloyal, and to show his contempt he had decided not to travel with them on the team bus but make his own way to the hotel in a symbolic gesture that cut him off from the squad. He was met by members of the radical supporters' group 'Ultras Sur', who unravelled a 60-foot banner near the entrance of the Sheraton. 'Mou, we love you', it said. When the squad arrived and the players began to file off the bus, one of the fans, hidden behind the banner, expressed the widespread feeling in this, the most violent sector of Madrid's supporters.

'Casillas! Stop blabbing and go fuck yourself!'

The suspicion that Casillas, the captain and the player closest to the fans, was a source of leaks had been formulated by Mourinho and the idea had penetrated to the heart of the club. Perez and his advisors claimed that for months the coach had insisted that the goalkeeper had a pernicious nature. When the suspicion was reported in certain sections of the media, the club did very little to rebuff it. The subject was the topic of radio and television sports debate programmes; everyone had an opinion on the matter except the goalkeeper himself, whose silence was enough to make many fans believe he was guilty. To complete his work of discrediting Casillas, Mourinho gave a press conference that same afternoon, suggesting that the goalkeeper was capable of trying to manipulate coaches to win his place in the team.

'Just as Casillas can come and say, "I'd like a coach such as Del Bosque or Pellegrini, a more manageable coach," he said, 'it's also legitimate for me to say the same thing. As the coach it's legitimate for me to say, "I like Diego López." And with me in charge, while I'm the coach of Madrid, Diego López *will* play. There's no story.'

The atmosphere at the Sheraton was gloomy that night, with contradictory rumours from England circulating about the retirement of Ferguson. The online pages of the *Mirror* and *Sun* offered a disturbing picture. Mourinho was certain that if Sir Alex had taken such a decision he would have at least called to tell him. But there had been nothing. According to the people from Gestifute who lent him logistical support he had not received as much as a text message. The hours of anxiety were slowly getting to him, and he made calls until dawn to try to confirm the details with journalists and British friends. Mendes heard the definitive news about Ferguson straight away from another Gestifute employee but did not dare tell Mourinho the truth – that he had never stood the slightest chance.

Mourinho was tormented by the memory of Sir Bobby Charlton's interview in the *Guardian* in December 2012. The verdict of the legendary former player and member of the United board had greatly unsettled him. When asked if he saw Mourinho as a successor to Ferguson, Charlton said, 'A United manager would not do what he did to Tito Vilanova,' referring to the finger in the eye incident. 'Mourinho is a really good coach, but that's as far as I'd go.' And as far as the admiration Ferguson had for Mourinho was concerned, the veteran said it was a fiction: 'He does not like him too much.'

Mourinho preferred to believe the things that Ferguson had personally told him rather than be bothered by what a newspaper claimed Charlton had said. But that night, the venerable figure of Sir Bobby assaulted his imagination with telling force. Mourinho had turned 50 and perhaps thoughts of his own mortality crossed his mind. There would be no more Manchester United for him. No more colossal dreams. Only reality. Only his decline in Spain devouring his prestige by the minute. Only Abramovich's outstretched hand.

In the morning he called Mendes, asking him to get in touch with United urgently. Right until the end, he wanted his agent to exert pressure on the English club in an attempt to block any deal. It was an act of desperation. Both men knew that Mendes had put Mourinho on the market a year ago. David Gill, United's chief executive, had held regular talks with Gestifute and was aware of Mourinho's availability but he was not interested in him as a manager. He had told Mendes in the autumn of 2012 that Ferguson's first choice was Pep Guardiola and had explained the reasons. At Gestifute, the message of one United executive seemed particularly pertinent: 'The problem is, when things don't go well for "Mou", he does not follow the club's line. He follows José's line.'

What most frightened Mourinho was that public opinion would conclude he had made a fool of himself. He felt cheated by Ferguson and feared people might stop taking him seriously. For years, the propaganda machine acting on his behalf had made quite a fuss of the friendship between the two men; this was now revealed to be a fantasy. To make these latest events seem coherent, Gestifute advisors told him to say that he already knew everything because Ferguson had called to inform him. On 9 May someone at Gestifute got in touch with a journalist at the daily newspaper Record to tell them that Ferguson had offered his crown to Mourinho four months ago, but that he had rejected it because his wife preferred to live in London, and for that reason he was now leaning towards going back to Chelsea. Meanwhile, Mourinho gave an interview on Sky in which he stated that Ferguson had made him aware of his intentions, but never made him the offer because he knew that he wanted to coach Chelsea. The contradictions were not planned.

From that fateful 7 May onwards Mourinho was weighed down by something approaching a deep depression. For two weeks he disappeared from the public eye and barely spoke to his players. For the first time in years, the Spanish and the Portuguese press – watching from a distance – agreed that they were watching a lunatic. On 17 May Real played the final of the Copa del Rey against Atlético Madrid. The preparation for the game made the players anticipate the worst. The sense of mutual resentment was overbearing. If Mourinho felt betrayed, the squad saw him as someone whose influence could destroy anyone's career. If he had jeopardised Casillas's future, the most formidable captain in the history of Spanish football, how were the other players to feel? A witness who watched events unfold from within Valdebebas described the appalling situation: the players didn't mind losing because it meant that Mourinho lost. It didn't matter to Mourinho, either, and so they lost.

On 16 May the manager showed up at the team hotel with a sketch of a *trivote* under his arm. '*Trivote*' was the term the players used to describe the tactical model that Mourinho claimed to have invented. It was executed by different players according to the circumstances. The plan, presented on the screen of the hotel, had Modrić, Alonso and Khedira as the chosen trio in midfield. This meant that the team's most creative player, Özil, was shifted out to the right to a position where he felt isolated. Benzema and Ronaldo were up front. Essien, Albiol, Ramos and Coentrão were to play at the back, with Diego López in goal.

Mourinho's team-talks had always been characterised by a hypnotic inflammation. The man vibrated. Every idea that he transmitted seemed to be coming directly from the core of his nervous system. That day this did not happen. He had spent a long time isolated in his office – absorbed, sunken-eyed, pale, melancholic. The players were at a loss as to why. Some interpreted it as sheer indolence, others saw him as quite simply lost, as if he were saying things he did not understand.

'He looked like a hologram,' recalled one assistant.

'All that was missing was a yawn,' said another.

The room fell into a tense silence. The coach was proposing something on the board that they had not practised all week. Incomprehensible, maybe, but a regular occurrence in recent months. He told them that after years implementing this system they should understand it so well that they didn't need to practise it. They would have to content themselves with understanding how he wanted them to attack. As usual, the most complex job was allocated to Özil. The German had to cover the wing when the team did not have the ball. When possession was regained he had to move to a more central position and link up with Modrić.

The players understood that to gain width and get behind Atlético the logical thing would have been to put a winger on the right, somebody like Di María, leave Özil in the centre and drop Modrić back into Khedira's position. But the coach believed that because Modrić lacked the necessary physical attributes, he needed to support the defensive base of the team with Khedira. No one spoke up against the plan. For years the communication between the leader and his subordinates had been a one-way street.

This time, however, it was because there was just nothing to say. The team-talk was brief. The players were left wondering why on earth they had to defensively reinforce the midfield with Khedira against an Atlético side who were hardly going to attack them. But, mute, they merely obeyed.

For the club with the largest budget in the world, the Copa del Rey was a lesser objective. Finding out that the final would be played in their stadium distressed the directors. After losing the league and the Champions League, the season had little left to offer. A final against

Atlético in Chamartín was in many ways a no-win situation. The joke had been doing the rounds since the team beat Barça at the Camp Nou to qualify, that the president had been heard to say that a final in the Bernabéu against Atlético was about as attractive as a 'punch bag'.

The ticket prices fixed by the clubs and the Spanish Football Federation set a new record. Despite the economic crisis that was crushing Spain this was the most expensive cup final in history. Prices ranged from €50 to €275. Attending the FA Cup at Wembley cost between €53 and €136, and German cup final tickets went from between €35 and €125. At the Coppa Italia the price ranged from €30 to €120. That afternoon, as was to be expected, there were empty seats.

Ronaldo headed in a Modrić corner, putting Madrid 1–0 up in the 14th minute. Following to the letter instructions that were now three years old, the team retreated to protect the lead, giving up space and possession to their opponents. Their opponents' situation looked impossible. Madrid had a more expensive constellation of star players than had ever been brought together. And against them they did not have the Atlético of Schuster, Vizcaíno, Donato, Manolo and Futre that had faced them in the final of 1992. Here instead were was Koke Resurrección, Gabi Fernández, Mario Suárez, Falcao, Arda and Costa. For an hour and a half, both teams cancelled each other out in the most extravagant manner possible. They tried to see who could go for longer without the ball. It was a fierce competition. Atlético dropped their level of possession to 40 per cent. Madrid had the remaining 60 per cent, but did not know how to manage it because Marcelo had been marginalised, Alonso was tired, Özil was suffering off-radar and Khedira was unable to channel the team's attacks. Atlético took cover and in two lightning counter-attacks settled the match. First, Diego Costa scored after Falcao had taken advantage of a mistake by Albiol.

Then, in extra time, Miranda headed in to make it 2–1, after Diego López made an error coming off his line.

Albiol had replaced Pepe, left out and watching from the stands because of his insurrection. Pepe called for more 'respect' to be shown to Casillas and in response was cleansed. Within hours the defender went from being the manager's right-hand man on the pitch to becoming the object of a public trial.

The emergence of rising star Varane was the excuse. 'It's not easy for a man of 31 years, with a standing and a past, being steam-rollered by a child of 19 like Varane,' said Mourinho. 'But it's the law of life.'

Varane could not play in the final because of injury. Even so, Pepe watched the game from the stands, giving up his place to Albiol, who had not played regularly for months. Some of the players believed they recognised in this decision the clearest evidence that part of Mourinho's selection-process was based on a dark code of loyalty even when it was to the detriment of the functioning of the team.

When the referee sent Mourinho off for protesting, Pepe went down to the bench and, in complete violation of the regulations, installed himself in the technical area. It was unprecedented behaviour as he took over from Aitor Karanka, the assistant coach, giving instructions to his colleagues from the touchline as if he were the manager. Not that it prevented an Atlético victory.

Karanka remained confused all evening. His boss had departed the stage, leaving him alone. Breaking protocol, Mourinho did not go up to receive the medal that King Juan Carlos had prepared to honour the coach of the losing team. Instead, it was Karanka who came up the stairs in front of the defeated players. On seeing him, the king grabbed the piece of silver and turned to the Spanish Football Federation president Ángel María Villar, seeking clarification:

'Shall I give it to him?'

And so it was an embarrassed Karanka who received the salver, while Mourinho went to the press conference room to pronounce his final words as the official representative of Madrid. Three years of stirring rhetoric, shrill speeches, sessions of indoctrination, warnings, complaints and entertaining monologues were interrupted by a confession. There was no hiding from the fact that in his final year he had won nothing.

Never in the history of Real Madrid had a coach been more powerful and yet more miserable; nor one more willing to terminate his contract with the club, happy to end an adventure that had become a torment.

'This is the worst season of my career,' he said.

CHAPTER 2

EYJAFJALLAJÖKULL

'It is easy to see thou art a clown, Sancho,' said Don Quixote, 'and one of that sort that cry "Long life to the conqueror!"'

MIGUEL DE CERVANTES, *Don Quixote*

The objective qualities of José Mourinho the coach were not what led Real Madrid to sign him in 2010. It was more that they considered him to be a magical, providential figure blessed with an unfathomable and mysterious wisdom.

Madrid's director general, José Ángel Sánchez, was the main driving force behind the recruitment and the process took years to reach its conclusion. Perhaps it started in the first months of 2007 when Sánchez made contact with Jorge Mendes, Mourinho's agent, to negotiate the transfer of Pepe. Képler Laverán Lima, nicknamed 'Pepe', was the Porto defender who cost €30 million, becoming the third-most expensive central defender in history after Rio Ferdinand and Alessandro Nesta. It was the highest price ever paid for a defender who had not played in his national team, and the first transaction concluded by Mendes and Sánchez, laying the foundations for a new order. From that moment on the super-agent began to redirect his strategy from England to Spain, those ties of friendship with Sánchez paving the way for the change.

Mendes did not delay building his relationship with Ramón Calderón, Madrid's president between 2006 and 2009. Bold by nature, the Portuguese agent made him the inevitable offer: he would bring his star coach – at the time, running down his third season at Chelsea – to Madrid.

'Once you get to know him you'll not want to hire anyone else,' Mendes encouraged. 'If you want to prolong your spell at Madrid, you'll have to bring in the best coach in the world.'

That is how Calderón remembers it, recalling how Mendes tried to organise a dinner with Mourinho. They promised him a lightning trip to a meeting in a chalet on the outskirts of Madrid in the dead of night to avoid photographers and maintain absolute secrecy. 'José Ángel was utterly convinced,' recalls Calderón, who says he looked into the idea with the director general and with Pedrag Mijatović, who at the time was Madrid's sporting director.

'This guy is going to drive us crazy!' said the president. 'With Mourinho here you won't last a minute, Pedrag!'

Calderón did not employ any particularly logical reasoning to reject Mourinho. He simply thought of him as a difficult character with outdated ideas. 'He's like a young Capello,' he said, vaguely alluding to a way of playing the game that bored the average fan. The ex-president did not account for the importance of charisma in arousing a crowd eager for Spanish football to regain its pre-eminence. A multitude increasingly in need of a messiah.

Mendes's capacity for hard work is renowned. He promoted Mourinho in various European clubs when he had still not ended his relationship with Chelsea and continued to offer him around with even greater zeal from the winter of 2007 to 2008. At that time Barça were looking for a coach. Ferrán Soriano, now the executive director of Manchester City, was Barcelona's economic vice president. Soriano explains that the selection process began with a list of five men and came down to a simple choice: Guardiola or Mourinho.

'It was a technical decision,' emphasises Soriano. 'Football is full of folklore but in this instance you cannot say that it was an intuitive choice. Instead, it was more the product of rational and rigorous analysis. In Frank Rijkaard we had a coach who we liked a lot but we could see that his time was coming to an end. Frank took a team that was nothing and won the Champions League. He inherited a side with Saviola, Kluivert and Riquelme that had finished sixth, and then he won the league and the Champions League.

'The following year the team's level dropped a little. A 5 per cent drop in commitment at the highest level creates difficulties and Frank didn't know how to re-energise the group. In December we decided to make a change. Mourinho had left Chelsea and there were possibilities to bring him in in January but we thought that it made no sense. We had to finish the season with Frank and give the new coach the opportunity to begin from scratch. Txiki was charged with the task of exploring alternatives and he went to various people: to Valverde, to Blanc, to Mourinho ...'

Joan Laporta was the Barça president who conducted the operation and Txiki Begiristain, ex-Barcelona player and the then technical director, organised the interviews. Txiki met Mourinho in Lisbon and, after hearing his presentation, told him that Johan Cruyff would have the last word. The legendary Dutch player was at the time the club's oracle. In the political climate that had always enveloped Barcelona, the presence of a figure whose legitimacy transcended the periodic presidential elections served to prop up risky decisions. The only person who enjoyed the necessary prestige to play that role was Cruyff.

Impatient ahead of the possibility of a return to the club in which he had worked between 1996 and 2000, Mourinho called Laporta:

'President, allow me to speak with Johan. I'm going to convince him ….' Laporta got straight to the point and confessed that the decision had already been taken. The new coach would be Pep Guardiola. The news completely threw Mourinho, who told him that he had made a serious mistake. Guardiola, in his opinion, was not ready for the job.

Soriano describes the decisive moment: 'After going through all the coaches that Txiki had examined, the conclusion was that it came down to two. In the end there was a meeting in which it was decided that it would be Guardiola, based on certain criteria.

'We had put together a presentation and produced a document: what are the criteria for choosing the coach? It was clear that Mourinho was a great coach but we thought Guardiola would be even better. There was the important issue of knowledge of the club. Mourinho had it, but Guardiola had more of it, and he enjoyed a greater affinity with the club. Mourinho is a winner, but in order to win he generates a level of tension that becomes a problem. It's a problem he chooses … It's positive tension, but we didn't want it. Mourinho has generated this tension at Chelsea, at Inter, at Madrid, everywhere. It's his management style.'

In his book *The Ball Doesn't Go In By Chance*, published in 2010, Soriano details the principles that led the club to choose Guardiola: 1. Respects the sports-management model and the role of the technical director; 2. Playing style; 3. Values to promote in the first team, with special attention to the development of young players; 4. Training and performance; 5. Proactive management of the dressing room; 6. Other responsibilities with, and commitments to, the club, including maintaining a conservative profile and avoiding overuse of the media; 7. Has experience as a player and coach at the highest level; 8. Supports the good governance of the club; 9. Knowledge of the Spanish league, the club and European competition.

Guardiola did not meet the seventh criterion, but then neither did Mourinho. What is more it was very unlikely, given past behaviour, that Mourinho could do the job without violating the second, third, sixth and eighth criteria.

The naming of Pep Guardiola as the Barça coach on 29 May 2008 marked Spanish football's drift towards politicisation. This was paradoxical because Guardiola, one of the coaches most obsessed with the technical details of the game, an empiricist whose strength lay in his work on the pitch, began to be perceived by a certain section of Madrid supporters as an agitator, a manipulative communicator whose propaganda needed to be countered off the pitch. Distracted by this misconception, Madrid would expend much of its institutional energy on taking the necessary steps to wage war in the media.

While Guardiola started an epic landslide that would transform football across half the planet and contribute to reinforcing Spain's national team as it conquered the world in 2010, institutional and social peace at Madrid became ever more scarce. Calderón, who hired Bernd Schuster, resigned a year and a half later amid accusations of corruption. Florentino Pérez, returning to the presidency in 2009, prompted a criminal investigation that led only to a ruling that Calderón had been the victim of slander and that he was not corrupt.

The return of Pérez to the Bernabéu signalled major changes. The president of the multinational construction firm ACS possessed an incomparable combination of determination and influence. In 2010 *Forbes* classified his fortune as the tenth largest in Spain. His origins, however, conform more to the petty bourgeoisie. A graduate of Madrid's School of Civil Engineering, he formed part of a line of technocrats who have nurtured Spanish administration over the last two centuries. Affiliated to the Union of the Democratic Centre (UCD), he entered politics in 1979, becoming a Madrid councillor, director general of the Ministry for Transport and Tourism, and undersecretary at the Ministry of Agriculture between 1979 and 1982. In 1986 he abandoned politics to begin a career in the private sector.

Unorthodox and adventurous in the management of sporting affairs, Pérez's reputation was being increasingly challenged by his followers. Madrid had followed a downward trajectory under his direction between 2000 and 2006. From the initial peak of winning two league titles and a Champions League, the club had stagnated. After three years of failing to win a trophy, he handed in his resignation in February 2006, claiming that he had indulged his players like spoiled children and that it was necessary to install another helmsman, who, without the same sentimental attachment, would be capable of purging the dressing room. Never before in Madrid's history had a president resigned in the middle of his mandate. But with a stubbornness to regain control of the directors' box, and an avowed sense of mission, he returned to the club in 2009, although he was not chosen by members because the absence of any other candidates meant there was no election. He was 62 years old and assured supporters that, thanks to his intervention, Madrid had been saved from administrative crisis and financial ruin.

Back in power, Pérez set about hiring a new coach. He began the selection process advised by his right-hand man, the sporting director Jorge Valdano. After failed attempts to sign first Arsène Wenger and then Carlo Ancelotti, Pérez signed Manuel Pellegrini. The Chilean's switch to Chamartín was preceded by suspicion and disaffection. He had still not completed half a season as first-team coach, and the idea of signing Mourinho was occupying Sánchez's mind more than ever. The operation had been thought through over a period of several years and he was now close to convincing the president to take the plunge. In meetings with friends the director general sighed: 'I love him!'

Valdano, however, insisted on protecting Pellegrini. The coach had been the subject of a smear campaign in the press, encouraged from within the club. During internal debates Sánchez identified Pellegrini as being inherently weak and too fragile to resist the rigours of the Madrid job. To convince Pérez, the director general reasoned, 'Pellegrini needs protection because he's weak. A strong man would not need protection.'

Sánchez took a two-pronged approach. He maintained contact with Mendes and he established a direct line of communication between the Inter coach and Pérez. When some raised suspicions over the suitability of Mourinho's technical footballing knowledge to the Madrid team, Sánchez confessed that he believed Mourinho's personality alone would make him worthy of a blockbuster production, while producing statistics to support his technical expertise.

'I don't know how much he knows about football,' he said, 'but a man who's not lost a home game in six years must have something. Six years without losing in his own stadium! If he doesn't know anything about football then he must know a lot about human beings. In his last game for Chelsea both Terry and Lampard ran to embrace him. That's just not normal. Both of the team's leaders!'

Sánchez is the mastermind behind the project that, between 2000 and 2007, turned Madrid into the richest football institution on the planet. His keen sense of humour co-exists with his zeal for his position. On one occasion in 2010 he presented himself in the following written terms: 'I have been an executive director general for the last five years. Before that I was marketing director general for five years. My responsibility is corporate: the administration, the management, the resources, the facilities and infrastructure of the club, the general services, the purchasing, the information systems and technology, the human resources, the commercial and marketing department, areas of content, internal media, use of facilities, sponsors, etc. I am responsible for 141 of the 190 employees at the club. I am responsible for the economic results, the accounts, etc. I direct the club in these areas and take a certain pride that for six years we have topped the income ranking, including in the bad years or through periods of institutional crisis. I have negotiated the signings and the sales made by the club over the last 10 years … maybe 70 transactions in total. I negotiate the players' contracts, the tours, the TV rights. I represent the club in the LFP (Professional Football League) and in the relevant international bodies. I have a certain disregard for the role of protagonist; I would even say I resent it … I have worked with different presidents, something that is significant in itself. In this transition (certainly an unusual experience in football) you make many friends, from Platini to Rummenigge, from Galliani to Raúl, from the president of Volkswagen to Tebas through to Roures, or a government minister, many businessmen, and football agents … That expanse of contacts just a phone call away is one of the strengths of the club.'

A philosophy graduate who cut his teeth in business administration with Sega, the electronic games company, serving as head of operations in Southern Europe, Sánchez is the most influential executive in Spanish football. When Pérez hired him for the club in the spring of 2000 he was 32 years old. Nobody imagined then that Pérez was preparing the ground for the development of someone who would dominate the Spanish league with an iron fist from 2006 onwards, contributing to the rapid enrichment of Madrid – and Barça – and, as a consequence, putting the finances of the other clubs in the Spanish league at serious risk. If the unequal distribution of TV income in Spain is something unique in Europe then that is in large part thanks to Sánchez's ability to take advantage of the entanglement of delay, carelessness and incompetence spun by the three institutions that should be ensuring football's economic health: the Ministry for Sport, the Spanish Football Federation and the Professional Football League.

Madrid's chief executive since 2006, Sánchez radiated all the enthusiasm of a young lover as he considered Madrid's future: the possibility of fusing the economic power of the world's most popular club with the taste for propaganda of a coach capable of surpassing the publicity extravaganzas of any of the companies with which he had previously been involved. His spirit of curiosity was intrigued. Enthusiastic by nature, this master of marketing understood that he had uncovered possibilities hitherto untapped in the world of sport. It would be a pioneering experiment.

Sánchez needed to finish convincing Pérez when events took an intimidating turn. The elimination of Madrid from the Champions League last-16 against Lyon in March 2010 began to erode the president's normally serene spirit. Barcelona were still on their way to a final that this year would be played at the Bernabéu. The possibility of an arch-rival – and Guardiola – winning their fourth Champions League in Chamartín was an outrage for Madrid's more closed-minded supporters and an unbearable affront to Pérez.

Barcelona's advance shifted the balance of power in Spanish football away from the capital. For the first time in 50 years Real Madrid, the club with the greatest number of European trophies, were no longer the reference point. This change in dominance, just when the Spanish national team was enjoying a golden era at all levels, led to inevitable political consequences. In many sectors of Spanish society, heavily influenced by nationalist sentiment, the presence of a Catalan club at the vanguard of the most popular sport in the country inspired a dark malaise.

UEFA had given the 2010 final to Madrid as a reward for Calderón's efforts to improve the institutional relations between the Spanish Football Federation and the officials of European football's governing body, headed by Michel Platini. For Pérez, since taking over as president, the organisation of the event – an uncomfortable inheritance from his predecessor – had become an unpleasant obligation and, ultimately, a trap.

The Madrid president's overriding concern that Barcelona would end up playing in the final meant Mourinho became an object of veneration as soon as the draw had been made. If Barça wanted to get past the semi-finals they would have to overcome Inter, the team managed by the director general's favourite. At this point, disappointed with Valdano after Pellegrini's failings in domestic cup competition and in Europe, Sánchez and Pérez began to share the same technocratic feeling. A type of force-field united them in one vision in which football as a business was far too important to be left in the hands of mere football people such as Valdano, the sporting director and principal sporting authority at the club.

Valdano had an extensive CV. A world champion with Argentina in 1986, a league champion and UEFA Cup winner as a player, and a league winner as a coach, he knew all the mechanisms that moved Madrid. He used to say – and his opinion was shared by those agents who knew all concerned parties – that neither Pérez nor Sánchez had any deep analytical understanding of the game. Both marvelled at the stand-out players, the most elegant or the most skilful ones, but they struggled to understand why things happened the way they did during a match. In a crisis, under pressure, they would end up rejecting anything that didn't dazzle and simply rely on their intuition. The models, the formulas and the sixth sense that had made them renowned executives fused with the historical necessity of stopping Barça. Mourinho, the man with the wistful gaze, was seen as the providential hero.

The repetitive discussions about Mendes and Mourinho had hit their target. There is no doubt that Pérez met with his future coach when Mourinho was still working at Inter. And even more certain is that the president had to listen to his director general explain why Mourinho was a great coach. 'He has an intelligence for football that I've never seen in anyone else,' said Sánchez at the time. He insisted that Mourinho knew exactly what each player could give and that he was able to anticipate what was going to happen in a game – that he was able to predict what would take place after half an hour, an hour, an hour and a half of play. He was 'amazing'. Sánchez's awe for a man he described as an omniscient magician always seemed genuine. Mourinho never went into too much detail, at least not in public. He never talked about what the training sessions were like or what his principles were, or what exactly was to be expected of his teams when planning matches. The only thing he knew for sure was that he had won a lot. Why ask so many questions when the trophies speak for themselves?

The eruption of the Eyjafjallajökull volcano in the south of Iceland on 20 March 2010 was an unexpected stroke of good fortune. The ash ejected into the atmosphere meant European air space was closed and Barcelona had to travel to Milan by bus. The team took a day getting there and spent two nights sleeping in hotels before the match. That would be significant in terms of performance levels in a competition decided by the smallest details. The 3–1 win from the first leg and the 1–0 defeat in the return gave Inter victory over 180 minutes of football in which they rarely dominated Barça. The fact that Inter finished the second leg with 10 men, hemmed into their own area, desperate, saved by the incorrect ruling-out of a Bojan goal, was not enough to make Pérez and Sánchez suspect that luck had played an important part. Barcelona's defeat was such a relief to the president that he immediately closed the deal with Mourinho, convinced he was acquiring two magic spells for the price of one: the universal antidote to failure, and the 'know how' that would destroy Guardiola's team.

'*Ilusión*' is the key word in all of Pérez's public addresses since first becoming president. It means 'excitement', 'hopeful anticipation', 'enthusiasm'. In his speech after winning the election on 17 July 2000 he said, 'We have in front of us, just as we said in our election campaign, an exciting job full of *ilusión*.' On 13 May 2009, when he presented his candidacy for the presidency, he spoke beneath a poster that displayed the project's slogan, 'The Ilusión Returns', as if everything that had occurred since he had been away had been turgid and sterile. In his speech at the Salón Real at the Ritz Hotel he confided that he felt capable of 'almost everything', and warned he had 'spectacular' plans. The word 'spectacular' appeared five times in his speech. The day he announced the signing of Mourinho he insisted, 'What I love about Mourinho are the same things that you are going to love: *ilusión*, effort, professionalism, motivation, aptitude … everything that makes him the best coach.'

Pérez's communications advisors understood from the outset that he set great store in the concept of fantasy. *Ilusión* and the spectacular are connected concepts. The dictionary defines the word 'spectacular' as an adjective applied to things that, because of the 'apparatus' that accompanies them, impress whosoever is in their presence. The meaning can even be extended to imply 'gimmicky'. The first definition of '*ilusión*' in the Royal Academy's *Dictionary of the Spanish Language* is emphatic: 'concept, image or representation without an actual reality, suggested by the imagination or caused by a delusion of the senses'.

José Luis Nueno, professor of commercial management at the IESE (Institute of Higher Business Studies) and author of a study of Madrid's business model for Harvard Business School in 2004, questioned the logic of the choice of Mourinho and considered that in a traditional enterprise his signing would at the very least be seen as unorthodox. It would be an error, says Nueno, 'for a company to imitate another in terms of who its leader is: to believe that one person is responsible for everything is like believing that the carrying out of one task is responsible for everything. It's like saying: if I buy the shop-window displays of Zara I am Zara. Or even, if I copy everything that Zara does I am Zara. You miss the relationships between all the bits and pieces in the system. And you lose the acquired experience of developing that system.'

Traditional industry is less sensitive to the mythology that fills the minds of football fans. Inter's defeat of Bayern to win the Champions League gave Mourinho another trophy, but, more importantly, it gave him a magical glow in the eyes of many Madrid supporters and the feeling that they had finally found their essential authoritarian patriarch for these difficult times. Somebody who could part the Red Sea. Is there anything more exciting, more full of *ilusión*, than beautiful superstition?

Nobody knew how to exploit this better than Mourinho, ever more conscious of the fact that his collection of trophies gave him an incalculable capacity to influence the minds of fans and directors: two Portuguese leagues, two English leagues, two Italian leagues, a Portuguese Cup, an English Cup, an Italian Cup, a UEFA Cup, two Champions Leagues … Success is exciting. Continual success, skilfully promoted, is persuasion's most seductive calling card. It is then that 'magical thinking' comes in to play.

In *The Golden Bough*, the anthropological classic published in 1890, James Frazer writes that primitive societies linked themselves to a 'magical man-god' who exercised 'public magic', primarily to provide food and control the rain. We don't expect anything less from the director generals who control the big multinationals, nor of certain football managers. Frazer argues that magic works by imitation: what appears to be, influences what appears to be. Like causes like. If you want more muscle, eat more meat; if you want to fly, eat birds; if you want success, attach yourself to someone successful, touch him, ask for his autograph. Magic works through symbols and symbols work by metonymy and metaphor – Mourinho is a symbol of the social leader and a metaphor for triumph.

Magical thinking establishes a mystical relationship that very few people in the world of football are capable of resisting, as nobody is wholly free from superstition. Players can't stop themselves, always taking their first step onto the pitch with their right foot. Roman Abramovich cannot suppress it, trying to import the Guardiola model to Chelsea, but without the 'Masia', without the culture of youth development, without the Camp Nou, and to an environment completely different to that of Spanish football. Neither could Pérez restrain himself when he coupled his desire to win the Champions League to a coach who had won it twice.

Champions League statistics brought Mourinho closer to Madrid. But those same numbers made it mathematically less likely that he would win it again. Bob Paisley is the only coach to have won three European Cups, and he did it from within a very stable club: the Liverpool of the seventies and eighties, a club that had been built on the firm foundations laid by Bill Shankly with a continuity that went back to 1959.

Mourinho himself must have noted a degree of rage from within the club when two months after arriving in Spain, after an unexpected 0–0 draw on his league debut in Mallorca, he felt obliged to clarify that he was not a magician.

'Look,' he said, 'I'm a coach. I'm not Harry Potter. He's magic but in reality magic doesn't exist. Magic is fiction and I live in the football world, which is the real world.'

Mourinho wanted to lower the levels of expectation. But he always knew that his signing was intimately related to marketing, a science that studies how to take advantage of expectations for economic ends. Harry Potter is not just a fictional character. He is a commercial system learned in the business schools well known to José Ángel Sánchez. When Madrid signed the Brazilian forward Ronaldo in 2002 the director general compared his impact on the economy of the club to the bespectacled boy wizard, saying that 'Ronaldo is Harry Potter'.

The commercial model of the Madrid brand that Sánchez inspired when he joined the club is the same that Disney used to promote *The Lion King*. Following a sequence outlined by the concept's inventor, Professor Hal Varian, Google's chief economist and a specialist in the economics of information, Disney developed an exploitation chain that multiplied the number of times a product could be offered to the public. The way a product was presented was expected to evolve, generating new expectations and new demand. Varian called these 'windows'. The first window of a film is at the cinema. The second is the showing of the film on passenger airlines; then, the release of the DVD; next, the barrage of articles with the image of the characters on patented toys, games, electronics, textiles, furniture, etc. And finally, the musical, or any other commodity that the imagination is capable of conceiving.

'Disney is a content producer, and we're another content producer,' Sánchez explained during the *galácticos* era, as he maximised profits from Figo, Zidane, Ronaldo and Beckham as if they were characters in a cartoon series. The director general glimpsed a universe in which supporters were transformed into 'audiences' and became consumers of legend. During a game, these excited customers could be divided into three blocks, according to how they consumed the product. In the stadium are those who have paid at the turnstiles; the people who have bought a private box, the companies that hire out their boxes; or private individuals who have hired VIP areas, everyone in their consumer 'window'. In the second block outside the stadium are companies paying broadcasting rights for live and subsequent transmission on TV and the internet.

But the spectacle does not finish at the end of the game: the club's in-house media, Real Madrid TV, the official web page and the various club shops go on drawing in a third wave of customers. In this last block are the sponsors. The players lend their image for the promotion of companies who have contracts with the club, such as Audi, Telefónica, Coca-Cola, adidas, Babybel, Nivea, Samsung, Bwin and Fly Emirates. And then comes the film, a climax promising to break through the final frontier. *Real: The Movie*, released in 2005, was the ultimate example of putting Varian's theory into practice. At this point Real Madrid were more like Disney than Disney could ever be like Real Madrid.

More than creating new icons capable of raising the market value of the product, from 2000 Sánchez and Pérez were looking for people who were already famous, established celebrities prepared to incorporate their own mythology into the club. Before signing for Paris Saint-Germain, a Brazilian international was offered to the club, his name Ronaldinho Gaúcho. A high-ranking Madrid official, however, dismissed the idea after passing judgement on the player's prominent teeth. Ronaldinho was – within Disney parameters – an absolute unknown and the casting was not being done by a football expert. As a result, David Beckham was the only signing of the 2003–04 season. The Englishman possessed an image that had, in the words of the president, 'universal projection'.

Along with the sale of the land on the Avenida Castellana to build skyscrapers where the old training ground had stood – a real-estate operation that transformed Madrid's horizons dramatically – Sánchez and Pérez's formula helped the club make a great deal of money. In the financial year ending in 2005 Madrid became the highest-grossing club in the world. The sum of €276 million entered the Bernabéu coffers, €30 million more than that earned by Manchester United, until this point the world's most financially powerful club. Negotiation of TV rights in 2006 concluded with an unequal distribution of funds, to the detriment of all first and second division clubs apart from Barcelona and Madrid, who were blessed with the biggest contracts in Europe.

Not even when the economic bubble burst did the club's income stop growing. At the end of the 2011–12 season it exceeded €500 million, and Pérez was also able to show off a league title, his first as president since 2003. It was the first and last Spanish league won by Mourinho.

CHAPTER 3

MARKET

'You are Peter, the rock on which I will build my church, and the gates of Hell will not prevail against her. To you I give the keys to the Kingdom of Heaven; and what you bind on earth shall be bound in heaven, and whatever you loose on earth shall be loosed in heaven.'

MATTHEW, 16:18–19

'The foundations of this our city are as firm as the convictions of all who love Real Madrid. An institution that respects its past, learns from its present and is firmly committed to its future.'

Inscription on the foundation stone at Valdebebas

Football nights at the Ciutat de València stadium have a distinctive feel. The salty sea air, the smell of sunflower seeds from the stands, the penetrating aroma of liniment on the ceramic-tile floors of the dressing rooms, boots scattered on the ground, incandescent lamps giving off slightly less light in the visitors' dressing room than in the home one, the kind of lamps you find in hospital rooms, lighting up the face of Pedro León as he gets changed, reasonably satisfied after the game on 25 September 2010.

28

MARKET

The crowd had just applauded him off the pitch in recognition of the time he spent at Levante three seasons ago. He had been Madrid's best player and had done what his coach had asked, or so he thought.

Mourinho had brought him on after 61 minutes in place of Di María in an attempt to break down Levante's defence. He told him to hug the touchline, to open up the pitch, to take people on and try to get around the outside of the opposition's defence; and if there was space to do so, to make diagonal runs inside, combining with Benzema and Higuaín. The substitute carried out his coach's instructions although from the bench he was being stared at by a clearly annoyed Mourinho. Furious, he grabbed a bottle of water and threw it to the ground. Despite the fact that he had created a chance for himself and served up another simple opportunity for Benzema to score, the match ended 0–0.

Pedro León was preparing to go to the bus when Mourinho stopped him in the dressing room and, calling the attention of the other players, pointed the finger of blame at the hapless Spaniard.

'I've heard you're going around like a star, saying you have to be starting games and doing whatever the hell you like. Your friends in the press, that Santiago Segurola … they say you're a star. But what you've got to learn is to train hard and to not go around saying you have to be a starter. You're going to be left out of the squad for several games. On Monday you won't be going to Auxerre …'

'I didn't say that,' the accused responded, stunned. 'Tell me. Who have I told that I should be starting? We should talk in private. Please, boss, let's talk in private …'

Mourinho sneered before turning around. The dressing room was electrified. The players did not understand what had happened to suddenly make the coach ruthlessly belittle someone who seemed so vulnerable. A 23-year-old newcomer to the team. A talented footballer who the group saw as a solution to the creative problems the team sometimes faced in away games. A player who had just shown against Levante that he was up to the task had been accused by the manager of being a kind of traitor, based on some idle gossip that it seemed only Mourinho had heard.

On Monday 27 September Madrid travelled to the French city of Auxerre to play their second group game in the Champions League. The absence of Pedro León caught the attention of both directors and journalists. That evening, during the official press conference, someone asked Mourinho the technical reasons behind his decision not to call up one of the players who had most impressed in the previous match. The question was either to be evaded or invited a football-based refection, but the answer Mourinho gave suggested the most powerful man at the club was almost out of control.

'Speculation is your profession,' he told reporters in a steely, inflexible tone that was then new but which, over time, would become almost routine. 'In very pragmatic terms I could say that Pedro León has not been called up because the coach didn't want to call him up. If President Florentino comes to ask me why Pedro León hasn't been called up I have to answer him. But he's not asked me. You're talking about Pedro León as if he's Zidane or Maradona. Pedro León is an excellent player but not so long ago he was playing for Getafe. He's not been called up for one game and it feels like you're talking about Zidane, Maradona or Di Stéfano.

'You're talking about Pedro León. You have to work to play. If you work as I want you to, then it will be easier to play. If not, it will be more difficult.'

Mourinho spoke with a mixture of cruelty and pleasure. The sadistic nature of the rant unsettled the squad. It was the first time that the players felt their manager represented a threat. Gradually, they began to follow his every public appearance: on TV, on the web, via Twitter, with iPhones or BlackBerries. They didn't miss a single appearance because they understood that in the press room a different game was being played out, one that would have a major effect on them professionally; a game that could ennoble or degrade them, place them in the spotlight or bury them with indifference, conceal their misery or entirely disregard their merits – a ritual of four weekly appearances that they only had access to as spectators.

Real Madrid's statute book establishes the board as the executive body of government responsible for directing the administration of the club. In practice, it works as a small, homogeneous parliament that meets regularly to discuss issues proposed by the president for approval. With the exception of the group closest to the president, whose position enables direct channels of inquiry, the confidential information handled by board members is usually limited to sources in the offices of the Bernabéu, offices well removed from the football team. Because directors are hand-picked by the president, Florentino Pérez, he has never met with overwhelming opposition and, except on rare occasions, the board unanimously agrees.

José Manuel Otcro Ballasts, recognised by *Best Lawyers* magazine as the top intellectual property lawyer in Spain, is Professor of Law at the University of Alcalá de Henares, a former dean of the Faculty of Law of the University of León, author of detective novels and one of the 17 members of the board of directors. Asked in November 2010 about the character of José Mourinho, this most intellectual of Madrid's directors turned to the Bible for reference:

'When Jesus named the man who was to lead his Church he did not choose the even-tempered calm John, but Peter, the passionate, hot-blooded fisherman. Mourinho plans everything, everything, everything … his intelligence enables him to analyse the reality of a situation and project his own solutions. I had never before heard Casillas say that a coach had been "great" during half-time [the goalkeeper said this to the media after the victory in Alicante in October

2010]. They all adore him. He's a communicator. He encloses the players verbally. He's been successful in all the signings. It's the first time I've seen this level of calm at the club.'

José Ángel Sánchez, the corporate director general, offered an equally complimentary account of Mourinho:

'The coach,' said Sánchez, 'is like Kant. When Immanuel Kant went out for his walk in Königsberg everyone set their watches because he always did it on time. When the coach arrives in the morning at Valdebebas everyone knows that it's 7.30 a.m. without looking at the clock.'

Sánchez felt that Madrid had its first coach who could be trusted to sign wisely. He cited the example of Khedira and Di María, whom the coach – showing what a clinical eye he had – asked for before the 2010 World Cup. He argued that his compendium of virtues made him exactly the solid figure that the club had needed for so many years. Mourinho, in the opinion of the chief executive, had 'brought calm' to Madrid.

The sports complex Valdebebas, known as Real Madrid City, is one of the most advanced centres of football technology in the world. It occupies an area of 1.2 million square metres, of which only a quarter has been developed, at a cost of some €98 million. The work of the architectural studio of Antonio Lamela, it has 12 playing fields, a stadium and, at its heart, a 'T-shape' of standardised units whose functionalist design of flat layers and clean lines projects a mysteriously moral message.

The main entrance, at the foot of the 'T', is at the lowest point of the facility. From there the complex unfolds, beginning with the dressing rooms of the youngest age categories (8- to 9-year-olds) and going through, in accordance with age group, the dressing rooms of each category, using the natural slope of the hill on the south side of the valley of Jarama. The architects, in collaboration with the then director of the academy, Alberto Giráldez, gave the main building an educational message for young people: the idea of an arduous climb from the dressing rooms of the youngest to those of the professionals. On top of this great parable of conquest – and indeed of the whole production – sits the first-team dressing room. And above the dressing room, with the best views of all, sits the coach's office, defining its occupier as the highest possible authority. As Vicente del Bosque said of his predecessor as head of the academy, Luis Molowny: 'He was a moral leader.'

Something in Mourinho's arrival at Valdebebas surprised those who worked there. As well as Rui Faria, fitness coach, Silvino Louro, the goalkeeping coach, Aitor Karanka, the assistant coach, and José Morais, the analyst of the opposition, the Portuguese coach brought his agent and friend, Jorge Mendes. Gradually, the squad became convinced that Mendes worked in the building. Not so much as another one of the coaches but as the ultimate handyman.

Impeccably fitted out in a light woollen Italian suit, with a tie that never moved and a fashionable but unpretentious haircut, tanned even in the gloomiest of winter days, Jorge Paulo Agostinho Mendes was the first players' agent who saw himself as a powerful business-man, often speaking as a self-styled agent of the 'industry' of football. Mourinho also used the term 'industry' in his speeches, seasoning his turns of phrase with expressions from the world of financial technoc-racy. For many other football agents, this was an artificial pose. 'They think they're executives at Standard & Poor's,' said one Madrid play-er's FIFA agent.

Born in Lisbon in 1966, Mendes was raised in a working-class neighbourhood. His father worked in the oil company Galp and he won his first trophies selling straw hats on the beach in Costa Caparica. He played football at junior championship level and, determined to make it as a professional, migrated north to Viana do Castelo. He ran a video rental store, worked as a DJ and opened his own nightclub in Caminha, before discovering that he had a gift – the talent of first being able to gain the trust of players, and then being able to value them, generally above market prices. His first major transaction was the transfer of goalkeeper Nuno from Vitória de Gimarães to Deportivo de la Coruña in 1996. With the commission obtained from the deal, the foundation was laid for Gestifute to become the football industry's most powerful agency, with subsidiaries such as Polaris Sports, dedicated to the management of image rights, marketing and advertising, and the promotional agency Gestifute Media.

Mourinho and Mendes shared an office straight away. The agent set himself up in the suburb of La Finca in Pozuelo. He went to Valdebebas, along with his players and his coach, almost every morning, accompanied by various assistants. When it was training time he would sit in Mourinho's chair and look out of the window from his own private agency to follow the progress of the team from up on high.

The sight of Mendes in his dark-blue pinstripe suit sitting behind the glass, drinking coffee and looking at everything from behind the mask of his sunglasses, sparked the imagination of the players every morning as they warmed up. There was no shortage of jokes and laughter. Especially when jogging as a group, they had the feeling they were being watched from above.

'There's the lord and master of the club,' said one. 'There's the boss.'

Mendes entertained his business partners in Mourinho's office. There they organised their interviews with other agents. Juanma López, the former Atlético player, who was now a players' agent, appeared one morning. It was a topic of conversation for the naturally curious players. 'Mendes has his office here,' they commented. Lass Diarra did not understand what all the fuss was about: 'Who's that?' he said. The Frenchman had never seen López play.

MARKET

The first stone of Valdebebas was laid on 12 May 2004. During the opening Pérez gave a visionary speech: he imagined a huge theme park that club members could access daily and in which they rubbed shoulders with the players.

'The new "City of Real Madrid" has an inclusive character,' he said. 'It will be open to all who love the sport and want to enjoy all the possibilities for entertainment around it.'

The old Ciudad Deportiva 'Sport City' on the Avenida Castellana, which finally closed in 2004, had been an accessible complex. Anyone, in exchange for a few pesetas, could get in to admire their idols as they trained. In Valdebebas the club forbade fans entering on weekdays. Even club members, whose contributions to the budget, mainly through ticketing, subscriptions or contributions, make up a third of Madrid's income, were denied access.

The first-team training sessions were closed to the public before Mourinho arrived at the club. But for the new coach, living in a cloister was not enough. So the ban was extended to relatives and agents of the players. If the father of Sergio Canales, who was then 19, wanted to see his son train he had to apply for a permit with three days' notice. The same thing happened to the agents of Casillas, Alonso and Arbeloa, among others. Before the end of 2010, Mourinho had extended the ban to Jorge Valdano, previously the highest sporting authority at the club. The doors of Valdebebas were now only unconditionally open to one person outside the club: Mendes.

There were now 300 players represented under the Gestifute banner. In some cases, the company merely represented them in the presence of third parties. In other cases, and under Portuguese law, the only European legislation that permits it, Gestifute acquired partial ownership of players through investment funds, and this enabled them to speculate in greater volume. When a Portuguese club sold a player whom it co-owned with Gestifute, the company charged its share of the transfer.

In the autumn of 2010 Mendes represented Mourinho and four players in Madrid's first team. Pepe and Ronaldo, on the club's payroll since 2007 and 2009 respectively, and Carvalho and Di María, signed on the recommendation of the new coach. Angel Di María was the player whom Mourinho had called for most fervently throughout the summer. Pérez found it difficult to accept the outlay of around €30 million, believing that the Argentinian left-winger, despite his success at the World Cup, did not have enough public appeal to justify his price. But Mourinho insisted that he was a good strategic signing.

The acquisition of Di María was more expensive because Benfica held no more than 80 per cent of the player's rights. Since 2009, the Lisbon club had been ceding percentages of players' rights to the Benfica Stars Fund, managed by Banco Espírito Santo. In return for greater liquidity, Benfica were required to transfer players only when their sale value ensured a profit for private investors. The sale of Di María marked the first profit in the history of the Benfica Stars Fund. Other equally profitable transactions would follow: the transfer of Fabio Coentrão to Real Madrid for €30 million in July 2011, David Luiz to Chelsea for €30 million in January 2011 and Javi García to Manchester City for €20 million in 2012. It is not known if Mendes participated in all these deals through the fund. He says that he did not and the Banco Espírito Santo guarantees investors' anonymity. The fund manager, João Caino, provided no documents but said that the participants are a group of companies and rich individuals, but not football agents.

* * *

MARKET

The summer of 2010 was full of high expectations. José Ángel Sánchez could at last count on a friend in the club, a true collaborator with whom he could shape the future from the same dressing room and with equal power. After two years of major investment in players, the board rubbed its hands at the prospect of infallible, charismatic certainty, unanimously agreeing that Mourinho was the missing piece. Inspired by stories that had actually been conceived in the board room, the press and fans dreamed of the wonderful adventures of a team full of stars and led by a secret-weapons scientist of a coach, permanently cloistered inside the perimeter of the impenetrable Valdebebas training complex.

Madrid's pre-season sessions were held behind closed doors, with the exception of one. Mourinho organised every day's work meticulously. He was busy with the most diverse of self-imposed tasks but, like many British managers, did not always personally take training. The players remember that on the evening he opened the doors to the press he had spent four days in his office, leaving the training-ground work to Karanka. This time, however, he appeared with renewed vigour on the pitch. Under the gaze of journalists and cameramen stationed on the balcony with their cameras, Mourinho was frenetic, urging a surprising level of movement for the middle of summer. Players laughed, saying that it seemed as if they were training to play the final of the Champions League the following day. This extrovert show aside, sessions were quiet affairs, the press only permitted for 15 minutes as the players left the dressing room and warmed up before beginning work.

One of the routines that most caught the attention of training-ground staff occurred when security guards locked the doors and ushered out the journalists. It happened a few times while it was hot. Mourinho took off his shirt, displaying his naked torso, and let Rui Faria and Karanka supervise the warm-up while he strolled off onto another pitch, walking alone, disappearing into the westerly distance before finally stopping to put his shirt down on the grass and lie or sit on it to sunbathe. Always the same. Methodical. Most players feigned indifference. The only one who dared to interrupt him was Dutchman Royston Drenthe.

'Boss! What are you doing?'

'I think my tan is fading,' came the reply.

Those days at the end of August were the most serene of all Mourinho's time at Madrid. He dreamed of the huge undertaking he was facing, a work of unknown dimensions that went far beyond his work as a mere coach. Not a press conference went by in which he did not use the word 'construction'. From the moment he, along with Mendes, began negotiating his contract with Sánchez, he was moved by a determination to start something that would climax in administrative greatness. After winning his second Champions League he felt ready to do more than just coach. His role model was Sir Alex Ferguson. Mourinho did not originally conceive Chamartín as merely a stepping stone. A trusted ally of Mendes said that Mourinho's plan was to install himself there for good: 'He believed that at Madrid he would be the emperor. He thought he would retire in Madrid. He believed that so strongly that he got ahead of himself.'

Mourinho did not sign until he was completely certain that Madrid would give him total power to redesign the club as he saw fit. The coach thought this was only logical, since he was leaving Inter after winning a Champions League, and it was Madrid who needed him and not vice versa. He and Mendes established their requirements and the club agreed to the two fundamental conditions requested. First, he wanted control over what the press published, and second, absolute power in team affairs. Having complete discretion over who would be sold and who would be signed was as important as controlling the information that was produced about him and his team.

Gestifute say Madrid promised Mourinho he would enjoy the support of 95 per cent of the media.

The project mapped out by Mourinho and Mendes as they negotiated his departure from Inter included the signing of Hugo Almeida, at the very latest in the winter transfer window. At six foot three and dominant in the air, Almeida was the classic target man. He was the perfect choice to complete the direct style of play – long balls bypassing midfield – that would provide an alternative in attack and a shortcut when more elaborate football was not possible. As a goalscorer he was not on the wanted list of any of the top clubs in Europe. Averaging just 13 goals a season in four years at Werder Bremen, he had a worse record than both Higuaín and Benzema. But Almeida had an added feature that made him particularly attractive: he was the most important number nine on Gestifute's books. And there seemed no market for him. The best offers he had received so far were from Turkey.

There were people at Gestifute who, upon learning of Mourinho's desire to push Madrid into signing Almeida, tried to persuade Mendes against it so as not to lose credibility with Pérez. They argued that the president might end up thinking that Mourinho was more interested in doing business than building a competitive team. In the opinion of these experts, the most prudent business plan would consist of three stages. First, signing excellent players. Second, winning major titles. Third, with the endorsement of the trophies, buying ordinary and perhaps even overrated players.

Mourinho broke with this plan of progressive action. He was so sure of his power that he tried to advance to third base in the first attack. According to close observers the coach had already taken enough risks with Di María and Carvalho. To sign Almeida, too, would constitute negligence. When the following year he showed off a minor trophy like the Copa del Rey to demand the signing of Fabio

Coentrão he took a definitive wrong turn. To pay €30 million for Coentrão, a weaker left-back than Marcelo, would constitute a record fee for a substitute. It was not only the directors of Madrid who began to be suspicious. Those trusted by Mendes noted that from then on the press and clubs were put on guard. And not only in Spain.

The freedom of movement enjoyed by Mendes at Valdebebas contrasted with the prevailing restrictive climate at the training complex. The players ended up wondering if Mendes might not appear from behind the work-out machines one day and surprise them in the middle of a meeting. That never happened but, apart from in the gym and in the dressing room, the man went where he wanted to. After Mourinho's office, his natural habitat was the cafeteria, where a free buffet was available every morning. He breakfasted and dined with the coaching staff, and went from table to table joking with the players, especially with Ronaldo, Di María and Pepe, with all of whom he shared a personal relationship. It was also where Mourinho mixed with everyone. He liked to tell jokes, to laugh. It was where he was at his most loquacious.

'You cannot imagine the money this man has,' he said, pointing Mendes out to a few players as they ate their breakfast one day. Most thought it strange but made an effort to be friendly. Casillas was unfazed. The captain would soon begin to tire of it all and be less than friendly.

Mendes and his entourage would often attend the last part of the training sessions, sometimes with foreign guests whom Mendes wanted to present to players. Having finished training the players would encounter him on their way back to the dressing room, waiting on the edge of the pitch. Players would stop to talk. Ronaldo would say hello, followed normally by Pepe, Di María, Carvalho and Marcelo. Each player, except for Marcelo, was under the administrative umbrella of the Portuguese agent and would regularly have things to share. The group exchanged pleasantries in front of the puzzled looks of the rest of the squad, who gradually became more familiar with what was going on. The Spanish contingent would also greet the agent. Almost everyone, in one way or another, sought to live with the situation as politely as possible – apart from Casillas. The goalkeeper ignored Mendes, pretending that he did not exist. At 29, the captain felt that he had fulfilled his quota of formal commitments. As he once said, winning the World Cup had helped release him: 'I've earned the right to say "no".

Casillas believed Mendes's activity at Valdebebas was invasive and discriminated against the majority of the players, whose agents, friends and family had first to pass through the filter system imposed by Mourinho under principles that were not really clear. The Spanish players and the older employees of the club all believed that the new order was tailored to those who had ties to Gestifute.

What the squad could testify to after just a few months of living together was that Mendes stood at the top of the food chain, the only one who paid homage to no one. The only person Mourinho was docile in front of was his agent. What the president of the club or the players thought did not bother Mourinho. He was at ease. He was not averse to displaying a bit of nonchalance. When he got behind the wheel of one of his cars – the Aston Martin, the Ferrari or the club Audi – he was prone to bravado. Especially if he thought someone was watching him. Revving the engine, putting his foot to the floor as he pulled away, burning tyres in a cloud of white smoke and the smell of burning rubber, it was all part of the spectacle for whoever was lucky enough to coincide with him in the parking area. Mourinho saw himself as an outstanding amateur rally driver.

It took two months for Mourinho's spiritual well-being to start to evaporate. That was probably as long as it took him to realise that Madrid would not give him all the power that they had promised. On

16 September the first signs of this appeared when Gilberto Madaíl, president of the Portuguese Football Federation, travelled to Madrid to personally request that Mourinho take charge of Portugal in the qualifying rounds of the 2012 European Championships. The unusual thing was not the request itself. The truly exceptional thing was that Mourinho made it public before admitting in a press conference that if he was unable to work for his national team it was not for lack of desire but because the Madrid directors had refused to allow it.

'Madrid has every right,' he said, 'to put an obstacle in my path, and if they do – however small it may be – I cannot go.'

The coach added that he saw no difficulty in reconciling the two jobs, because in the two weeks that FIFA had set aside for international matches there would be very few players left at Valdebebas for him to train.

'If I go with Portugal I'll be going with three Madrid players: Pepe, Ronaldo and Carvalho,' he said. 'And if I stay here I'll be with three players: Pedro León, Granero and Mateos'.

This was a stunt to remind Pérez that he did not sign a contract just to train players but also to manage the club. If he was the manager, then fine. If he was just the coach, then why not go with Portugal when there was no one left at Valdebebas to coach. He told the president that he was delaying giving him the power that he had demanded as a condition of signing the contract. He wanted to reform Madrid from top to bottom and if they did not let him, then he would go elsewhere.

Contracts for Carvalho, Di María, Özil, Khedira, Canales and Pedro León for a total of €90 million did not satisfy Mourinho. First, because it would mean keeping Benzema rather than signing Hugo Almeida. Second, because he had not signed Canales or Pedro León, but had only approved what were sporting director Jorge Valdano's proposals, seeing them as obstacles to his project rather than reinforcements. Third, because it bothered him that Valdano continued to act as the club's presidential advisor and spokesman. Mourinho wanted to appoint a spokesman he trusted. He also wanted to move Pepe and Di María up the salary scale above Ramos and Alonso. But Pérez was not committed to any of this. He was shrewd enough to suggest he would support Mourinho completely, while at the same time not doing anything to translate that support into anything concrete. He played for time, waiting to test the effectiveness of the methods proposed by the coach. He also played with two hands – in front of Mourinho he showed his condescending, entrepreneurial side. But later his influence would be a delaying and conservative one.

Along with Granero and Alonso, the Murcian Pedro León Sánchez belonged to a long line of Spanish midfielders who had emerged over the previous decade. He was one of those players whose style of play had provided Spain with a distinctive footballing identity. In the pre-season with Madrid he had given the impression of being physically ready to fulfil the potential that scouts from Chelsea, Barça and Milan had all glimpsed in him. His development at Getafe in the 2009–10 season – that combination of vision, creative audacity and a clean strike of the ball – had placed him among the top players in the league with nine assists. Only Alves (Barcelona) with 11 and Navas (Sevilla) with 10 were ahead of him, and he was level with Valero (Villarreal), and Xavi and Messi (Barcelona). Pedro León had succeeded in Getafe, a small team on the outskirts of Madrid, without the attacking players around him that he would have had at Barcelona, Sevilla and Villarreal. When Madrid paid €10 million for him no one seemed to think it was a bad deal.

His way of dominating the ball, the co-ordination of body and object, his subtle touches – these were all a throwback to another era, to a time when children had no TV, no consoles, no McDonald's, no mobile phones or Dolce & Gabbana – only footballs. For José Luis

Mendilíbar, his coach at Valladolid, the lad seemed to have stepped out of a time machine.

Mendilíbar, born in Vizcaya in 1961, gets excited just thinking about it. 'There are no players like Pedro León anymore,' he says. 'He's from the last century. He's like a child. Throw him a ball on the street and he'll start to play with it. I had to practically call him in from training sessions.'

Pedro León was always a boy with slightly old-fashioned habits. Born in Mula, an inland town in Murcia, he had the reserved nature typical of highland people, and had had a strict upbringing from his father, a retired policeman permanently disabled after being the victim of a terrorist attack, possibly by ETA. There was a spartan regime in the house and sacrifice, physical courage and discretion were valued above all other qualities.

Pedro León detested jokes and abhorred electronic games. He paid very little attention to social life, to music, to bars or admirers, and settled down with his first girlfriend. Vicente del Bosque once said of Pedro Munitis: 'Football is his vice.' Football was also Pedro León's vice, and he left evidence of his weakness wherever he went. When he played for Levante in the 2007–08 season, he trained with his teammates in the mornings in Buñol and then travelled 200 miles to Mula to play indoor football with his friends.

The summer he signed for Madrid, after a somewhat inactive holiday period, he enrolled in a seven-a-side football championship despite running the risk of injury. It was one of those tournaments that lasts for 24 hours without interruption, like 'The 24 hours of Caravaca'. A marathon. It began on a Saturday and ended on Sunday after some early-hours-of-the-morning play-offs. The Madrid scouts whose job it is to check out the private lives of potential signings could not have been clearer in their reports. Valdano shrugged his shoulders: 'The boy is clean-living to the point of being naive.'

Pedro León possessed the spirit of an amateur but that contrasted with Mourinho's rather industrial notion of football, where players were aseptic pieces on an assembly line to be put together as the coach saw fit. Pedro León would never put in an indifferent spell at training, despite the fact that his coach hardly ever used him for competitive matches. It was a new experience for the youth. Never before had he had such a peripheral role in a team and it burned him up inside. He was going to Valdebebas every morning like someone on his way into battle. Teeth clenched, he worked as if each session were his last chance to win his place in the team. His aim was to occupy the right wing, where the most expensive signing of the summer – the first transfer that turned a profit for Benfica Stars Fund – played: Angel di María.

That night at the Ciutat de Valencía – when Mourinho accused Pedro León of displaying a vain and selfish attitude in front of his team-mates – was only his second game of the season. In five rounds of league matches and one round of Champions League fixtures he had only played 60 minutes; Di María had already played 340. The press conference in Auxerre was the most explicit public attack that Mourinho had launched against one of his own players. It is probable that after hearing what he said Mourinho realised he needed to make what had happened seem like nothing special. Who better for the job than Pedro León himself?

Mourinho spoke to him two weeks after returning from Auxerre, asking him to give a press conference that he himself would supervise. The procedure was the same as he used when Karanka spoke in public and more often than not when one of his players held a formal press conference: he would meet the player in question, he would formulate the questions that he imagined reporters would ask and suggest answers, as if in a face-to-face interview. What Mourinho asked Pedro León can be worked out from the repetitive answers the player gave in the press room.

'I spoke with the coach after the game against Levante and I knew I'd done some things wrong,' he said, without specifying exactly what his mistakes had been. 'There's been no punishment. I'd even say I feel protected by my coach. He's the boss. I know that when the boss gets along well with someone he usually tell them these things. At no time have I felt bad or offended. If I have to ask anyone for advice, then, with the friendly relationship I have with my coach, I ask him.

'I get along with him very well. I've a very good relationship. I know that everything he does is for the good of the group and for me. And the team's good …'

This was positive propaganda that favoured the powers that be. But still, Mourinho did not like some of the words used by the player. In time, the coach would forbid Madrid players from giving press conferences – something that they had hitherto done on an almost daily basis.

His public appearance did little to enhance Pedro León's career prospects at Madrid, and he played less and less. On 3 October at the San Siro in the fourth round of the group stage of the Champions League, Milan led 2–1 when the coach brought him on with 10 minutes remaining. His contribution was explosive: he got the equalising goal in the last attack of the match. But there was no reward. This goal was the last thing Pedro León did on the pitch for a long while as he did not play a single minute in any of the following six league matches.

Murcia lawyer José Sánchez Bernal, one of the 16 men who sat alongside Pérez on the board, was quick to offer the official version of his fellow Murcian in the newspaper *La Verdad de Murcia*. 'I have to clarify the fact that our coach has not put a cross against his name,' he said. 'I'm sure Pedro León will end up playing many games for Real Madrid and have lots of success.'

Sánchez Bernal's vision offers up an idea of the type of information available to the board. The reality for Pedro León at Valdebebas was very different. His future in Madrid was unfeasible. Chelsea and Manchester City made contact with Valdano in December and January to inquire about the footballer, checking the possibility of a loan until the summer. Hearing this, Mourinho rejected the idea, saying he needed him. In the second half of the season, however, he used him even less.

For players, and for employees close to the first-team squad, the reasons for the relegation of Pedro León are the same ones that inspired the demotion of Kaká and Canales. Because of the way Mourinho lined up his team, the presence of these players would have been a serious threat to Di María's place in the starting line-up. Since the Argentinian winger clearly could not compete with Ronaldo or Özil, it became clear that he had to play on the right wing. In order to keep Di María there, Mourinho had to edge out all serious competitors who performed well on that side of the pitch.

By Christmas 2010 Mourinho was fully aware that Pérez was withholding the power and the conditions from him that he had demanded to carry out his grand task. It was not enough for him to have converted Valdebebas, that once public exhibition of all things Madrid, into a fortress whose inhabitants increasingly believed that the interests of a privileged few were being served above all others. He needed much more power and something told him it would not be possible to progress in his mission without first causing a long conflict. The pacification of the club, which José Ángel Sánchez had spoken about, could not be achieved without violent transformation.

CHAPTER 4

FIGHT

'In short, there is nothing mysterious, romantic or necessarily laudable about leadership. Indeed, some of the most effective leaders have been those who, merely through having more than their fair share of psychopathic traits, were able to release antisocial behaviour in others. Their secret is that by setting an example they release a way of acting that is normally inhibited. This gives pleasure to their followers, thus reinforcing their leadership.'

NORMAN DIXON, *On the Psychology of Military Incompetence*

José Mourinho skirted the technical area and, covering his mouth so no one could read his lips, turned to the Levante left-back and insulted him.

It was about 8.30 p.m. on 25 September 2010 and Madrid were playing their fifth league match of the season. The Levante left-back, Asier del Horno, had gone to the touchline to take a throw-in late in the first half. He held the ball in his hands when, from the visitors' bench, Mourinho could be heard directing a tirade of abuse his way, referring to his private life.

Del Horno tried to ignore it but the coach hammered him through-out the whole match, making del Horno feel sorry primarily for the coaching staff and the substitutes. Just a few feet away, sitting on the bench, the players looked on, perplexed and embarrassed. They could not believe Mourinho was capable of so viciously insulting a footballer.

That night at the Ciutat de Valencía stadium they began to realise that the most powerful man at the club, the person they would depend on professionally in the coming years, had a mysterious and chaotic side. Something that verged on the delinquent. Granero, Mateos, Dudek, Pedro León, Lass and Benzema, lined up in the dugout and almost all stunned at what they saw, said they had never had a coach like this before. This taunting of an opponent was a new experience. The only one who was not surprised by his behaviour was Lass, who between 2005 and 2007 had played for Mourinho at Chelsea.

The game provided a summary of some of the main problems that Madrid would face from there on in. The league championship, with its draining routine, would be psychologically exhausting, as they would mainly be up against against modest opponents who would be inclined to give up all attacking ambitions.

In the Ciutat de Valencía tactical situations were encountered that, despite their extreme simplicity, were not easy to resolve. With Levante having fully retreated and seeming impenetrable in their own penalty area, Madrid had no choice but to try to pass their way around their opponents until a gap finally appeared. Committed to playing on the counter-attack, as had been the case since pre-season, it was not long before Madrid displayed symptoms of extreme slug-gishness. The distance between Levante's back four, led by Ballesteros, and the goalkeeper Reina was minimal.

Mourinho was immediately aware of the situation. That opening-day draw against Mallorca had left his team only one point ahead of Barcelona. They could lose their lead over Guardiola's side, who were playing in Bilbao at 10 p.m. that evening.

The nerves in the Madrid camp were palpable, even at the team hotel. That same morning a group of journalists, alerted by Mourinho's entourage, had gone to the stadium to discuss and film the state of the pitch. Levante's press officer, Emilio Nadal, was astonished to see them take out a ruler and measure the exact length of the grass, which was long and dry to slow down the ball. It was nothing new in the catalogue of tactics employed by smaller teams to deprive their more skilful opponents of the advantage of a fast pitch. Nothing illegal. A detail, however, that hardly helped keep Mourinho calm. Once the game started it was not long before he left his seat. Seeing Del Horno clearly irritated him.

What Del Horno really liked was *pelota vasca*, a traditional, fast-moving Basque sport played with a small rubber ball. Football was not so much his passion, more his trade. He had always been a formidable athlete and stood out at youth level for his strength, his power and his ability to arrive late in the penalty area. He was a tenacious man-marker and was surprisingly good in the air. He also stood out for his audacity, both on and off the field. The qualities that enabled him to face any game without the fear of failure also allowed him to live carelessly. A native of Biscay – and wholly attached to the town of Gallarta in the mining heart of the Somorrostro Valley – he would do anything so as not to miss the annual local festivities. One day he signed for Chelsea, Mourinho having personally requested the signing.

'I signed for Chelsea for four years in 2005,' he recalls. 'In 2006, after a season in London, Valencia offered me the same salary but for twice as long. It was an important club – it was Valencia – and it meant returning to Spain. The offer was very good and, although it was a difficult decision, I accepted.'

For the Basque, Mourinho was the coach who opened the doors to the Premier League, the most attractive market in world football, a showcase that allowed him to transform his career. 'Mourinho was a very accessible coach who took care of everything,' he says. 'He was great with me and my family when we arrived in England. I have a very good memory of that year because I had the opportunity to win two trophies. I was very young, and the truth is that he and the people working with him welcomed me and helped me. I'll always be grateful for the opportunity he gave me to be part of a team like Chelsea. For the way he took a chance on me and how he behaved towards me.'

Between 2006 and 2008, Del Horno became the best left-back in Spain. He was regularly called up to the Spanish national squad by Luis Aragonés, participating in the process of qualifying for the World Cup but missing out on the final cut. Sources from the Spanish Football Federation confirm that he suffered a chronic inflammation in his right Achilles tendon during his season at Chelsea, the kind of injury that requires rest to prevent the irreversible deterioration of the affected tissue. The player played on with pain-killing injections. A year after signing his contract at Stamford Bridge, Del Horno could not jump without experiencing severe pain. He did not go to the World Cup but joined Valencia for €8 million. The tendon was badly torn. The two operations that he had on it could, at best, only prolong his career a little, and at great cost. He would have very few games left by the time he came to play Madrid: just 34 more matches in the top division.

On the night of 25 September an enduring football discovery was made as to how to frustrate Madrid. Levante's game plan was an exercise in renunciation, a strange approach in the Spanish league, where pride in retaining possession of the ball usually prevails over any recognition of inferiority, any dedication to defending or playing on the break. Directed by Sergio Ballesteros, Levante sat back, allowed their opponents to have the ball and dug an impassable trench. They had just three shots on Casillas's goal, each going wide. But Madrid only managed two shots on target. Never again that season did they have fewer than three shots at goal, proof of the success of Levante's tactics, and a symptom of the deficiencies in Madrid's functioning that would persist in subsequent years. These were the reasons for Mourinho's exasperation and why he turned his anger towards Del Horno. But unlike his colleagues and several members of the opposition, the player did not take Mourinho seriously.

'Everybody knows,' says Del Horno, 'that everyone takes their own path, and when you come together on a football pitch things completely change. That day we had a chance to get the draw; they just couldn't figure us out. They weren't counting on dropping two points at a ground like Levante's. We made things difficult for them and in order to do that we had to use all the weapons available to us. Just as Mourinho used the weapons available to him. He saw he could unsettle a player to get a response from his own team, that's all there is to it … He is a coach who likes to be close to the players, the matches … Well, he looks after his own interests.'

Mourinho's attempt to rebuke his former player caught everyone's attention as the night went on. Del Horno clashed with Ronaldo, claiming a foul, and provoking a free-for-all involving players from both teams. The Madrid coach intervened again against his former player. They exchanged insults. The tension continued until the end. Violence is contagious.

But referee Carlos Delgado Ferreiro only dared to send off Dr Juan Carlos Hernández. A sports medicine specialist with over 10 years of honest service to Madrid, if there was one thing you would never associate with Dr Hernández it was brawling.

More attentive to the developments than Delgado Ferreiro was Sergio Ballesteros, the Levante captain, who had just turned 35. His story is one of local boy made good, although he had to first leave his home town before he could enjoy success. Emerging from somewhere in the 'Garden of Burjassot' in Valencia, his talent honed in the harbour club's youth team, he made his début in 1994 and then went in search of his fortune: four years in Tenerife, one at Rayo Vallecano, three in Villarreal and eight in Mallorca. Then he returned home, well worn both inside and out. He signed a contract with Levante in the summer of 2008, after the club filed for bankruptcy. The alternatives were both extreme: end his career surrounded by debris and decay, or get the team promoted against all odds. On 13 June 2010 the impossible happened. The club with one of the lowest budgets in the second division, and still in administration, won its fourth promotion. At the head of the company stood Ballesteros.

Long and wide like a piece of industrial pipe, Ballesteros stands six foot two. His body resembles a turret from which a leathery head sticks out, turning, featureless, on his not inconsiderable neck. The nickname of '*Papá*' sums up everything he means to the dressing room. Ballesteros is their natural leader: his presidential voice, his watchful green eyes commanding respect. Everyone see him as the great provider. He misses nothing – and that includes the provocations from the Madrid coach, to whom he quickly conveyed a simple warning. At the final whistle he approached him in the tunnel and repeated it several times.

'Respect your fellow professionals,' he said. 'Respect your fellow professionals …!'

In the 2010–11 season Levante's players were the lowest paid in the first division. According to a report by Professor José María Liébana Gay for the University of Barcelona, spending on Levante's staff for that year amounted to €7 million in total. This was followed by €11.7 million at Almería, and €14.4 million in salaries and bonuses at Real Sociedad. All a world away from Barcelona, who set aside €240.6 million of their budget for the payment of salaries, and from Madrid, with €216.1 million as the second highest spenders on personnel in the league behind Barça. Mourinho's salary alone – about €14 million – was double the wage bill of the Levante team. In this time of fiscal crisis Levante were the club with the smallest total debt to the government. The bankruptcy action had forced them to settle their accounts with the tax authorities.

'The professionals' to whom Ballesteros was referring live according to the law of the marketplace; a law that is crueller to the smaller clubs. Eight of the eleven Levante players who played against Madrid in 2010 were in the final days of their careers in the top flight. Del Horno has been without a club since 2012; David Cerrajería, right-back, signed for Cordoba in 2011; Sergio González Soriano, midfielder, retired in 2011; Xisco Nadal signed for Alqueires in the third tier in 2011; Nano, who played in the centre of defence alongside Ballesteros, went to Guizhou in the Chinese league in 2012; the goalkeeper Manolo Reina ended up at Atromitos, a team on the outskirts of Athens in 2011; Nacho González, midfielder, played for Standard Liège and in 2012 signed for Hércules in the second division; after a brief period in the Chinese League, Rubén Suárez, the striker, returned to play for Almería in the second division.

Levante's training ground is located in the Comarca region of Hoya de Buñol on a plateau surrounded by mountains, dotted with almond trees and lined with ditches. The horizon is marked by the giant metal cylinders of the Cemex cement plant, closed due to a lack of demand. In early 2013 the future of the 150 workers at the plant hung in the balance of rather grim negotiations. Dust particles of crushed materials floated in the air. It was a cold February day with a chill wind, normal in the microclimate of the plain of Buñol, and Vicente Iborra sat in a small room next to the dressing room to explain what kind of club he served.

'We're aware of our limitations,' says Levante's second vice-captain. 'The club cannot pay transfers and we're forced to wait for loan players or free transfers. Because the club that pays the most is the first to choose, we have to wait until the end of the summer. It's an uncomfortable situation because you start the season with only half the squad guaranteed, and after the league starts two or three more players come in.'

Born in Moncada, Valencia, in 1988 and brought up through Levante's youth team, Iborra spent his formative years at the club during that crucial time of administration and promotion. Since he was 24 years old he has been a loyal lieutenant to Ballesteros and Juanfran, sharing a sense of administrative duty and talking about the club with the solemnity of an entrepreneur speaking about his investments. Listening to Quico Catalan, the president, was not much different to listening to the players. In his conversation he referred to the crisis, the austerity and the structural problems that constitute the daily struggle in the vast majority of Spanish clubs.

'We often resort to players who don't have an important role at the clubs they're at and who are keen to continue enjoying their football,' Iborra says. 'They come here and I think the club's friendliness is a great calming influence – and now we also have economic stability. People who come feel very comfortable, and they perform to a much higher level. It's very easy to become committed to the cause.'

The match on 25 September plotted the course for the years ahead when Madrid would come up against many teams who surrendered most of the pitch, together with the ball. It was also an indication of how Mourinho would go about explaining such bad results. The coach's explanations of the draw in the press room at the Ciutat de Valencía drew subtly on his players' lack of accuracy in front of goal, obscuring the fact that Madrid had had fewer chances to score than he acknowledged: a meagre balance of just two shots on target meant Mourinho had to avoid recognising that his team had played poorly.

'I'm concerned about not turning so much attacking football and chances into goals,' he said. 'It's not normal to need so many opportunities. If from six chances we score two or three goals, then OK ... But this has been happening from the first game. It was like this against Mallorca, Osasuna ... And now against Levante we had some big opportunities but didn't take them.'

In the draw for the knockout stages of the Copa del Rey, Madrid again found themselves up against Levante. The first leg was played at the Bernabéu on 22 December. If Mourinho had shown signs of nervousness in September, three months later he was bordering on neurotic. After the 5–0 rout suffered against Barcelona at the Camp Nou on 29 November he had embarked on a flurry of team-talks and training sessions that kept the team on constant alert. The preparation for matches had become a continual source of surprise for the squad; the resources drawn on by the coach to motivate the players amazed them and the close proximity of Christmas provided new ammunition to fire up the team. In the dressing room the players interpreted Mourinho's preparations as his revenge for the two points they had dropped in the league.

Taking advantage of the fact that it was the last game of 2010, Mourinho promised to prolong the Christmas holidays in proportion to the number of goals put past their opponents. To complete the message, he named most of his first team: Casillas, Lass, Pepe, Albiol, Marcelo, Alonso, Granero, Di María, Özil, Ronaldo and Benzema all started. The pre-match team-talk was a masterpiece of motivation. Even the most sceptical of players took to the pitch like men possessed.

Benzema, Özil, Benzema, Ronaldo, Benzema, Ronaldo, Ronaldo and Pedro León scored in that order from the fifth minute to the ninetieth to deliver a historic win: 8–0. The process was painful for the Levante players. Some said that Di María, Marcelo, Özil and Pepe had openly mocked them, repeating the phrase 'Don't touch the shirt. You'll make it dirty,' which to the ears of the visiting players sounded like a rehearsed insult. Nobody at Madrid would acknowledged this to be true, but the accusations were never officially denied.

'We were a little annoyed that when they had already scored six goals, the seventh and eighth were celebrated with such enthusiasm,' recalls Iborra, although those involved in the game itself were not so aware of this. But the watching Levante directors were amazed by the public reaction in the stadium. The Bernabéu, as electrified as the players, celebrated the thrashing and called for Levante to be relegated with the familiar chant: 'To the Second! To the Second ...'

'I'm very happy with the attitude of my team,' Mourinho said in the press room with uncharacteristic serenity. 'I'm happy with the way the year ended. A 2010 that for me, personally, has been fantastic. It's ended in the best way possible. And also for us – because we played 25 official matches, we won 20, we drew four, and we lost one [the 5–0 against Barcelona] ... It's a very nice record.'

'I didn't know that Madrid were that annoyed by Levante,' confessed their perplexed coach Luis García. 'We're a small club but with big values. I'd like it to be remembered that a team with a budget of €450 million drew against one with the most limited budget in the division. Thanks to that point we're out of the relegation zone and they're not leaders.'

Madrid were through to the next round but in the Levante dressing room there remained a prevailing feeling of humiliation. Luis García had given the result up and rested Robusté, Xavi Torres, Javi Venta, Juanlu and Ballesteros.

The game was played on Thursday 6 January. Mourinho watched Madrid concede two goals before the final whistle. It was the team's second defeat of the season, after the 5–0 at the Camp Nou. The aggregate result, however, assured Madrid of a spot in the quarter-finals of the cup.

It was all Levante could do to finish the season in 14th position. Not many teams are better prepared for the annual routine of resistance. It is hard to imagine a club any further removed from Madrid. Their matches played against each other in the league are sporadic clashes that, rather than cranking up any fierce rivalry, have historically served to cement a sense of fraternity. Most of the Levante directors are *Madridistas*. The family of Vicente Boluda, a former president of Madrid, comes from a long line of Levante directors. As with many provincial clubs, fans' sentiments are split. The older supporters remember with admiration the visits of the Madrid team of Di Stéfano in the sixties. They were festive occasions. The matches were held at the Mestalla to maximise the size of the crowd, and fans mixed in an atmosphere of brotherhood.

'We've only spent a few years in the first division and people want to follow a team that fights for titles, wins leagues and Champions Leagues,' says Vicente Iborra. 'Many Levante fans also follow Madrid or Barça because, after all, they're the biggest clubs in Spain – and supporting nearby Valencia is out of the question. When they come here to play, the ground is invariably full of people backing those teams. We have no choice but to accept it and play well on the pitch to increase our own support base.'

Madrid returned to the Ciutat de Valencía to play the fourth game of the 2011–12 season on 18 September. They lost 1–0 in what was another heated match. With new coach Juan Ignacio Martínez in charge, Levante refined the approach they had taken the previous year.

'We knew that if we went after them they'd be better than us both physically and in terms of quality,' recalls Iborra. 'We tried to deny them space because we knew that on the counter-attack – and especially in one-on-one situations – they're the best team out there. We tried to stay very close together on the pitch, help each other, be very committed and take our chances. Fortunately, it went well. We were able to beat them, and other teams realised that if you play them on their terms then you lose 99 per cent of the time. It's an intelligent way to play them. Don't allow them space, until they end up feeling uncomfortable. Perhaps in that sense Barcelona are a better side; they know how to find the space while in possession, waiting for the opportunity. Madrid don't, and teams have realised that you can't allow them space to run into.'

That second stumble against Levante renewed Madrid's rivalry with them, hardening the grudge held by Mourinho. He kept up the provocation, although he pursued it via other means, employing Pepe to irritate opposing players and prevent them from concentrating on competing during the game. Casillas's appeal to colleagues in the Levante dressing room to try to end the resentment between the teams had very limited effect. By the time Madrid showed up at the Ciutat de Valencía to play a league match on 11 November 2012, Ballesteros and his team-mates had identified whom they considered to be the Madrid coach's enforcers. In particular they singled out Pepe, but also Ronaldo, Di María and Coentrão, all represented by Mendes, Mourinho's agent and friend, calling them 'Mourinho's puppets'. In the first minute Navarro went for a loose ball with Ronaldo and gashed his opponent's eyebrow with his elbow. Ronaldo took it very sportingly; the bleeding was stopped, a bandage was fixed and he began to play football as best he could. He even scored a goal.

Levante lost the game 1–2. After the match the home players say they saw Pepe dancing in the tunnel. 'It was as if he were dancing the "*jota*",' said a witness, referring to a traditional Spanish dance, usually accompanied by castanets. 'He was yelling, "Take that! Take that!

Take that …!'" When he heard about this, Ballesteros went straight to the dressing room and found Pepe heading for the treatment room. Versions of what happened next are conflicting. The Madrid players say Pepe fought bravely, but the Levante players say their captain grabbed Pepe by the neck with one hand while repeatedly hitting him in the head with the other. When he released him, Pepe ran for cover. 'Dance now!' roared Ballesteros. 'Call your boss to defend you.'

The small medical room quickly filled up with about 30 people. Adán, the Madrid goalkeeper, was the first to intervene on Pepe's behalf, aided by his team-mates. Soon, all the Levante squad were there. Some Madrid players, like Casillas and Albiol, tried to separate the scuffling players. Others took the opportunity to settle old scores. Ballesteros was going around warning Madrid players, 'Tell Pepe that today he's laughed and danced, but in two weeks' time when you go to Barcelona we'll be the ones laughing.' Ballesteros, for his part, denied being part of any fight when he was interviewed by several radio journalists as he left the stadium.

The melée had cooled when Juanfran, Juanlu and Iborra exchanged words with some Madrid players. Someone remembered Mourinho.

'Do you notice that there's one person missing here? We're all killing each other and the one who started it all is nowhere to be seen!'

Barça won 0–4 two match days later on the same stage. Levante turned in a serious and rigorous performance, but there were no over-the-top challenges, the two teams exchanged shirts, and at the end of the game Xavi, Puyol and Iniesta asked the senior Levante players about the situation at the club. As ambassadors observing the basic rules of etiquette, they knew that showing some warmth also made practical sense.

The victory helped Barça consolidate their lead in the table on what was a particularly happy weekend for the team. The day before, on 24 November, Madrid lost 1–0 in Seville against Betis, dropping 11 points behind in the table. It was still a month before Christmas but the league was virtually resolved – and Madrid were facing an unexpected crisis. Ever since Sunday morning, Pérez had been making calls to various figures at different levels of the club, from the offices of the Bernabéu to Valdebebas. He consulted officials, technicians, players, as well as his friends and advisors, people who were not legally tied to Madrid. He asked everyone if they believed sacking Mourinho would solve the problems of a squad that was sinking fast in the league.

The games against Levante – the most unlikely of direct rivals – and the Madrid supporters' urgent need for success meant that the team's directors, instead of processing serenely as usual through good times and bad, had responded with all the fervour of a firebrand preacher. Ramón Calderón had behaved in a similar way when he took the stand to celebrate his election as president one hot evening in 2006 in the Plaza de Lima. All around, the talk was of the need to copy Rijkaard's Barcelona, who had lifted the Champions League a month earlier, and the new president was busy trying to please voters by announcing that the hiring of Fabio Capello would guarantee success. Excited, he proclaimed that in 2007 the fans would go to the Plaza de Cibeles to celebrate winning the league 'any way we can!'

Calderón did not have any written speech but spoke from his heart. The words read by Pérez the day after he began his third term on 1 June 2009, a week after Guardiola's Barcelona had won their first Champions League, were unusually melodramatic for an executive who had made modesty and calm his trademark between 2000 and 2006. But in the new era there was no room for formalities.

'We must recover our dreams, our stability and the time we have lost as soon as we can,' said the new president. 'Real Madrid has to leave all doubts behind and tirelessly work towards the lofty goal that should always be present in its spirit – to endeavour at all times to be considered the best club of the 21st century. For this board, contributing to the achievement of that goal will be a real obsession.'

Pérez acknowledged that his strategy had two elements: first, the urgent need to make up lost ground on Barcelona, whom he did not name; second, to act with restraint in order not to harm the club's heritage.

'Our club has been – and still is – an essential part of football's history and therefore we must always set a good example,' he warned. 'Do not forget that our reputation and our image are the most precious treasures we have earned over the 107 years of our history.

'In this club our ethics will always be unyielding,' he concluded. 'Solidarity will forever be the basic reference point for our behaviour. The challenge that's now beginning for all of us is possibly the biggest and toughest we've ever taken. But I assure you that we'll make this Real Madrid a great symbol and an example.'

A year and a half after this pronouncement, and spurred on by the coach he had hired to put an end once and for all to Barça's dominance, Madrid set forth on a series of riotous confrontations with Levante. 'It was like Madrid wanted to win any way they could,' recalled Iborra, 'because they feared that Barcelona were getting away from them.'

For young Iborra the astonishment was clear. He had grown up in a club in administration and could not conceive of being so passionate about anything other than keeping his job. Barcelona, in any case, pulled away from the field in the 2010–11 season. Perhaps because of the strains of competition and the tensions thereby generated, the breaking of the code of co-existence between the two teams seriously threatened to destroy the majestic image that Real Madrid had maintained for over a century.

CHAPTER 5

HUMILIATION

'Machiavelli says that whosoever wants to cheat, will find somebody who allows themselves to be cheated, proving that if there are no more lies, it is not for want of somebody who would believe them, but for the difficulty of finding he who is resolved to lie.'

LUCIO V. MANSILLA, *An Expedition to the Ranquel Indians*

Sunday 28 November 2010, and staying in the hotel Rey Juan Carlos on the Avenida Diagonal in Barcelona is a true believer, a man of unshakeable conviction. A native of Vitoria, pale skinned, with a prominent nose and wavy hair, the man is pleased to be where he is, in this uniform, with this badge, and following the orders of a visionary leader. Aitor Karanka believes in José Mourinho.

The assistant seemed animated by a childlike excitement. With his contralto voice conveying a devout enthusiasm, he confessed his faith to all those on the trip – at the airport, on the bus, in the dining room, in the meeting room, in the glass elevator of the giant hotel hall, as the hours passed that would lead inexorably to the Camp Nou.

'We're going to give them a footballing lesson,' Karanka repeated to his listeners. 'We're going to give them a footballing lesson.'

The passion of Mourinho's assistant contrasted with the scepticism among the Spanish players when the coach met them at 11.00 a.m. on the 29th to give the team-talk before the first *clásico* of the season. The coach was displaying all his usual self-confidence – the body language, the seductive poses – conscious that his talk was merely a way of getting his own players on his side, infusing them with the same mixture of pleasure and fear as in an initiation ritual. One of them joked, 'He thinks he's George Clooney!' While the meeting was going on, nobody spoke. No one commented or questioned anything as Mourinho told them how they were going to ambush Barcelona.

Mourinho asked them to press in what he called 'low-block', except at those times when they would go higher up the pitch, pressing in 'medium-block' at goal-kicks, throw-ins and attacking corners. He reminded them to maintain 'medium-block' only while Barcelona were trying to play the first and second pass. On the third pass they were told to return to their own half. To bear out this approach he showed them a video of a recent game between Barcelona and Villarreal that Barça won 3–1, in which Villarreal could be seen pressing their rivals in their half, trying to ensure that the periods of possession enjoyed by Xavi and the others were short and uncomfortable. The players recall Mourinho being absolutely certain that he had the answer and citing Villarreal as an example of exactly what not to do: 'Maybe Barcelona think we're going to press them high up the pitch like those fools from Villarreal ...'

For Mourinho, the fundamentals of 'pressing' came from the principles – and with the terminology – of Victor Frade, retired Professor at the University of Porto and Director of Methodology at FC Porto. Frade was known by coaches across Europe for creating the 'tactical periodisation' method, which took over in importance from the methodologies that had previously dominated team sports until the 90s. Pioneers such as Frade in Portugal and Paco Seirul-lo in Spain concentrated their training session on playing with a ball, dispensing with linear-based, non-ball-playing exercises derived from athletics. The new theorists such as Frade argued that players only get better if you invite them to solve complex problems during a game situation, and not when they are just repeating a mechanical formula on a piece of apparatus. As a coach and driver of this new trend, Juanma Lillo said, 'If there's one thing that's not linear it's a human being.'

Guardiola and Mourinho drank from the same theoretical spring but their methods were quite different. Guardiola was a virtuoso when it came to organising the attack and defence to the point where they harmonised, as if there were a wholly natural transition between the two. Mourinho's talent, by contrast, lay in building defensive models. Guardiola built his defence on the way his team organised themselves with the ball; Mourinho built his attack on the way his teams defended. Pressing can be understood as a collective, synchronised movement to win back the ball. It is a defensive exercise that can also be used as an offensive tool if applied in the right places and at the right times.

Mourinho gave lectures on pressing with all the poise of someone who feels they are an innovator in the field. He insisted to his players that possession of the ball does not have value in itself and, if not treated with extreme care, at times can be dangerous. He said that the more resources opposing teams had, the more caution should be shown when moving the ball through the middle of the pitch. 'The more the ball circulates in midfield, the more likely it is that the other team will dispossess us,' he could be heard repeating to his players. The saying had a reverse logic – the more the opponent had the ball in midfield, the greater their exposure and vulnerability to well-applied pressure. Using Mourinho's tactics, Madrid spent many hours practising retreating to create space for the opponent to enter into, as one might lure someone into a deep gorge. The players called these movements 'decoys'. The opposing team had the ball, moved with it into the space that was offered to them, and when they stepped into the middle of the pitch near the centre circle, the pressure activated by Madrid robbed them of possession and they were hit by a counter-attack. That last part of the strategy was what least worried the coach, who emphasised the need to channel the offensive movement to the flanks if possible, and requested that it be done at speed. More than three passes could pose an unreasonable risk.

Using Frade's terminology, Mourinho understood that pressing is divided into three categories – low, medium or high – depending on the part of the pitch in which it is applied. The low-block consisted of putting the defensive line and the midfield on the edge of the area. The medium-block was practised 60 feet further forward. The high-block meant putting the defensive line on the edge of the centre-circle, sometimes as far up as the halfway line, the midfielders pressing the opponent's half. For Mourinho, the high-block was the climax of attacking football. The team regularly used it for opposition throw-ins in the opposing half, and for attacking corners. He also used it frequently in emergency situations. If time was running out and the team needed a goal, the high-block was the solution. But against strong opponents, especially against Barcelona, pressing with the high-block was considered a risky and seldom-used tactic.

Casillas, Alonso, Ramos, Albiol and Arbeloa knew Barça better than Mourinho. Not only had they faced Guardiola's team a few times. They had won a World Cup playing with Xavi, Iniesta, Villa, Busquets, Pedro, Piqué and Puyol, and they understood their way of thinking. They sensed that the best way to hurt them was suffocating them at source, pressing the first pass out from Valdés. Mourinho did not see it like that at all, so among the players there was a sense of fatalism. 'We're going to sit back,' they said. 'Barça will have control of the ball 20 metres from our goal, and sooner or later ...'

HUMILIATION

Xabi Alonso offered the most incisive analysis, based on an informal meeting with some players at the hotel. At 29 years old, the Basque midfielder was the latest in a line of highly respected players in his family. His father, Periko, had been a midfielder for the national team and Barcelona, and he himself was instrumental in Spain winning the World Cup in South Africa. His experience in the Premier League as an important player for Liverpool in 2005 when they won the Champions League earned him extra credit among his colleagues. Alonso told his team-mates that Mourinho's vision had lost its relevance months ago. He recalled that in the semi-finals of the Champions League in 2010, when Inter beat Barça, the interfering presence of Ibrahimović in Messi's space disrupted Barcelona's ability to play the final pass. Barcelona did not have that problem any more. Alonso observed that Mourinho's plan could work against the Barça of Ibrahimović, a relatively immobile centre-forward who was easy for central defenders to mark, but Ibrahimović was not playing at the club now and Iniesta had just recovered from a long period of injury that had kept him out of the 2010 semi-final. The mobility of Pedro, Messi and Villa, with Iniesta and Xavi appearing from behind, would leave the defence without a reference point and turn the 'low-block' into something close to suicide – Barcelona's passing options were so multifarious that it would be impossible to close off all routes to goal.

'Today, we're going to have to run a lot,' he said.

At 3 p.m. on 29 November Mourinho gave his fourth pre-match team-talk. He announced that Benzema would play up front on his own and that Ronaldo would move to the right wing, switching positions with Di María, who would become the custodian of Alves on the other flank. Those present say that the instructions directed at Mesut Özil took up much of the meeting, Mourinho always reserving the most complex list of demands for the German midfielder. Not only was he assigned the mission of playing passes to the forwards and arriving in the box himself. He was also given the job of working defensively in three or four areas.

Given that the general plan predisposed Madrid to defend mainly in their own half, there was a risk that the team would be over-stretched once their own attacks had broken down. To avoid that, Özil had to be alert so he could stop Piqué coming out with the ball or Busquets and Xavi receiving it, depending on where he found himself on the pitch when Madrid lost possession. In brief, he had to cover the spaces between the defenders and the strikers; he had to be decisive in attack; creative in looking to pick out Benzema and Ronaldo; and, when possession was lost, capable of pressing high up the pitch against whoever was on the ball, before coming back and lining up to assist Alonso and Khedira. These were Özil's tasks, and nobody else was given such physically demanding and tactically diverse responsibilities by Mourinho.

The success of Inter in the semi-finals of the 2010 Champions League was influenced as much as by events outside of football as by the technical decisions of the two coaches and Mourinho's conservative tactics. However, Mourinho seemed convinced that the final result was a consequence of his organising genius alone. He simply replayed his old plan, ignoring any new information available to him. As if he had not contemplated the effect of the eruption of the Eyjafjallajökull volcano, forcing Barça to travel by bus to Milan, affecting them physically; as if he did not take into consideration the fact that Iniesta could not play and that his place in the team was taken by Keita – as if Iniesta's return and Villa's signing had not changed the nature of Barça, making reassessment necessary. In short, as if he thought Madrid's players would respond as Inter's had, giving on the pitch what really proved so decisive in the semi-finals: the desperate self-sacrifice of players who knew they were on the verge of achieving something unique. The Inter players, veterans at the very start of decline, knew that there would be no more shots at glory. The Madrid team was full of inexperienced players, too tender – and too talented – to really put in such a shift against Barça. Mourinho's contempt for thinking that anything had fundamentally changed was something his own players saw before stepping out on to the Camp Nou pitch to experience what Ricardo Carvalho described to a team-mate as 'the most embarrassing match of my life'.

In the ninth minute Xavi burst through, lifted the ball above Casillas and scored. In the 14th minute Pedro put away the second. Madrid's plan was already officially useless.

Wrapped in a black coat and standing under an incessant down-pour, Mourinho reorganised his team. He ordered them to press higher up the pitch and swapped the positions of Di María and Ronaldo so they were both coming inside on their stronger foot – as they had been doing all season – because it made them more comfortable when they shot at goal. Until the break, however, the game belonged to Barcelona. On returning to the dressing room the players expected a major intervention from Mourinho, urging them to turn the match around and offering them tactical solutions. But the coach was restrained. His decision to put Lass on in place of Özil was a clear indication that he was more interested in defence than attack.

The overriding feeling in the squad was that no Madrid player was more skilful than Özil. At 22, the young midfielder from Gelsenkirchen was a rare case in the world of elite football, which was defined as much by jealousy, individualism and internal competition as by camaraderie. Özil, who hardly spoke any Spanish but understood everything that was said to him, was admired by his team-mates. In every training session they saw him do things that other players could not do. His controls, his feints, the ease with which he played in confined spaces, his ability to find ways of passing through labyrinthine defences, his excellent touch with both feet – all these made him a player without equal. He had arrived in Spain just four months earlier and had won over the group in a short time. Removing him from the pitch was little more than capitulation. It was Mourinho's way of admitting the superiority of Barcelona and his inability to offer any sort of solution.

If the players had expected a rousing speech when they went back to the dressing room at the break, all they found was Casillas, close to despair. It was shocking for players who had only been at the club a short time to see the captain, usually so introverted, pleading:

'Let them see that we're at least running. Right now there are millions of people watching TV, millions who won't sleep tonight. At least let them see us running.'

The re-start had a special significance. The decision to line up Lass, Khedira and Alonso in midfield constituted the start of a long – although ultimately failed – experiment. Here was the first sighting of what Mourinho called the 'high-pressure triangle'. Conceived, as the name suggests, to exert pressure by having players covering more ground, this tactical model worked better without the ball than with it. Once the team had recovered the ball, the pressure was unnecessary but the triangle remained, as an invasive presence, obliging the team to play their passes around the scaffolding of a building in ruins, or to hit longer, higher, less considered passes. The 'high-pressure triangle' took 12 minutes to fail, the time it took Villa to put Barcelona 3–0 up.

Under teeming rain, the Camp Nou echoed to chants of 'Come out from the dugout, Mourinho, come out from the dugout …' Since the restart he had been sitting on the bench under the transparent roof looking out on to the technical area, when on the hour he made a substitution that he would increasing rely on: Marcelo off and Arbeloa on in his place. He was discarding one of the world's best attacking full-backs for an obedient man, a pure defender, someone reluctant to cross the halfway line. The substitution was meant to prevent an even heavier thrashing, but all it succeeded in doing was ending all hope of a comeback – it also did nothing to guarantee any more defensive security. Madrid had four shots on goal in the first half and one in the second. But Barça kept on attacking, more frequently and to greater effect. They had seven shots in the first half and eight in the second.

Villa made it 4–0 after outwitting Pepe with four dance steps: he walked the 'ledge' of Madrid's offside trap, went past his marker and then came back before darting diagonally towards the goal and on to a pass from Messi. The fifth goal went a long way towards illustrating the limitations of Madrid's second-half tactical response.

Mourinho had put on Arbeloa to challenge hard – to foul if necessary – as the first act of pressing after losing the ball. Arbeloa squeezed up near to the halfway line, then raised his boot to Iniesta's head height, narrowly missing the midfielder. It was a foul, but referee Eduardo Iturralde González played the advantage and Iniesta delivered a pass to Bojan, who had come on for Villa in the 75th minute. Bojan raced down the right, and Madrid's pressing game wilted: the newly deployed two banks of four markers could not close down the space when Bojan changed the direction of play. Neither Khedira nor Lass, nor Di María, got back quickly enough; it was one of those situations that Mourinho had tried to avoid at all costs: four on four. Bojan, Iniesta, Messi and Jeffren against Arbeloa, Carvalho, Pepe and Ramos. Madrid's defenders were tilted towards the left – freeing up the right flank – and they had no time to readjust. Jeffren received the ball in space behind Ramos, whom he turned easily before scoring.

When Mourinho sat in the Camp Nou media room he radiated the serenity of the Buddhist monk Bodhidharma. He had been at Madrid for five months and no one had ever seen him so quiet.

'It's the worst defeat of my career. I've never lost 5–0. There's no doubt about that. But it's an easy defeat to digest. Because it's a defeat where there was no chance of winning. It's not one of those defeats where you're left with a bitter taste because it's difficult to accept, because you've not deserved to lose but you've lost, or you've lost because the referee has influenced the result, or because you've hit the post, or because of bad luck. No. It's none of these things. A team have played to their potential and another team have played badly. A deserved victory, and a very deserved defeat.'

Few press conferences from Mourinho were as measured as this. The calm surface, however, concealed a murky whirlpool. The argument he presented for the changes he had made hinted at the pessimism he felt at the half-time break, the certainty that the best he could do was avoid a thrashing because the lead held at the 45th minute could not be pegged back.

'When you're 2–0 down against a side that's very dangerous and very quick on the counter-attack, you have two options. You either say, "I'll take 2–0" or you say, "I'm going to try to press higher up the pitch, I'm going to give the opposition more space and then they hit you on the counter-attack and score more goals …" I tried to help the team during the break; the only thing I wanted was that the team didn't lose its balance in midfield and that it continued to play with dignity until the end … I've always said that Barça are the finished product. And I've always said that Madrid are not the finished product; and they're a long way from being so.'

In the days before the *clásico* a cloud of frustrating unease formed around Mourinho, with the coach feeling that he lacked support. He saw the presence of Valdano as a threat. He thought the club required too much from him and gave back very little in return. He thought that Pérez ignored him every time he asked for a centre-forward, such as when he put forward the name of Hugo Almeida. The recent good news meant these concerns had been temporarily sidestepped. In the two months between the 0–0 at Levante and their visit to the Camp Nou, Real had put together a string of good results. The thrashings of Deportivo (6–1), Málaga (1–4), Racing (6–1), Hércules (1–3), Atlético (5–1) and Ajax (0–4) seemed to show that the team was developing successfully. This was probably the most brilliant period of play for Mourinho's Madrid. The cohesion with which his team attacked, the absence of the restrictive tactics that would later become standard fare, the freedom afforded some players – all this made the fans think that the coach had tried to develop a mode of play that coincided with Spanish fans' tastes.

The results were reflected in Mourinho's mood. When he was in a good mood he transmitted it immediately. After pre-match meals, he would call everyone's attention, raising his voice and telling jokes. 'He's a showman,' the players said. 'Here comes the showman again!' But on 29 November – after the Barça game – the show was over and the his mood changed dramatically. He became irritable and unpredictable. Players found that he had a bottomless capacity to provoke difficult – and unprecedented – situations. Valencia, Zaragoza and Sevilla, the three games that followed before Christmas, involved one confrontation after another.

Valencia's visit to the Bernabéu on Saturday 4 December, five days after the 5–0, caused one of those unexpected moments. When Mourinho brought the group together to talk tactics, the players found a man on the verge of a nervous breakdown. According to the testimony of some of those present, the coach talked about the ups and downs of the team in the first person, as was his strange habit:

'Today is not a tactical team-talk. Today what matters is the heart. Today what matters is my son. This week my son is home from school, crying because I was beaten 5–0! Today we've got to play for the pride of my son!'

The boss's son José Mario Mourinho was named after his father. He was aged 10 and the players knew him well. Sometimes the coach would bring him to Valdebebas, and he used to go down to the dressing room at the Bernabéu after watching matches from behind the bench. But for Mourinho to include the boy in the team-talk baffled the players, almost as much as his team selection. He dropped his centre-forward and picked the *trivote* – Khedira, Alonso and Lass – to start for the first time.

Only the sending-off of Albelda in the 65th minute brought calm to a team who had played the most turgid first half of football seen at Chamartín that season. Up against 10 men, Özil and Ronaldo were unstoppable. Ronaldo scored both goals in the match, one in the 73th minute and one in the 87th.

Mindful of the media reaction to his ultra-defensive line-up – and well aware of how it might be seen as an affront to footballing good taste – Mourinho used the subsequent press conference to justify himself. Sigmund Freud would have said that when Mourinho spoke of the self-esteem of the team, what he was really doing was recognising his own inner weakness:

'Today, we were lacking in a bit of self-esteem and confidence, and the most important thing was to start the game without suffering too much. That's why I changed the team: with the intention of not suffering. Because I could imagine what would happen to my team and to the fans if we lost control of the match early on. We have problems at the back, and with conceding the first goal. That could have finished off what little self-esteem the team had. For that reason I decided to play with a fuller, more defensively capable midfield.'

Casillas, Arbeloa, Pepe, Albiol, Marcelo, Khedira, Alonso, Lass, Di María, Özil and Ronaldo made up the strikerless formation. For Mourinho, it was both a way of pointing the finger of blame at Benzema for his disastrous showing at the Camp Nou and of insisting that the club bring in another number nine. Mourinho also explained to those closest to him that the 5–0 had served to confirm his worse fears. For as much as the public and the press demanded attacking football, the last *clásico* had shown that the team were not mature enough for such a proposal. That rout had reaffirmed his fundamental principle: pressure was the most important part of the game and the team could not face strong rivals without the right players to apply it. Inside him, both a phobia and a fondness were developing. A phobia of Benzema and a fondness for the *trivote* as a lucky weapon against Barça.

From the time of the Greek historian Polybius in *The Histories*, there has been no shortage of public figures who have explained their success by their pragmatism. One of Mourinho's most repetitive claims during his first months at Madrid was that he thought of himself as a pragmatist. He used the term 'pragmatic' to explain a tactical decision, as a slogan or as a clinching argument. He would often preface his reflections by noting the empirical-utilitarian vision of his coaching work: 'I'm very pragmatic …' In April 2012, during an interview with *Audi Magazine*, he verged on self-parody when he said: 'From a pragmatic point of view, I consider myself a great coach.'

Laying bare his empirical approach he distanced himself from other idealistic coaches, famous for seeing things only through their own dogmas. Time, however, showed that Mourinho was also wrapped up in principles that he could not easily shake off. One of these principles was 'mental aggression'.

At the end of November a back injury put Higuaín out of action for several months. The Argentine forward was the coach's favourite striker and in the summer he had announced that he would play him more than Benzema. Mourinho had become exasperated with the

Frenchman's sluggish character, his apparent compliance in any situation and his indifference to all advice or warnings.

Pérez, however, liked Benzema more than any of Madrid's other strikers. The president had personally overseen his signing from Lyon in 2009, paying €35 million for him after visiting his home and speaking with his parents. The boy had the reputation of being a genius and at youth level had been talked of as a future Ballon d'Or winner. At the end of 2010 he was about to turn 23. As fascinated by rap music as he was by football, the game more than anything seemed to stimulate his sense of hedonism. Some players shine thanks to the rage they have accumulated over the years, others because they are motivated by pleasure. Benzema was in the second category and his attitude clashed directly with the principle of 'mental aggression'.

The three goals that Benzema scored against Auxerre in the last group match of the Champions League did not convince Mourinho. On 12 December, before travelling to play Real Zaragoza at La Romareda, the media asked the coach if he wanted to sign another number nine. In reply, Mourinho bemoaned his helplessness working alongside Valdano, and criticised Benzema, stressing the need for a centre-forward whose style would be more to his liking.

'The subject of signings is something that concerns people who are higher up in the club and doesn't go through me,' he lamented. 'I already said in the summer that it would be difficult to go through a season with only Benzema and Higuaín. And if I have to face the second part of the season with just Benzema it will be even more difficult. I'm just the coach, nothing more. If you have a dog to go hunting with, you catch more; if you have a cat, you catch less, but you can still hunt. We only have one attacker, and that's Benzema.'

Ronaldo's omission from the list of strikers was as strange a move from Mourinho as his downgrading of Benzema in his own personal zoological scale. But what the dressing room found most repugnant was Mourinho's behaviour on the bench at La Romareda. He spent half the game closely following Benzema, criticising his every move with volleys of abuse. Mourinho lost control after Benzema showed how uncomfortable he was playing with his back to the central defender, receiving long passes to bring down and lay off to the advancing midfielders. 'This is a disgrace,' he shouted. 'He's not even a cat. He's a rabbit!'

With every mistake on the pitch, Mourinho would turn to his assistants in search of agreement, or he'd look enquiringly at the substitutes, as if he were waiting for a sign of approval. His outbursts of anger became so frequent that, to spare themselves the aggravation, his players ended up fighting over the seats that were furthest away from him. No one wanted to be party to the ill-treatment of a team-mate. Madrid won 1–3 at La Romareda, but it was the penultimate step on the road to a looming internal crisis.

Madrid played the last game of the year at the Bernabéu against Sevilla on Sunday 19 December. It was a bad game. Alonso's absence had stripped the side of the one player capable of imposing order on the match, and when the referee signalled the break the score was an unsettling 0–0. The players were together in a group in the tunnel when Silvino Louro, the goalkeeping coach, went for Cristóbal Soria, the Sevilla official. He acted with such violence that neither friends nor enemies were spared. There was a charge, a shove and a fall. In the melée Agustín Herrerín, the Madrid pitch official, was pushed to the ground. At 75 years old, the man was an institution among employees of the club. Herrerín defended Louro, claiming Soria had taunted the home bench with the open-hand sign that referred unambiguously to the 5–0 defeat at Barça.

Di María's goal in the 77th minute, after referee Carlos Clos Gómez had sent Carvalho off, did nothing to end the unrest in the home dugout. In the heat of the moment, Mourinho threw a passionate –

albeit coldly calculated – fit of rage. When Miguel Pardeza, the director of football and right-hand man to Valdano, went down to the dressing room to congratulate the players, the coach, witnessed by the squad, launched into a barrage of abuse:

'You lot say that this is a noble club but this is a fucking shit club. Now you can go and you can say this to the president and his friends … Now I'm going on holiday. If you want to sack me, then that's fine by me, I won't come back. I'll be happy to go because this is a fucking shit club.'

Pardeza maintained his composure and denied that what Mourinho had just said was true. The coach seemed beside himself as he headed off to the press room, holding a piece of paper.

'They've given me a list with 13 serious mistakes,' he said, taking out a folder with the supposed errors of referee Carlos Clos Gómez. 'Today. They asked me in the last press conference if I was tired of the pressure. I'm not tired of the pressure because I don't feel pressured doing the things that I like to do. And I like to coach and I like very much to play matches. What I'm a little bit tired of is this, for example. That they give me a list of 13 serious mistakes from the referee and I defend my team. My team has to be defended because my team deserves to be defended. Not just today but many times over. And if I go ahead with this list, the story will be the same. I will be on the front pages: "Mourinho suspended". We have a club, a structure, an organisation. And I want people to stand up for my team, as it's not always going to be about me. I just want to say that I have an out-of-this-world team, with an out-of-this-world character. We have achieved what seemed impossible … I prefer not to talk about it anymore. I prefer to request a meeting with the president. I would rather talk to the president.'

Speaking about referees has always been one of Mourinho's favoured tactics over the course of his career. In December 2010 he spoke about them for two reasons: they were the perfect alibi when his team played poorly and they enabled him to question the role of Valdano at the club. Annoyed that Valdano was opposed to the signing of Hugo Almeida, Mourinho sought ways to attack him, suggesting that Valdano would do well to spend more time criticising referees.

That night Pérez went to bed in the early hours with some unpleasant things on his mind. According to a close associate, it occurred to him that if he sacked the coach he would not have to pay any compensation: the contract stipulated that in case of termination, no one had a duty to compensate anyone. But he also asked himself the fateful question: If not Mourinho, then who? Who else can lead Madrid if we bid farewell to the man I myself have described as the best coach in the world? Without Mourinho – and even with him – a deserted landscape dominated by Barcelona lay before him. More unprecedented failure – with nobody to blame but the president, the author of the signing, one that would mark his mandate for better or for worse. A president who ought to have taken more care of his image, his aura of being a solid leader, solvent, with convictions. He could not turn his back, after just six months, on the biggest gamble of his presidential career since the signing of Beckham. The following day he would be playing host at the club's traditional Christmas dinner with both the football and basketball squads. A director explained away the previous night's nightmare with some soothing words: 'Mou's soul is still wounded by the 5–0 …'

Mourinho appeared calm as he sat at the table with captain Casillas, the honorary president Alfredo Di Stéfano and Pérez. As if nothing had happened, he smiled and tucked in to the pheasant served with caramelised onions. Pérez took the microphone and, before starting on the congratulations, entered into a dialogue with Di Stéfano, by way of digression:

'There are people who think that they're qualified to work in any business, but not everyone is. Real Madrid is the biggest company and represents the biggest challenge. You, Alfredo, you came with me when FIFA gave us the trophy for being the best club of the twentieth century. There's the trophy … It's not easy to cope with this pressure. You have to live under the pressure within the club to really know it. I understand that some find it impossible and end up going crazy. Because this is not a pressure for everyone …'

Di Stéfano nodded his head: 'Of course …' Casillas blushed with embarrassment. The basketball players followed the speech without really understanding what was happening. Mourinho stared into the distance.

The private meeting – a dinner – between Mourinho and Pérez was held in late January. The president told his friends that the coach was insistent on renewing Pepe's contract and the need to sign Hugo Almeida to replace Higuaín, and explained his wish to coach Portugal's national team, something he considered feasible only if his sole responsibility was training Madrid's first team. But none of the issues that the coach touched on made the president very excited. The coldness of the meeting prompted Mourinho to come up with one of those statements that would circulate through the offices of the Bernabéu that winter:

'I'm not the coach you thought I was, and you're not the president I expected.'

Pérez realised that his coach did not just want to coach. 'He's not happy just training,' he said after the dinner. The defeat at the Camp Nou had helped remove the mask successfully worn Mourinho up until that point. Mourinho required the complete transformation of the club, saying that the need to resist Barça was a compelling reason for this. He argued that to win a trophy against them, whether it be the league, the Copa del Rey or the Champions League, he would have to beat a team that had just inflicted the worst defeat of his career on him. There was no way to avoid the confrontation. For the first time in many years he felt seriously threatened by a failure that had the potential to haunt his path for ever. Distraught and unable to focus, his reaction was unsurprising: put pressure on his players, pressurise the club and come up with excuses later to explain away the predictable outcome.

The need to counter Barça coloured all his requests to Madrid. He asked for powers to direct sports strategy, co-ordinate the ins and outs at the club, and reform the chain of command. He wanted to be the one who chose which players joined the club and which were transferred. Without interference. There were to be no more lists imposed by the club. He argued that Valdano was expendable and he continued to suggest signings from the portfolio of his agent Jorge Mendes. And he remained insistent on the need to buy Hugo Almeida.

Pérez, however, dealt with the situation in his customary way. He did not say yes or no, but promised to give all these things some consideration. He did not rule out Hugo Almeida, nor did he defend Valdano. Moreover, he won time for himself, trying not to show any of his cards until the end of the hand. Every time he needed to justify a delay he said that Madrid belonged to its members and that there was a process that needed to be followed. Mourinho, shrewd like few others at detecting weaknesses in his counterparts during face-to-face exchanges, found these arguments hard to rebuff. Whether at Porto, Chelsea or Inter, he had never encountered such administrative obstacles – for him the club's presidential system was a useless extravagance.

Pérez consulted his advisors as he mulled over a decision. The people the president listened to most were Valdano; José Angel

Sanchez, the corporate director general; Enrique Pérez, director and his own brother; Manuel Redondo, the director general of the presidency; and Fernando Fernández Tapias, the vice president. Another name may be added to the list, a friend who ended up influencing Pérez far more than the others over the years: Antonio García Ferreras, head of the TV channel laSexta, and one of the most influential men in Spanish political journalism.

The 5–0 defeat, an abject failure from a coaching point of view, was transformed by Mourinho into a political triumph. Something that had originated in serious tactical errors ended up strengthening Mourinho's position, extending his powers to a level that had only ever been previously enjoyed by Madrid's president. Sensing that any gesture of taking responsibility for the defeat would weaken him, he acted with unusual political skill to transform a momentous defeat into an opportunity for personal empowerment. Here he employed public mockery, veiled threats, propaganda and – in no short measure – audacity. He used the 5–0 as a lever to remove everything that seemed inconvenient to him within the club. The uproar that began after 29 November lasted until the spring. It was a sustained crisis, with not a moment's rest. As one player said, 'There's trouble here every day.'

In the midst of the conflict over signing another number nine, Valdano said he was banned from Valdebebas and from official flights. The signing of a centre-forward, Emmanuel Adebayor, on loan until June, failed to bring an end to the skirmishes. Tensions continued into January, February and March, and news was leaked from the dressing room that favouritism, capriciousness and division between the privileged and the not so privileged – all according to their proximity to Jorge Mendes – were rife. Every time a player's agent called the club to bemoan the influence of Mendes over the decisions of the coach, the answer from Pérez's entourage was the same: everyone knew that Mourinho would bring confrontations with the press and the referees; what no one foresaw was 'the other'. 'The other' was the code name for all matters linked to Mourinho's tendency to direct operations towards outcomes that apparently favoured the interests of the Mendes group, to which he himself belonged.

In early March 2011 news spread in the president's inner circle that Pérez was preparing a back-up plan, just in case Mourinho did not win a trophy and he was forced to fire him. 'There's a 90 per cent chance that the coach will not continue next season,' Pérez told a friend. The factors against the coach included his mismanagement of people, the damage he inflicted on the club's image, the poor football played by the team and, above all, the limited chances of winning a trophy that would justify the extravagance of the project.

'This way of playing does not guarantee trophies,' the directors told each other in the corridors of the stadium. They let slip to Valdano that they would never allow Mourinho to take over all managerial duties and that sports policy would remain the exclusive responsibility of the club. Valdano and Pérez began searching for a possible emergency coach. Juan Carlos Garrido, at the time having a good season with Villarreal in the Europa League, Rafa Benítez, who maintained frequent contact with Pérez, and Alberto Toril, coach of Real Madrid Castilla, were considered as alternatives.

The relationship between the players and the coach deteriorated. Pérez said many players called him complaining that Mourinho was unjust in his decisions. And it was not only the players who complained. The president said that the coach had serious problems even with the doctors and cooks.

Every time Mourinho felt threatened he responded with propaganda and agitation. He used his presentations in the press room like a surgical instrument, a case in point being when he took advantage of the visit of Manuel Pellegrini's Málaga on 3 March. Pellegrini, who had been his predecessor in the Madrid dugout, provided the combustible material. Asked if his situation was comparable to the Chilean's in the previous year, Mourinho blazed, 'No, because if Madrid get rid of me I'll not end up coaching Málaga. If Madrid get rid of me, I'll go to a big club in England or Italy. I'll have no problem in ending up back at a big club.'

Fernando Fernández Tapias was one of the directors most offended by these words. The shipping magnate requested his immediate dismissal as the only way to restore the club's institutional image. More than just offending Málaga, what upset several members of the Madrid board was the lack of respect shown to Madrid. It was the coldness with which he had said that it was all the same to him whichever 'big club' chose to hire him. Pérez believed the words to be 'inadmissible', telling a close friend that if Madrid were knocked out of the Champions League against Lyon he would start a campaign to bring down Mourinho and replace him at the end of the season. The next day, during the pre-match meet-up in the Sheraton Mirasierra hotel, Pérez made the coach aware of how badly the board had taken his comments and asked him to retract them in the post-match press conference.

There are moments that determine the mood of an entire era. The meet-up on 2 and 3 March was the first time that the players had observed the coach adopt an attitude that mixed melancholy, a generalised resentment, suspicion and indolence. Suddenly, he was not even acknowledging people. He treated as strangers those he had previously treated as friends. There were no more jokes. He did not talk with people who not so long ago he had playfully teased. He felt he could be betrayed by the people around him. In the dressing room a rumour started that over the years would become recurrent, periodically spoken, like a litany: 'He wants to leave.'

HUMILIATION

The 0–0 draw in the Riazor on 26 February left Mourinho contemplating a distressing idea: that the team was being swamped in the early parts of matches, and was then not able to come back and win games. In the team-talk before the match against Málaga he emphasised this point: 'We're not going to give away the first half.' This kind of team meeting usually lasted 45 minutes but now it was cut drastically short, being over in less than 10 minutes. It seemed scandalous to many of the players to suggest that they were starting games with reduced intensity, especially taking into account the fact that it was the coach himself who insisted on inviting the opposition forward by using the medium-block.

Most of the dressing room began to feel a crippling fatigue. Players used the word 'burnout' to describe the permanent state of mental exhaustion brought on by the complaints of a coach who not only never seemed satisfied, but also hinted that he did not appear to believe in the honesty of the group. Ricardo Carvalho, who had worked under Mourinho for a decade, reassured his team-mates, explaining that Mourinho had done the same at Chelsea. He summoned trouble up out of nothing just to introduce more pressure.

Madrid beat Málaga 7–0. But, rather than being a joyful occasion, Mourinho's post-match press conference was loaded with bitter irony. There was no end to the caustic messages aimed at the directors who had earlier rebuked him, begging him to offer up a public excuse. He began by complaining about the conspiracy mounted by TV schedulers, who in his opinion designed a deliberately difficult calendar that had been meekly accepted by the club:

'News reaches me that we'll probably have to play against Lyon on Wednesday and then against Atlético Madrid on Saturday, which will be just fantastic after the others [Barcelona] play on Tuesday and Sunday. But, of course, for the sake of the club's image we should not report this type of thing. So we keep quiet and pretend everyone's very happy, and on we go.'

He was asked if he had considered apologising to Málaga, but he apologised to himself instead:

'If you ask those who work in the top clubs if they'd go to Málaga, they'd answer you: "Why not?" But it would not be true. They would not go! If I have to apologise I will, but the truth is I responded without hypocrisy. In a hypocritical world, not being a hypocrite is seen as a defect … Obviously, I've nothing against Málaga, neither the club nor the professionals who work there; I simply responded honestly without hypocrisy. It's not a problem for me. I've said from the start that the day that people are not happy with me I will go. It's not a problem. The fact that they don't want me is not any pressure for me.'

Pérez saw the press conference as a direct confrontation. Even José Ángel Sánchez moderated his defence of the coach. The corporate director general had previously argued that Spanish society was not mature enough to assimilate the pioneering vision of Mourinho. Now, however, he admitted that if Mourinho did not win a trophy he would become an unbearable burden for the club.

Mourinho has never looked so suffocated as he did in the first week of March. It was then, however, that he began to gain the full support of Pérez – for reasons that even those closest to the president have not been able to clarify.

Mourinho thus began his advance towards the power that had until then been the exclusive prerogative of the man chosen every four years at the polls. The president was careful not to reveal what was said, and from the directors' box it was whispered that only the two people involved knew of the reasons for the great change. Suddenly, Pérez, previously so reluctant to support the coach in his attempts to wrestle more power – and such a jealous guardian of the club's institutional image – became docile. Gradually, he began to allow the club itself to allow such allegations, both formal and informal, against the integrity of Barça's players, against referees, against UEFA and against TV schedulers. At this point Valdano was being moved back into the shadows without knowing it. His head was soon to be served up on a platter.

The speech that sealed the deal was given by Pérez during a ceremony to award medals to some of the club's oldest members. There, the Madrid president formally reformed the scope of the notion 'Madridismo' by reclassifying a phrase that had until now had not applied to Mourinho: the 'señorio' of Real Madrid. Until then this word, meaning nobility or dignity, had summed up an ideal of sportsmanship that was treated as an unshakeable and distinctive principle of the club. The old hymn reflected this ethos in the verse, 'If you lose, shake hands'. Señorio necessarily implied a self-control that went against the coach's desire to operate without restrictions. Sánchez, together with Antonio García Ferreras, head of the TV channel La Sexta, a close friend and advisor to Pérez, applauded the initiative. But it was Pérez himself who put his face to the change, reading the following words:

'This institution is proud of what we call señorio. Señorio is recognising the merits of the adversary, but it is also defending what we believe is right and denouncing irregular conduct, whether inside or outside the institution. Defending Real Madrid from what we think is unfair, irregular and arbitrary is also Madridismo. And that is precisely what our coach José Mourinho does. What José Mourinho says is also Madridismo.'

The final reconciliation between the two men was staged before the workforce. On 15 March Mourinho invited Pérez to dinner with the team on the eve of the second leg of the second-round Champions

League match against Lyon at the Bernabéu. The point was to win something. Winning a trophy. Any trophy. This was the message to Mourinho, a condition of granting him those ultimate powers that he had requested. The coach realised immediately that his fate rested in the hands of the players. To persuade them to offer him their support he conceived of a surprise encounter. During the pre-match meet-up ahead of the game against Atlético at the Calderón on 19 March, he called everyone to attend what they thought would be a tactics talk but was instead 20 unforgettable minutes. Mourinho, said one of the directors, is 'a speaker who binds his players up with his talk'. That is exactly what he did in a monologue that an assistant recalled as follows:

'I'm going to tell you something. I think you should know. I hate to be hypocritical. I'm honest. I'm not a liar. At the end of the season, either Valdano goes or I go. I cannot bear him and it's been that way from day one. If I stay the only thing I'll not be taking care of is the basketball and the financial side of things. But if I stay then I'll have maximum responsibility for everything related to the football. And the people who have the key to all this are you. If we win, I'll stay and he [Valdano] will be got rid of. If you lose, he stays and I go. And so, from here on in I'll be observing who's with the team and who's thinking about other things.'

The players were stunned. Most felt as if they were being put in an impossible situation. There was a makeshift parliament. According to one of those present, Alonso and Lass took the lead. 'We've got into a very strange situation,' they said. 'This is not professional. What's happening? Do they want us to be accomplices? Do they want us to be the judges of Valdano? If he goes it's because we've got rid of him, and if not, we're the motherfuckers [who have got rid of Mourinho].'

They soon realised that they were trapped. Anyone who had a bad day – in any game – would automatically become a suspect. If the team won, Mourinho would use the fact to show the president that the dressing room was with him and not with Valdano. There was no honourable way out.

CHAPTER 6

FEAR

'If I were to judge the worth of emotions by their intensity, none would be more valuable than fear.'

HORACIO QUIROGA

The Madrid players said that the meat they ate every day at Valdebebas was good. But Mourinho, a man with a discerning palate, disagreed.

Beef shank or sirloin, chuck steak or hump meat, loin or shoulder top – each cut required its own special preparation. According to Mourinho, this was not being carried out with the necessary skill. Hump meat in the pan, sirloin on the grill, shoulder top in the oven. The chefs had to work with dedication to cook it properly. Otherwise the meat would toughen, and one's teeth would encounter an unpleasant resistance, followed by cartilage with the consistency of rubber and nerve tissue whose elasticity required a lot of tedious chewing. If this was what was served up, there were two possible explanations: the chefs did not know how to prepare the beef or the suppliers were cheating the club.

As the winter of 2011 passed without his complaints being resolved, the manager ordered Madrid to sack their chefs and change their butchers. He said the meat had a 'very high percentage of nerve tissue'.

FEAR

Mourinho was living days of prolonged and convoluted pain. Everything spoke to him to him of an unavoidable destiny. At the end of the season, Barcelona awaited – the team that had provoked Madrid into hiring him, the team that would later call into question his competence in the job with the 5–0 and even his status as a visionary. Who knew which nerve, which muscle, which minor occurrence would alter for ever the course of history?

The way a team plays is determined by the quality of the squad and the message of its coach. The worse the quality in the squad, the more important the message. This message comes in the form of a flow of daily information from the coach, a combination of thousands of notes, images, reactions, suggestions, orders, jokes, rewards and punishments, and acts of rejection, disdain or approval. The first conclusions the Madrid players drew after the first few months of living with Mourinho was that they had to remain in a permanent state of alert, in constant tension, just like the chefs at Valdebebas.

The nervous system of an elite footballer is a marvellous composite. It is capable of resisting environmental and social pressures that would be unbearable for most people, and it can achieve levels of abstraction and co-ordination inaccessible to the average professional athlete. In psychomotor terms it is capable of offering a more highly tuned response than the nervous system of any other team-sports player. The unnatural essence of football leads to the exceptional. Adapting an organism designed to use its hands to manipulate things rather than its feet implies, in itself, a selection. Those who have stuck it out after passing through the filter of the local neighbourhood, the school, the youth academy and the professional system are frankly extraordinary cases.

This privileged organism is sensitive to one thing above all others: the threat of inactivity. The absence of offers of work, a serious injury or a coach who has other plans constitute every player's damned trilogy. The brevity of a footballer's career and the anxiety of youth magnify the drama. Mourinho knew how to master these psychological anxieties to the extent that he made them his main instrument of government.

To what extent is it traumatic for a professional not to play for a long time because of the coach's decision? Patricia Ramírez, an expert in professional sports psychology who worked with the staff at Real Betis, says the real trigger for anxiety is uncertainty.

'Not playing can generate a lack of confidence and insecurity,' she says, 'but if a player knows the reason why he's not playing, it allows him to make a change or look for a way out. The greatest insecurity comes from a lack of information, when the player is left to contemplate possible reasons … when the player doesn't know why the coach has not picked him.'

If information provides security, its absence can create doubts, fear or panic. Players are usually enclosed in a small universe that tends to magnify even the most mundane issues. They are also incapable of expressing their identity if they do not feel that they are integrated in the team. Mourinho knew perfectly well that the fear of marginalisation was the most flammable fuel in his players' psychic engines. To manage his players, he turned the control of information into a fine art. Not only inside the dressing room; in addition, he demanded exclusive control of the club's communication policy, of what each player said when facing the press, and the selection of the club's spokesmen. Inside the dressing room his behaviour oscillated between two extremes: friendship and indifference. With some players he behaved like a friend you could talk to every day. With others he was distant, even treating them with disdain. There were players such as Kaká to whom he was warm and friendly for months and then suddenly, overnight, would not even acknowledge. No more 'Good morning', no more niceties. Kaká never understood the reason.

His team-mates realised that if it could happen to Kaká, it could happen to any of them.

The punishments began in the autumn of 2010. At the same time as the media was optimistically exalting the marvellous qualities of the new coaching staff, the players began receiving threatening signals from Mourinho. These came without any apparent cause; there was never any act of misconduct that justified them, nor anything in the code of conduct that suggested to those targeted that they needed to swallow their pride. The surprise was part of the method, which would culminate in an invitation to go up to the coach's office. There, the uninitiated sat at a table on which the trophy for FIFA Best Coach of the 2009–10 season sat. Behind the table was a magnetic board and something approaching a shrine. A photo of Mourinho lifting the Champions League trophy with Inter and a black and white portrait print in a heroic pose stood out among a panoply of trophies, memorabilia and souvenirs.

The players' attention was most drawn by the portrait print. They used to comment on it. That smouldering gaze, chin up, as in the famous Alberto Korda photograph of Che Guevara, provoked comment.

'He's posing like a model,' they said.

One young player who went up to see the coach spoke of his unusual body language. Sitting behind the desk, the manager remained motionless like a sphinx or a yogi, showing off his prodigious ability to disengage his facial muscles, fix his gaze on his guest without blinking, and just move his lips – and evidently his tongue – to express his opinion in a metallic voice. Threats of total marginalisation, straightforward tickings-off or confessions of disappointment were given in the straight monotone of a robot. Whatever they were, his revelations were usually preceded by a formula of powerful resonance: 'I am José Mourinho ...'

Xenophon tells how, when King Croesus went to consult the oracle of Delphi, the god's answer was final: 'If you are human, try to think of human things.'

Ubaldo Martínez is Professor of Social Anthropology at the National University of Distance Education in Madrid. Over the course of his long career he has taught at the Autonomous University of Madrid, at Columbia University, in Baltimore and at the London School of Economics. He lives 200 yards from the Bernabéu in one of those streets leading to the stadium that is filled with fans on match days. Mourinho's reliance on the most primitive ways of influencing other people struck him immediately.

'We're convinced that we've become rational but we're still more persuaded by magic than by reason,' he comments. 'Everything that Mourinho says, that sort of austerity he imposes on players, that continuous punishment thing, that takes you down a certain path – it's what the shamans do. Here, fear plays a tremendous part. Fear is everything. In this case, fear that they'll throw you out of the club, that they won't let you play … everything. Fear is a way of imposing discipline on people. The theoretical problem that we encounter is that these guys, these players, are untameable. They're cocky. How do you dominate that?'

Football coaches seek to unite the individual into the collective. To want to create a new entity from many wills suggests a certain desire for omnipotence. Mourinho set out on an extreme path. On 23 January 2011, after a match against Mallorca at the Bernabéu, he proclaimed his absolutism:

'I am the team.'

Mourinho designed a three-level programme of indoctrination – football, psychology and propaganda – with each of these requiring a different type of language and role from the coach. The programme's main audience, but not its only one, were the players. To understand Mourinho's work it's impossible to dissociate the tactical from the technical, the purely footballing from the attempt – through suggestion – to permanently involve people. The multitude of areas in which he attempted to extend his influence turned the whole thing into a sort of play. Gradually he devised character roles for himself, each with their own script and voice. He was inspired by the work of Anthony Hopkins in *The Silence of the Lambs*, the actor and the role that, according to those close to him, he most admired.

The style of Madrid's play between 2010 and 2013 will leave fewer recognisable traces in the future than the multifarious character assumed by the team's coach to extend his power over the staff, board and fans. The tactics that Mourinho preached were not nearly as original as his theatrical mode of power management that owed as much to Neolithic sorcerers as to Dr Hannibal Lecter and reality TV shows.

'Mourinho became the master of putting on a show,' says the semiotician Jorge Lozano, Professor of the General Theory of Information at the Complutense University of Madrid. 'He's an exceptional expert in strategies of space. He has it perfectly organised. He's very disciplined. Always maintaining the same antagonisms is difficult. It's over-acting. But he's a faithful disciple of Stanislavski, he breaks the fourth wall. He puts himself up there and acts for different audiences. And the performance differs according to the situation. First, in front of journalists, he wears a mask behind which there's always mystery. Always the same. The mask emphasises an exaggerated solemnity. It makes no concession to communication. He's there because it's his only option. If he could leave, he would. He presents himself as afflicted. Bored. Full of disdain. Ignoring everyone else. In front of the public he's Coryphaeus, the leader of the chorus in Ancient Greek drama, the cheerleader of the most radical supporters, emphatic, celebrating goals to the limit, running through and past everything. He acts for the referee, but the referee is always the villain, whatever he does he's on the side of the opposition, he's bought, he's bad, he didn't see it, he's the evil fool. Mourinho is delighted when the referee orders him out of the dugout, gloriously proving that he, Mourinho, exists.

'Mourinho,' he continues, 'turns up and puts on a performance: when there's the need for emotion, he applies the emotion, but when it's time for zero emotion [that is what he delivers] … He puts on all kinds of shows. "Now I'll show you that I love this kid who's come up through the youth team, or this Portuguese player, but I don't want anything to do with this guy who I don't care about and who I'm offended by." And he has to be offended because he's the one who controls everything. He's very good at being able to pretend that he's experiencing feelings. This, like his performances, he does admirably. As to whether these feelings are sincere or not, I've no idea. But they do seem plausible. He could be on the big stage with a very narrow range of interpretation. Like Humphrey Bogart. It's admirable.'

Ubadlo Martínez was also struck by the similarity of his behaviour to that of a tribal leader. 'Madrid,' says the anthropologist, 'is something that many people have access to. It's influential, it's fun, it distracts and dazzles. And a man appears with all these self-same qualities, a man with a certain dimension of mystery. Because Mourinho, with his way of saying things, always comes out with something cryptic. It's not always clear what he wants to say. That much is obvious. He uses an arcane system of language, of religious mystery, of shamans. He doesn't say, "The player doesn't know how to take a corner." No. He comes up with something enigmatic that makes people think he knows more. He plants riddles. People say, "What the hell does he want to say?" He lets slip, "Something has happened here …" And he lets it hang in the air … so that people can think about it. This is typical of pseudo-religious, pseudo-mythical language. I find it fascinating.'

Mourinho represented the figure of the ambivalent legislator-rebel. He obeyed nobody. He created the rules. He broke them. Only he knew why, and from the confusion and bewilderment he always extracted benefits. It is commonplace for primitive religious figures to speak only through intermediaries. The god remains hidden, manifested in the priest. One way of interpreting his sudden absence from public events he should have presided over was that he was upset and wanted his assistant to talk. The process was calculated to have an impact, Mourinho remaining the remote, mythical figure and Karanka – like a priest – reproducing his words. Mourinho put across the idea that the team was more important than the individuals, as if the team were some sort of vaporous soul existing above all of them, as if he himself were not expressing his own desires and concerns but was speaking in the name of one unintelligible guiding spirit.

The manager assigned the same multidisciplinary functions to his assistants as he did to himself. Silvino Louro was goalkeeping coach and Casillas-watcher; fitness coach Rui Faria was counsellor to Ronaldo; José Morais, besides analysing rivals, had to establish friendly ties with the Portuguese contingent. Aitor Karanka's mission was not limited to overseeing Mourinho's programmed training sessions; he was also to gain the confidence of the Spanish players and the club's veteran employees. The entire back-room staff formed a well-ordered network of data collection that was fed back to the boss so that he could make decisions. Some of them made it their business, at Mourinho's explicit request, to maintain contact with certain journalists in order to give them prepared information. Karanka, furthermore, took on the task of representing the coach in the press room. His first appearance was on 18 December 2010 on the eve of the game against Sevilla. His press conferences were so devoid of content that they could be summed up in one solitary phrase: 'As the manager has already said.'

Until Mourinho appointed him his own personal priest at Christmas 2010, the players saw in Karanka somebody they could trust. He was then 37 years old, had finished his career not long before, and as a veteran *Madridista* and a former youth-team coach at the Spanish Football Federation had a dignified, familiar air. Alongside Casillas, he had been part of the Madrid team that won the Champions League in Paris in 2000. In time, however, even Casillas would start avoiding him. The once frequent chats at breakfast in the dining room between the Spanish players and Karanka took place less and less. The players saw him take a tray in the free buffet and waited for him to sit at a table so that they could sit at another table far away. All they said to him these days, in the majority of cases, involved the exchange of banal bits of information. It was getting more and more difficult to find a place in Valdebebas sufficiently far from the earshot of potential informers. Distrust rolled in like a mist. At first the players were only suspicious of Mourinho; then they suspected that his assistants were play-acting or responding to other spurious interests; then they felt that club employees were setting traps for them to reveal information. Finally, the players stopped trusting each other.

During the 2010–11 season the various groups were quickly delineated. The faction closest to the coach was composed of Pepe, Khedira, Marcelo, Ronaldo, Özil and Di María. On the other side – and not enjoying the same access, but with occasional contact with Pérez, the president – were Casillas, Ramos, Higuaín, Benzema, Pedro León, Lass and Canales. Between the two, an ambivalent group had formed: Arbeloa, Granero and Xabi Alonso. On a planet apart lived Carvalho, bound to Jorge Mendes. Carvalho was the great patriarch of the

Portuguese clan, but he could not take the coach seriously. With the passing of time, and according to changing interests and shifting political forces, the groups exchanged members or fragmented. Mourinho managed to impress the idea upon them that to enjoy his professional regard it was essential to fulfil every one of his precepts. And his precepts determined the style of football the team played.

Considering Barcelona to be the active team, Mourinho had to come up with the correct tactics as the reactive team. Barça's possession of the ball was the backbone of their organisation, so Madrid identified themselves with the hunter, with the wait, with surrendering possession most of the time and occasionally attacking. The players noticed this tendency from the pre-season tour of Los Angeles, when he would pontificate:

'Nobody in the history of football has closed down and covered as perfectly as Inter.'

Training sessions began with passing drills and simulations of games on pitches of various sizes. Four against four, six against six, eight against eight, three against two, four against three, etc. – more-or-less standardised exercises to loosen up the muscles with the ball, all at a very high and almost constant tempo. Then came the fine-tuning during the second half of the sessions: cycles of exercises working on pressing, closing down as a unit, and defensive movements co-ordinated so that each player knew when to hold his position and when to leave it so that he could press the ball. The exercises were done together with the so-called fifth defenders, Mourinho's name for those midfielders and forwards who trained specifically in covering techniques. In this, Di María, for his willingness, obedience and ability to cover so much ground, was the benchmark. Based on these exercises, Mourinho would turn to the tactics board when games came, adapting his tactics to the opposition's strengths, with the aim of neutralising them.

According to the squad, all of this was the bread and butter of Mourinho's methodology. In many training sessions he grouped the attacking players as far back as their own penalty area, 'put in the box', as they called it, and then rehearsed moving as one to reduce the opposition's space and launch counter-attacks. These moves would be repeated so as to make them automatic: two touches in midfield, a pass out wide, a cross and a strike at goal; ball to the forward, support from midfield, opening out to the wing, cross and shot … Systematised routines, quick passes through the midfield using multiple lanes: down the right with Di María; down the left with Marcelo and Ronaldo; and right down the middle with Higuaín and Özil.

The players complained that Mourinho tended to reproduce the same configuration over and again. The team trained to counteract imaginary adversaries who wanted the ball and who were prepared to put a lot of players in the opposition's half. Throughout the entire summer he did not devise a single plan for static attacking. Some players also complained that the drawback of this sort of training was that most teams they would face in the league and in the cup would sit back and wait for them to attack, forcing them to keep hold of the ball for longer in midfield to avoid being predictable and to find space. Very few teams would compete against them with the same weapons as Barça, but Mourinho only seemed to be preparing to play against Barça.

A part of the squad began to think that he was not conveying certain footballing ideas because he actually did not really understand them. But he did not seem bothered by the simplicity of his work in attack. He saw his strength – the key to his success – in the simplicity of his model, and he thought that introducing ideas about positional play and static attacking would complicate training. This was not what had turned him into such a well-regarded coach. He owed his fame and his fortune to his ability to get great results quickly in a range of different countries. Until then, his cocktail of virtues had been enough: his instinct for perceiving the vulnerability of his opponent, his gift of explaining to his players how to organise defensively and then how to counter-attack, and his acute power of persuasion were what made his ideas and his psychological penetration possible. His methods did suffer from important tactical limitations, but they offered a greater chance of rapid and efficient adaptation of both means and men.

As a confirmed winner, Mourinho had another decisive element in his make-up. Madrid had not contracted him to entertain the public with a highly evolved style of football. They had contracted him to stop the advance of Barça. To win. To reach this goal, as far as those in the inner circle of the coach understood it, it was enough just to apply his recipe. His agent, Jorge Mendes, repeated this to Pérez, to José Ángel Sánchez, to his friend Peter Kenyon, Chelsea's former chief executive, and journalists – 'José always wins titles. Always. And he's never had a squad with such quality as he now has at Madrid, so … the normal thing would be that here he wins even more.'

During the summer and autumn of 2010 Mourinho thought he should concentrate on creating defensive order. Everything else would be solved by the abundant talent in his squad and it would be enough that the players got to know each other on the pitch. They remembered him being excited by such a wealth of technique, monitoring the practice matches without shouting out advice about how to create space or pull away from markers. He just gave shouts of encouragement: 'Spectacular … Touch … Quality …!'

He ordered his team to defend in a certain way, but then, once they had recovered the ball, he told them to distribute it according to their intuition. He wanted to experiment with this idea in the friendly Madrid played in Alicante on 22 August. They lined up in a 4-2-3-1 formation, with Gago and Khedira in midfield, and Di María, Canales and Özil behind Higuaín in attack. To everyone's surprise, in the dressing room he said that he had come up with a new slogan:

'Occupy space however you want to.'

Madrid came back in at half-time 1–0 down after a half of complete chaos. Mourinho amazed the players again with a completely different message:

'This is anarchy. You can't all just do what you want.'

The simplicity and certainty of the way in which he organised his defence turned into vagueness and confusion on the rare occasions he dedicated any time to practising elaborate attacks. Over time, Mourinho stopped persevering along a path that he neither understood nor was convinced by.

On 20 November 2010 Diego Maradona visited Valdebebas. To a starstruck Mourinho it seemed a good time to leave the training pitch, let the players continue with their exercises and sit alongside the legend. Perhaps allowing himself to be carried away by the commercial value of the moment, he allowed a Real Madrid TV camera team to film the conversation. The film shows the Argentine hero lounging on the bench, his hands in the pockets of his leather jacket, rejoicing at the statements of the coach. Puffed up by the company, Mourinho confesses his principles:

'I score and I win.'

'Sure,' Maradona responds.

'And another thing – you score and you don't know if you win!'

If Mourinho's football philosophy could be summed up in a single aphorism, it would be those 14 words in which he boasted to Maradona: 'I score and I win, you score and you don't know if you win.' I score against you and drop deep to focus on protecting my goal to close down the game. I score and your hopes disappear, because I forget about attacking you unless you make a mistake. And if I don't score? Only then am I forced to attack, but only gradually, using more and more resources, rationing every advance. What if I still don't score? Then the limits of a model that fits into one slogan have been reached. The dark side of the theory was not revealed to Maradona, but the players eventually discovered it as winter turned into the spring of 2011 in visits to the Riazor, the Sardinero and the Vicente Calderón.

Madrid's line-up at the Riazor on 26 February invited fans to dream of a great attacking display: Casillas, Ramos, Carvalho, Pepe, Marcelo, Lass, Alonso, Kaká, Özil, Ronaldo and Benzema. If these same fans had heard what the coach told the players in the team-talk before the match they would have been confused. Madrid needed to face the matches ahead of them with resolution, in order to regain ground lost to Barcelona, topping the table with 65 points to Madrid's 60. But in La Coruña Mourinho called for caution. The phrases rained down on the players like a depressing drizzle: 'Don't take any risks in defence', 'Come out from the back with great caution' and 'Don't be aggressive in attack'. By now the word 'aggressive' had only negative connotations. The full-backs applied the handbrake, the ball barely touched the midfield, and the transition from defence to attack, rather than being fast, was just poorly timed. With 25 minutes left Mourinho made changes – Di María for Lass, and Granero for Marcelo – and ordered a charge. But it was too late. The match ended 0–0, with nobody explaining to the players exactly what it was that the coach had feared from Deportivo's forwards Guardado, Adriano or Riki.

Mourinho waited for the players in the dressing room to ask them to tell the press that the schedule imposed by the TV companies favoured Barca's recovery between games, while at the same time

Madrid were being physically worn down. But after taking a shower, Casillas took the microphone with something quite different in mind. The captain conscientiously expressed his dissatisfaction:

'We let the first half get away from us. We threw 45 minutes away. The team needs to give much more. We have to be more focused from the start and press a lot more because the league is running away from us.'

Mourinho deeply disliked his players failing to reproduce the soundbites that he prepared for them to give to the media after the match. As he saw that no one had given his account of the game, in his next public appearance he launched a hidden warning to the squad – and to Pérez:

'There are clubs that have a different communication strategy from ours. Here, I'm the one who comes [out to speak] and I never ask a player to be part of a communication strategy in which the coach is protected. There are other clubs in which players participate very well in a communication strategy, where the coach is protected, calmly playing a different role. Not here. Here it's me coming out to show my face. Not anymore.'

On 4 March Madrid travelled to Santander, Ronaldo's absence changing the mood of the trip. Mourinho usually set up the team to channel the attacks to Ronaldo and part of the squad felt that in the Sardinero they would be presented with the chance to prove that they could perform well without their star player.

With all the travelling and the staying at hotels, forced to rest and remain in their rooms, taking siestas and not staying up too late, footballers belong to a profession with more dead time on their hands than any other. These great stretches of inertia lead them to watch reality shows, go on their PlayStations, come up with nicknames and imagine possible conspiracies: Jorge Mendes's activities in Valdebebas, the fact that Mourinho treated his agent like an unofficial director of football and Ronaldo's role as standard-bearer of the Gestifute group were a cocktail too obvious not to arouse suspicion.

There was no doubt that Ronaldo enjoyed a unique level of protection, including tactical privileges. He was the only team member whom Mourinho had liberated from defensive duties and this allowed him to excel in attack. Most of the players came to the conclusion that this tactic, which increased the status of the Portuguese striker, had much to do with the common interests that linked Mendes to the coach. In these months, perhaps undeservedly, Ronaldo became a target for those alienated peers of his who felt marginalised by the Portuguese clan. Inspired by the constant frenzy to deify him, the Spanish gave him the satirical nickname *Ansias*, derived from the word '*ansioso*' – anxious.

Wary of Ronaldo's status, his team-mates decided to put on a show of force in Santander. An official meeting was called in the team hotel the night before the game. The men closest to Mendes – people like Pepe, Di María and Carvalho – did not attend. The dressing-room heavyweights spoke and the majority nodded at the calls for them to be respected by a coach who they felt discriminated against them.

'Tomorrow, we have to be clear. We have to go all out. If not, Mou will say in the press conference that without *Ansias* we cannot win,' said one of the players.

'What will his "dad" say if we win playing well without *Ansias*?'

On the night of 4 to 5 March, eight months after Mourinho's arrival at Madrid, the squad decided that enough was enough. The players were exhausted by a coach obsessed with political manoeuvring, a man seemingly intent on dividing the squad into tiers, which sometimes only followed lines drawn by loyalties and ties of kinship with his agent, someone who appeared to be just as concerned with making propaganda as with football. The ban on speaking in public – unless it was to parrot other people's ideas, most of which were in praise of the coach's leadership, or were complaints against referees or the broadcasters who had come up with the fixtures calendar – had exhausted the patience of more than a few players.

There were those in the team who now wondered aloud whether a players' boycott would lead to his dismissal; or perhaps it would be necessary for the team to allow themselves to be beaten, what is commonly known as 'making the bed' of the coach. The conclusion the leaders of the Madrid dressing room came to was that in Madrid this would be impossible. Not only because of the constant scrutiny of the media and fans, but also because when the requirement is to get trophies, failure is a stain on all those players who finish the season empty-handed. The only way to protect their contracts – and the privileged professional status they enjoyed in one of the world's highest-paid squads – was to win. Winning always, and without hesitation. For them. For their families. For their insatiable followers. Never for the boss. As one Spanish player said that night:

'If Mourinho were manager of Sevilla or Valencia they would have already made the bed for him.'

Mourinho gave between two and four team-talks before every game, lasting 10 minutes to an hour. The first talk he gave at the team's hotel in Santander lasted an hour. It was a monologue about his efforts to control the press. His voice was inflamed. He always spoke in the first person, without looking at the players. Club employees had never seen this kind of talk from a coach:

'I'm sick of the press telling me we don't win away from home … We have to win … We have to score more goals … We have to compensate for the stick the press are giving me … I'm sick of being criticised for us not scoring goals … I'm sure we'll win, for the press …!'

There were no references to Racing Santander, Madrid's opponents, until the following morning. Because of Khedira's absence, there was something new in Mourinho's line-up: Alonso would play in front of the defence, with Granero, Özil and Di María behind Benzema and Adebayor in attack. A 4-1-3-2 scheme was an innovation. They had never practised it in training but the manager was convinced it would organise itself spontaneously. All that he was worried about was that the players had understood what he had instilled in them defensively – everything else should come by itself. Following that way of thinking, in those months he spent many hours instructing his more attacking players how to play defensively. Before the team ran out onto the pitch in the Sardinero he spoke individually with Özil, Granero, Di María, Benzema and Adebayor. The subjects were the same for all of them: close down the space, pressurise and help the defence.

Mourinho gave three team-talks to the group before the game, disparaging the opposition in one of them:

'Racing are the most basic team I've seen in the league. They just get the ball out wide and then cross it ... Also, I know that we'll win here because we don't have "Cris". We'll surprise them without "Cris".'

'Cris', to his friends, was Cristiano Ronaldo. When the Portuguese striker was on the pitch Mourinho made the team sit deeper, allowing the opposition to advance, thereby generating gaps between their defence and the goal. In the absence of Ronaldo – and because neither Benzema nor Adebayor were as quick running into space – the coach moved the team further up the pitch to press higher. The effect was spectacular. The first part of the game saw probably the most comprehensive exhibition of football from Madrid in the 2010–11 season.

The team could have gone in at half-time five goals up. This was not hit-and-run football, just 45 minutes of considered passing, woven from the midfield to attack, with timing, precision and class. Adebayor and Benzema both scored brilliant goals but Mourinho, contrary to his usual custom, celebrated neither. The substitutes watched him from the bench. With the first goal he limited himself to taking a drink of water. After the second goal he remained motionless. All of a sudden, and in front of what certainly seemed like a spectacle worthy of celebration, Mourinho became taciturn. He had very much disliked one move in which Marcelo, Ramos, Benzema, Adebayor, Özil and Granero all advanced into the attacking half. On entering the dressing room at half-time he delivered the sort of tirade that over the years would become standard fare. In front of players proud of what they were achieving, he told them not to press so high, adding that they could not afford to give the opposition the chance to counter-attack. He insisted that no one put on any virtuoso displays. To complete his diatribe, he stuck the sword in:

'It's impossible for Racing to play so badly in every way as they did in the first half. Now they're going to attack us. They won't take us by surprise because it's impossible for a football team to play as badly as Racing did in the first half.'

Seeing that that he was taking credit away from them, some players complained bitterly before going back out on to the pitch.

'So what is it then? If there's no Ronaldo, then we don't know how to do anything? We've also played well.'

Top players usually get excited about the idea of imposing themselves on the opposition. But it was a disconsolate Madrid that emerged for the second half, a team that played under the flag of a coach who suggested that the Racing forwards Giovani and Munitis posed a potential danger. Granero went back to play alongside Alonso in front of the defence, there was a general withdrawal to their own half, and Racing almost managed a draw after Kennedy pulled a goal back.

Regulars on the Madrid bench say they have never before seen a coach display terror as obviously as Mourinho. The manager's body language during games reflected his understanding of the game as a fierce struggle. He rarely seemed satisfied, and was unable to show happiness without an added dose of rage. For him, the essence of coaching was not to offer solutions and provide a nice product. For him, the essence was not to lose. Losing, for Mourinho, was to suffer an unbearable misfortune. It was like a plane crash. That is how one player who was on the bench when Giovani almost inspired the equaliser in the Sardinero described it:

'Watching Giovani, Mourinho looked like a passenger with a fear of flying stuck in a small plane during turbulence.'

For a moment, you could begin to see the vertigo in his eyes, standing, then suddenly swaying, gripped by the struggle to stay upright. Livid, making a fuss, waving his arms and hands to ask for concentration, for players to drop back, for assistance, for compact lines and defensive intensity – he seemed to be calling for protection from the bottom of his soul. The issue was not the team. It was not football. It was Mourinho himself who felt exposed.

Benzema's goal in the 76th minute made it 1–3 and ended the torment.

As someone with a keen smell for danger, Mourinho felt that several players distrusted him. Alarmed at the approach of the season's most decisive duels, he sought the help of Pérez, and set Mendes and Sánchez to work at aligning all available forces for the job of constructing just the right media story. More than a few journalists and media organisations reproduced the same prefabricated phrases they were fed: the team is united, everyone is happy with 'Mou', 'Mou' is the best coach there is, the team is playing very well, etc., etc. It was as if the use of the words 'armoured' and 'united' – repeated over and over again in different forums – had been medically prescribed, echoing like a rattling snare drum: 'The dressing room is "*blindado*"'. The word means bullet-proof or armoured. But armoured against what? That was never made clear.

With the same totalitarian logic, a number of enemies were created. The Madrid mythology contained three fundamental demons: TV companies plotting to harm Madrid with adverse match scheduling that was favourable to Barcelona; referees who favoured Barcelona; and Barcelona themselves, subject to various slurs and innuendo from journalists based in Madrid.

Mourinho believed that if players publicly warned of the existence of a hidden plot it would give his campaign the stamp of legitimacy. To do this, he insisted that he had to 'co-ordinate' the 'communication strategy', underlining the notion of a team cursed by the power of institutions and deeply attached to the eminence of the coach. Under the pretext of safeguarding them from pressure, he stopped players giving interviews and individual press conferences, unless they allowed the content to be drawn up beforehand. At the same time, players were required to help him after every game in the mixed zone in denouncing referees and the fixtures calendar, or saying they completely agreed with the coach regarding these issues.

The Spanish contingent felt particularly ridiculous complaining about things they thought irrelevant. Whenever they could they avoided it. One day, gathered in the gym, they spoke about refusing to participate in the company's propaganda. They were talking when Silvino Louro, the goalkeeping coach, happened to pass by, and, coincidentally, began complaining about how easy the TV operators were making things for Barcelona. When the goalkeeping coach was gone, Albiol said what everyone was thinking:

'This is an embarrassment! They even believe it themselves!'

Alerted to the squad's scorn for Mourinho's psychological-warfare methods, in March Pérez called Ramos and Casillas in and asked them to back down. 'You must support the coach,' he pleaded. The president conceded that Mourinho's methods might be extravagant and difficult to follow but he asked them to stand behind their manager, whatever his instructions were, and to do so for the greater good of Madrid. Pérez reminded them that the fans – yearning for success, upset by the lack of trophies – deserved exceptional sacrifice. And, if they won the Champions League, the league or the cup, all of their efforts would have been worthwhile. He never said to the players that at the end of the season Mourinho would continue but he somehow led them to understand that the coach was not going to be an interim solution. Only once – and then through third parties – did word reach the dressing room that Mourinho would not still be there the following year. It is not known whether these messages were contrived or not, but the squad believed that Mourinho was not so important for the president.

To finish reassuring Mourinho, Pérez suggested that Casillas publicly endorse him. The captain did this in an interview on the radio station Onda Cero:

'Mourinho's a great coach. Today, he's probably the best in the world. You can like what you see on TV or not. It used to be strange to see him on TV, but of course, now I see him every day and know him, and I can tell you that I'll defend him and will give everything for him because I think as a person he's a "10 out of 10" ... and as a coach his record speaks for itself.'

Thanks to Pérez's intervention, the spirit and the routine of the team were moulded to fit the whims of the coach. Mourinho could not get Barcelona out of his head. He had them in mind when analysing every game against every opponent. The league derby against Atlético on Saturday 19 March 2011 served as a testing ground, the perfect occasion to put some of his ideas into practice. On the Friday the players gathered in the Valdebebas conference room for some instruction. As always, when what he had to say transcended the game itself, Mourinho spoke of himself. According to those in attendance, his team-talk went as follows. First, he addressed the issue of the TV schedules:

'I'll be honest with you. All this discussion about the TV companies, I've invented all of it. It's a lie. It's a lie I told you to distract the press. Because what difference does it make if we get two or three days' rest [between games]? Between us, it makes no difference at all!'

His audience remained silent, save for a few snorts of surprise. Mourinho continued, completely convinced by what he was saying:

'Stay calm, because next year Florentino will terminate the contract with Mediapro and will sign with another operator. From then on, I'll be deciding the schedule … Now I'm going out to the press room and I'm going to tell the journalists once again that we're hurting because of the scheduling of our matches.'

To conclude the session, Mourinho touched on the most personal topic imaginable, confessing that he had experienced a dreamlike trance. The players received this confidence in complete silence; there was not a single laugh, not even a murmur as the coach recounted his experience of the previous night:

'I want to say one thing. Last night I had a "feeling". When I have these very strong "feelings", they then take place in real life. I dreamed that if we won against Atlético we would win the league. I say this because I feel it. Otherwise I wouldn't say it. I have a "feeling" … And when these things happen to me … When I see things so clearly, they always seem to come true.'

The message sank into the players. Mourinho's team-talk – a long monologue full of esoteric points – linked technical instruction with an intriguing personal story. The squad were increasingly aware of the alibi – or the excuse – as a form of protection against failure. It was impossible to talk of purely footballing matters; everything else – his sense of distress, of persecution, of threats and conspiracies both on and off the pitch – was bundled in. The tasks that Mourinho gave to his players during that period reveal much about his way of seeing the game. According to those who witnessed it he would say:

'You must learn to rationalise the attacks. If you see that if you go up you're not going to be able to get back into position quickly, then don't go up. If you're not sure, regardless of what you might get out of it, stay put … I'm going to be checking this on the pitch.'

The word 'rationalise' soon became fixed in the minds of the players. During the game, if the coach saw a midfielder such as Khedira or a winger such as Di María go up the pitch, but then – exhausted by the effort – was unable to get back, Mourinho would be off the bench like a shot, shouting, 'What did I say?'

Mourinho granted freedom of movement to attacks so long as they ended successfully. If they failed he would curse those who had dared set them up. This attitude began to condition players to stay out of trouble, over the years developing reflexes and automatic behaviour patterns. When in doubt Mourinho's players did not try to take opponents on, did not play a pass, repressed any desire to elaborate. They just got rid of the ball.

Mourinho did not even calm down when Madrid thrashed other teams. He had great difficulty maintaining a good mood during games, and his levels of extreme stress would often turn into what seemed like sheer terror. At the bottom of his sliding scale of fearful situations he ranked losing possession while coming out of defence with the ball; then came one-on-ones between rival attackers and his own defenders; and finally, at the top, the one-on-one with his goalkeeper. The care that was put in to warn everyone that they must never forget about their opponents can be shown by one of his most persistent slogans, three words that the squad believed created the closest thing to a conditioned reflex:

'Watch your back!'

The return of the *trivote* was a sign of things to come: Casillas, Ramos, Pepe, Carvalho, Marcelo, Lass, Alonso, Khedira, Özil, Benzema and Ronaldo. Before the game, in the dressing room of the Calderón, Mourinho's assistants followed the protocol of such occasions. The state-of-the-art projector was installed and connected to a laptop, and the lights were dimmed. On-screen graphics reproduced Atlético's most typical movements and, with animated simulations, it was explained how best to counter them. Armed with a remote control and a laser pointer, Mourinho indicated a sign in the middle of the projection: it was a virtual Alonso, who when necessary moved between the central defenders as a fifth defender. He asked Lass and Khedira to press in midfield, squeezing Mario Suárez and Tiago. Behind them, Alonso would monitor Forlan and block him if he dropped into his zone. Mourinho warned that if Reyes dropped deep to receive the ball, it was up to Khedira or Lass to mark him, depending on whether he moved to the left or right.

'Be very careful, because if they score the first goal they will win the game,' he insisted.

Having outlined his defensive message, Mourinho moved on to the attack. He put his pointer on the Alonso icon and explained that the Basque should bring the ball out, looking to play it out to the full-back or forward to Benzema and Ronaldo. Then the program reproduced a situation in which Alonso's path was blocked by Atlético's players. Mourinho explained that when this happened the central defenders needed to come out with the ball from the back using the full-backs, so that they could play the long ball forward to Benzema. Benzema should receive the ball with his back to goal and look to play in Özil and Ronaldo. If the flanks were also covered, then the defenders should get the ball back to Casillas so he could kick it down the pitch straight to Benzema. The coach said that only Khedira, Özil and Ronaldo should go for the second ball, while Ramos and Marcelo had to 'rationalise' their forays forward.

Benzema opened the scoring on 11 minutes and, from the bench, Mourinho instructed Madrid to drop deep. Khedira was told to stop joining in attacks when the ball was played long up to Benzema and Ronaldo. There were now two blocks of players: the keeper and seven men back, with three attackers in front of them. A forward run by Marcelo, who, taking a risk, reached the byline and centred, enabled Özil to score in the 33rd minute.

At the half-time break Mourinho told his team to carry on with the defensive set-up, maintaining lines of cover in their own half and pressing in medium- or low-block. To simplify the attack even further, on 70 minutes he swapped Benzema for Adebayor on the principle that the Togolese striker was better in the air and would be more comfortable receiving long balls from the back. The natural reaction from Atlético was to advance forward into areas of the pitch that Madrid had surrendered. Agüero scored in the 84th minute and Madrid ended up struggling to hang on to the three points. When the players headed for the showers Mourinho seemed on edge and told them to stop shouting:

'Stop! Shut up! Stop! Stop! When you go out you have to tell the press that we sat back because we were dead on our feet. We were very tired by the scheduling of the matches. So the journalists talk about the match schedules.'

Aware that some of the press might criticise him for using a *trivote* or closing the game down, Mourinho lay down a smokescreen and asked his players to collaborate. Reluctantly, many did. But in the privacy of the dressing room most were convinced that this tactic was the coach's way of avoiding the shame he felt about playing in such a rudimentary style. The more experienced players said that the sophistication shown by Mourinho in the plans he made to cancel out the opposition vanished when he had to organise the team once they had possession. Without the ball it was difficult to attack.

On 5 April Madrid played Tottenham at the Bernabéu in the first leg of the quarter-finals of the Champions League. The build-up to the game was long and tense. What surprised the staff was the appearance of a new enemy in the long list of enemies: UEFA. In his team-talk before the game Mourinho issued an alarming warning. He said that UEFA were out for reprisals and warned his players to be extremely cautious when they went hard into challenges because referees were under instruction to dish out unduly severe punishments.

The elimination of Tottenham meant everyone's calendars were now marked in red – inevitable drama loomed. Madrid would play Barcelona four times in three competitions. In the league on 16 April, in the Cup Final on 20 April and in the semi-finals of the Champions League on 27 April and 3 May.

CHAPTER 7

PREPARE TO LOSE

'Fire, whatever its nature, transforms man into spirit. That is why the shamans are considered masters of fire and become insensitive to contact with the coals. The mastery of fire or incineration is the equivalent to initiation.'

MIRCEA ELIADE, *Shamanism: Archaic Techniques of Ecstasy*

The presence of a mole at Real Madrid worried Mourinho so much that between 2011 and 2012 he ordered two sweeps of the hotel where the team stayed to search for hidden microphones. The investigations were unsuccessful. The Sheraton Mirasierra was apparently clean.

The control of information was another thing that deeply exercised Mourinho; he assigned a group of people hired by Gestifute to carry out a daily analysis of everything that the media said about him. Every morning Mourinho received a package containing the summary. His day began at 8 a.m. in his office at Valdebebas, studying videos, articles and broadcasts. He realised that he and his colleagues were not the only sources of the content, and that certain things that were being published did not exactly project an image of infallibility. He began to suspect that there were leaks in his organisation. His anxiety to control everything that reached the outside world – and the realisation that he could not – made him think that there was a mole, or a number of moles, or even that there were hidden microphones recording his conversations.

The proximity of the *clásico* ramped up his sense of suspicion. According to club sources, the growing fear of leaks made Mourinho ask the directors to set up a study of the phone records of players and club employees. Some players were warned about this informally, as it was in their interest to be careful about whom they spoke to on their mobiles. The secrecy, however, did not prevent the boss's intentions becoming widely known. In fact they were obvious in every training session. The staff suspected that against Barça the coach would drop Özil, use the *trivote* and play with a single striker, although there remained some doubt about what kind of pressing he would demand. Alonso took the lead in the meetings the players held away from the coaching staff. The midfielder said that if they sat too deep Barcelona would destroy them. Equally, if they played with the *trivote*, even though it allowed them to press higher up the pitch, it would be difficult for them to move the ball around. Alonso thought that they had to prepare for what to do when they had possession if they were to have any chance of winning.

At 5 p.m. on 16 April 2011, shortly before Madrid's home league match against Barcelona, the newspaper *Marca* reported in its online edition that Madrid would play Pepe in midfield, along with Khedira and Alonso. The team selection was unprecedented: Casillas, Ramos, Albiol, Carvalho, Marcelo, Pepe, Khedira, Alonso, Di María, Ronaldo and Benzema.

When they took to the field to warm up, the two teams noticed something unusual underfoot. The grass was long and dry. The groundsmen had carried out perfectly the instructions of Mourinho, who believed this was the way to slow down the rapid movement of the ball that Barcelona needed to develop their game. In the event,

Madrid sat deep, defending with order and energy, and Barça tried to control the match rather than hurt their rivals. It ended in a 1–1 draw, the referee awarding two penalties, one scored by Messi, the other by Ronaldo. The Madrid players said that if the grass had been short and wet Albiol would not have needed to bring down Villa in the area. They explained that Busquets's pass from 50 yards would have gone out of play, but that the longer grass had kept it in and allowed Villa to run on to it.

The 1–1 did not help the home team's title chances but the crowd applauded their team off with a certain relief, Barça's last couple of visits having ended with scores of 0–2 and 2–6, and filed out of the stadium reasonably content. Not so Mourinho. He waited for the team in the dressing room before issuing a torrent of accusations and insults that distorted his face until he began to sob loudly:

'You're traitors. I asked you not to speak with anyone about the team selection but you've betrayed me. It shows that you're not on my side. You're sons of bitches. The only friend I have in this dressing room is Granero … and I'm not even sure that I can trust him any more. You've left me all on my own. You're the most treacherous squad I've had in my life. Nothing more than sons of bitches.'

Casillas did not wait for the outburst to finish. He pretended that nothing was happening, turned around and went to the shower; he was not the only one who ignored the commotion. But Mourinho was filled with such intense emotion that he grabbed a can of Red Bull and hurled it against the wall. It exploded and drops of the sugary energy drink ran down the faces of those nearest to him. Squatting on the ground – some say he was kneeling – he rattled off a further series of insults, then, getting up, he wiped the tears from his face and announced that he was going to speak with Pérez and Sánchez because they would be able to find the mole. He promised reprisals and also made an analogy between martial law and football:

'If I'm in Vietnam and I see you laugh at a mate, I'd grab a gun with my own hands and kill you. Now it's you yourselves who have to look for the one that leaked the line-up.'

Most of the players watched this display with disbelief, caught between embarrassment on the one hand and the fear of losing their jobs or contract on the other. For everyone present it was difficult to work out if what they had seen was a real loss of emotional control or a piece of spontaneous theatre. But they understood that theatrical or not, the threats were serious. The danger was real. By improvisation or calculation, Mourinho had ensured that everyone had been on edge ahead of the league *clásico*. The team had been emotionally stirred up and he had adjusted the final details of his grand tactical plan. All his work, all his energy, the planning of more than nine months, were now focused on one goal: to reach a state of ecstasy in the final of the Copa del Rey in Valencia on 20 April.

Alonso was asked on Madrid's official TV channel about Mourinho's work at this, the decisive stage of the season. He replied: 'In key moments, and for knockout games or finals, you've got to know very well how to prepare for matches, and work very hard on the psychological and emotional side. In this respect he knows how to connect with us.'

The day after the league *clásico*, the morning quiet at Valdebebas had been chirpily disturbed by the work of assistant coaches Karanka, Louro and Faria. They'd descended on the players like a flock of birds on to a recently sown field, each to a different group but each with the same message.

Club employees suspected that this type of synchronised choreography was Mourinho's work. The fitness coach Rui Faria went down one of the corridors and proudly proclaimed:

'Barcelona are going through many problems. They're scared shitless by what they saw yesterday. Their mental weakness shows when they have to face us. Today they've not slept and the fear will not leave them. We're going to sit back and wait for them, and we're going to put one player up front to hold the ball up … their attacks aren't as quick as ours.'

The players were stand-offish with Rui Faria, all except Granero, who – in agreement – said that he had seen the 'fear in the eyes' of the Barça players. The internationals felt that the fitness coach patronised them like a nursery-school teacher and were sure that their rivals had played within themselves. They also understood that when Faria spoke of a striker who would get on the end of all the long balls played out from the back and keep possession he was referring to the plan to put Adebayor in the starting line-up for the cup final. For weeks now, Madrid had been focusing in training on bypassing the midfield with long balls played forward to the strikers. However, in the Mestalla it would not be Adebayor but Ronaldo himself who would be the target man.

The days were filled with impassioned talk until finally 20 April arrived. All of the instructions Mourinho had given before the final in the Mestalla had permeated his players' minds so deeply that he now ran the risk of being repetitive. He talked about politics, about nationalism, about the inexorable division between the Castilian and Catalan peoples and of the illusion of coincidence. He told them that they had nothing in common with Barça. He knew, he said, because he had lived in Barcelona for many years, and was well aware of the local culture and the education that Catalan children receive. He explained that people like Puyol, Busquets, Xavi and Piqué had been taught from childhood to distance themselves from Spaniards such as Casillas, Ramos and Arbeloa.

He insisted that his players were wrong if they thought they had made friendships with the Barça players over their years together in the Spanish national team. The Barça players were not their friends because they took advantage of this supposed friendship by betraying the Madrid players, trying to snatch their prestige from them through their manipulation of the press. All the media propaganda, he said, favoured Barcelona and stigmatised Madrid. But they, the Madrid players, were not to participate in this charade anymore. They must accept their role as bad guys and should refuse to acknowledge their rivals. Mourinho warned his players that if he saw any of them shaking hands outside of the formalities of the game they would be turning their backs on him – and on their team-mates. Anyone making any such friendly gesture towards the opposition ran the risk of becoming something very much like a traitor.

Mourinho held a separate meeting with the players to discuss the referee, Alberto Undiano Mallenco. He said that they should always go in very hard, closing the Barça players down without too much finesse. He added that they should not worry about being penalised because Spanish referees – and Undiano was no exception – 'shit themselves' when it came to Madrid. And if the referee did blow for a foul by Madrid then the players who were closest – Alonso in particular – were to get right in his face, put pressure on him and complain. But the feelings in the team hotel were mixed. Casillas was telling team-mates he was tired of all the 'politicking'.

'We can't play like we did at the Bernabéu,' he said. 'I don't care if it's Mourinho or Capello or Pellegrini … I just want to win the Copa del Rey, and everyone else can fuck off!'

Before the game Emilio Butragueño, head of institutional relations at Madrid, called his contacts in the Spanish Football Federation at Mourinho's request to ask the groundsmen not to water the Mestalla pitch. But nothing was doing.

Pinto, Alves, Piqué, Mascherano, Adriano, Xavi, Iniesta, Busquets, Pedro, Messi and Villa lined up for Barça. The Madrid team was made up of Casillas, Arbeloa, Ramos, Carvalho, Marcelo, Pepe, Alonso,

Khedira, Özil, Ronaldo and Di María. Of all the decisions Mourinho made that week, possibly the most important was playing Ramos in the middle of the pitch. Ramos had been playing at right-back but more than anyone he felt comfortable directing the defensive line, perhaps because in addition to reading the game so well his distribution from the back was extremely secure. This enabled the Madrid defence to move 20 yards up from their own area, narrowing the space that Pepe, Khedira and Alonso needed to cover to block off Barcelona's passing channels, and effectively inhibiting Guardiola's players in their movement.

The match quickly descended into trench warfare. Madrid fought for every inch of the pitch, contesting every ball with exceptional aggression. Barça struggled to find space, and when they did they encountered Casillas. The goalkeeper saved his team with three memorable stops: one from Messi in the 74th minute, another a minute later from Pedro and the third from Iniesta in the 80th minute. The game went to extra-time, in which a towering header from Ronaldo crowned a move started by Marcelo and Di María. The match ended 0–1.

The way Madrid celebrated their victory was rather curious. Ronaldo, seemingly more proud than overjoyed, threw a few glances the way of his team-mates to suggest that he felt vindicated. Casillas wrapped himself in the Spanish flag and raised the cup, overjoyed to have secured his first trophy as Madrid's first-team captain. But the Barça players were startled that several Madrid players did not acknowledge them. Mascherano and Guardiola were particularly disappointed by the evasive attitude of Alonso. The Argentinian player, who had been friends with the Basque when they were both at Liverpool, did not understand what was going on. Something similar happened between Villa and Arbeloa, jeopardising their emerging friendship.

Iniesta told a friend that during the April *clásicos* there were times when his international team-mates on the Madrid side behaved as if they did not know him, as if they had become different people. They avoided looking him in the eyes so they did not have to say hello.

Someone said that during the final Özil looked like a ballet dancer in the jungle. Playing on the right, loaded with defensive duties, Özil was more concerned with tracking Adriano than attacking, and because of the *trivote* he finished up lost in the scrub. Replaced by Adebayor on 71 minutes without having contributing anything important, his team-mates say he was so upset with himself that he barely joined in the celebrations. The German suspected that Mourinho did not quite trust him because he was not a Mendes player, that hardcore group that the rest of the squad called '*los suyos*' ('theirs' or 'their own'). As one Spanish player said, 'Özil is the least "theirs" of "theirs".

Although after the medals ceremony, in the dressing room, Mourinho was surly and seemingly dissatisfied, by the time he caught the plane back to Madrid he was more relaxed. He puffed out his chest in the waiting-halls of Valencia Airport in Manises, repeating, 'This is football! This is football!' The final reaffirmed his belief that a very good way of playing football is to give the ball and the initiative to the opposition. Overcoming the Spanish public and players' resistance to football being played in this manner, especially at Madrid, had been one of his great challenges as a coach and he used the final to gain credibility for his methods. Supportive as ever, Karanka spent the return journey to Madrid maintaining that Barcelona were really not a very competitive team, echoing what Mourinho said: that their status was just an invention of the press.

On 23 April, four days before the first leg of the semi-finals of the Champions League, Madrid returned to Valencia to play their 33rd league game of the season. Mourinho was in an excellent mood, pacing the dressing room and encouraging the troops with some stand-up comedy. Once again they heard that Barcelona were a fiction constructed by the media, and that this owed everything to the semi-final they had unfairly won against Chelsea in 2009. During lunch at the hotel he approached the table where the Spanish players were sitting, from where he could be heard laughing at himself uproariously:

'You know what I'm going to do to Barcelona? I'm going to keep the grass long and I'm not going to water it. You'll see the look on their faces when they go out to warm up!'

'You bastard!' Granero said admiringly.

But only he – and Adán – found Mourinho funny; they were the only ones who appeared to admire the coach, even when he was not there. Granero's appreciation was so exaggerated that his team-mates changed his nickname from 'Pirata', meaning pirate, to 'Perota', merging *pirata* with the word *'pelota'*, an informal term for a sycophant.

By winning the cup and reaching the semi-finals of the Champions League Mourinho consolidated his power. Pérez began to let it be known among his colleagues that the coach would be staying at least another year and that Valdano's days were numbered. This had a startling effect on the dressing room: now aware of what had been decided at the highest level, the group of players pledging allegiance to Mourinho grew in size, although many at the club still doubted his theories. Of all the players it was Alonso who made the most surprising U-turn. The midfielder went from being Mourinho's sharpest critic to becoming an open ally. Only a few remained unmoved, Pedro León, Casillas and Lass prominent among those who continued to keep their distance. Lass told team-mates after the game in the Mestalla: 'I've known Mourinho for years and I can assure you that beating Barça's not the main thing for him. What he really doesn't want is to lose by many goals. That way he can blame the referee.'

These remaining tensions were discussed at the official directors' lunch. The Barcelona directors had asked Pérez to do something about Mourinho before any bad feeling spread to the supporters but the Madrid directors agreed that it was impossible to do anything with him. He was uncontrollable. 'You don't know Mourinho,' said one Madrid director. Pérez said nothing. The food was getting cold and soon everyone fell silent; shortly afterwards they left, without the traditional post-meal chat. The Barcelona representatives' anger was evident when one of them made an abrupt threat that Pérez took very seriously:

'Do you know what the dream of *Barcelonismo* is? It's to get you back for what happened with Figo. Because the damage that did to the club was irreparable ...'

The team-talk before the semi-final first-leg on 27 April was much like the ones Mourinho had delivered at the Mestalla. In part dedicated to the referee, it included instructions that the players thought were somewhat contradictory. After asking them to go in hard for the ball and try to physically overwhelm Barça, Mourinho stressed how they should realise that UEFA referees would not be as benign as Spanish ones. Pepe, according to team-mates close to him, said that Mourinho had given him a series of one-on-one talks in which he repeatedly mentioned the word 'intimidate'. Face to face with Pepe, he insisted that he should cultivate a frightening image in the eyes of the Barça players and that to achieve this, if necessary, he had to be violent. He warned him that he would come in for criticism but promised him protection. Whatever he did, however well or otherwise he played, if he did what he was told he would always be in the team.

The 5–0 in 2010 had made Mourinho so nervous that he cooked up the theory that the only way to stop Barça was to commit more fouls. He asked his team to be as physical as possible, suggesting the referee would not be able to blow for every single foul unless he decided to abandon the match.

The number of fouls that Madrid committed against Barcelona in the 17 *clásicos* of the league, Copa del Rey, Champions League and Spanish Super Cup during the 2010–11 and 2012–13 seasons are, in chronological order: 16, 22, 27, 18, 30, 26, 17, 22, 20, 29, 20, 13, 17, 16, 19, 13, and 21. In total: 346 fouls by Madrid against 220 from Barça over the same period.

The peaks of the Madrid graph were the 27 fouls of the cup final in the Mestalla, the 30 fouls of the second leg of the 2011 Champions League semi-finals and the 29 fouls of the Copa del Rey semi-finals in January 2011. The first leg of the semi-finals of the Champions League was, however, an exception: an unusually low number of fouls by Madrid and an unusually high number by Barça. It was the only *clásico* in the three-year series in which Madrid committed fewer fouls than their rivals: 18 to Barça's 20. The conservative approach of both teams led to a strange situation. Madrid played for a goalless draw, and although Barcelona enjoyed plenty of possession they did not commit themselves to all-out attack.

Guardiola admitted later that he did not think it possible that his team could win both the cup and the Champions League. The physical and mental exhaustion of his players at that point of the season was so extreme the Barça coach believed that only the anger following the defeat at the Mestalla could give them the energy to keep going.

The first leg of the semi-finals of the Champions League at the Bernabéu on 27 April 2011 was the most pitiful *clásico* of the lot. With the exception of Puyol, who had come back from injury, replacing Adriano at left-back, Guardiola picked the same team as for the cup final. Mourinho retained his system, covering the absence of

Albiol and Khedira with Carvalho and Lass. Once the game started, the spectacle left the crowd bemused. Half-paralysed by the exertions of the cup, Barcelona barely had the strength even to attempt controlling the game by maintaining possession. Their players waited for Madrid in their own half, displaying an obvious attacking deficit down their own left flank where Puyol found himself in his least favoured defensive berth. Far from exploiting the situation, however, Madrid were reluctant to press and limited themselves to launching speculative 50-yard through balls to Ronaldo, up front on his own. Neither team dared venture into the other's half without taking significant precautions, but Madrid's reluctance was the more striking. In the first half the home team did not force Valdes to make a single save; Casillas only made two, both from Xavi.

At half-time Mourinho further simplified his plan by introducing Adebayor for Özil. The German had burned himself out receiving the ball with his back to Puyol on the rare occasions when his team-mates had found him with long passes out to the right touchline. With the exception of Ronaldo, who spent the match gesticulating to his team-mates, urging reluctant midfielders to advance a few yards to support him, the Madrid players were resigned to what seemed like a truce. But there was no truce, as the tie suddenly descended into chaos. Tired after playing two *clásicos* in an unfamiliar position that required him to cover a lot of ground, Pepe began arriving late into challenges. An hour into the game, a challenge on Alves – studs-up, flying spectacularly towards the Brazilian's shinpad, and with no intention of playing the ball – left referee Wolfgang Stark with no choice. It was dangerous play, a straight red, and Pepe was given his marching orders.

This decision infuriated Mourinho. The coach, who had spent the game sitting on the bench, began protesting so furiously that Stark sent him off, too. Messi took advantage of the confusion to resume hostilities on the pitch, scoring twice in the last quarter of an hour. The match ended 0–2. Employees at the Bernabéu saw Rui Faria, Mourinho's right-hand man, yelling in the tunnel at the Barça players through the bars of the dividing barrier:

'Why don't you go and change in the referees' dressing room? You win everything because of the referees.'

Pinto, Puyol and Piqué invited Faria to carry on the discussion on the other side of the barrier. The Madrid players began to berate their rivals, with the Barça players responding that they had given Madrid another footballing lesson:

'That's how you play football.'

Celebrations began on the Barcelona side. People sang. Some scoffed. On the Madrid side Faria's voice continued to rise:

'You believe that you play football but what you really do is buy referees.'

Boiling point had not yet been reached when Faria encouraged Pepe to go into the Barça dressing room and tell them to shut it. Pepe, like a manic robot whose on-button has just been pressed, launched himself into the visitors' dressing room where all hell broke loose and a number of players from both teams started fighting. The Barcelona players, who throughout the season had endured veiled accusations of bribery, simulation and even doping, found that their international team-mates at Real Madrid were far more loyal to Mourinho than Mourinho himself believed – or at least said he believed.

Other coaches, with the same or similar resources, would have taken steps to try to turn the result around at the Camp Nou. This was not the case with Mourinho, for whom the decisiveness of the first goal had by now become almost a religious belief. Some employees and players at Madrid even speculated that the sending-off of the coach had been premeditated, in keeping with his policy of always having a ready-made excuse handy. Another theory came from his own dressing room: given the choice between an epic sporting achievement and some heroic propaganda, the coach would really rather prefer to be the underdog rather than the victor. He had more to gain from being the victim.

Mourinho showed his utter indignation when he proclaimed in the dressing room that his team had been robbed. He reminded the players that this confirmed his idea of a UEFA plot, and encouraged them to go to the mixed zone and denounce what had happened in their own words.

If shamanism is a desperate attempt to control the terrors of the world by imitating them, what Mourinho did after the defeat was a kind of exorcism in reverse. Perhaps he was resolved to put on a demon mask and stage a parody of a black mass, in what has to go down as the most outrageous press conference in the history of the Champions League. His greying hair, half messed up by the fever he had caught, his grey jacket, his mournful black shirt – all these gave him the look of a troubled priest as he delivered his now-famous denunciation of the institutional conspiracy within UEFA and the Spanish Football Federation, one that favoured Barcelona:

'If I tell the referee and UEFA what I think and what I feel, my career ends today. And I cannot say what I feel but I leave a question that I hope one day will have an answer. Why? Why Obrevo? Why Busacca? Why De Bleeckere? Why Stark? Why? Why in every semi-final does the same thing always happen? We're talking about an absolutely fantastic football team. I've said it many times. Why Obrevo three years ago? Why could Chelsea not proceed to the final? Why did Inter have to play with 10 men for so long? Why this year have they tried to finish the tie in this match, when we could be here for three hours and it was still going to finish 0–0 … We were going to put Kaká on for Lass and we were going to try to get a little bit further up the pitch, but the strategy of the game was that we were not going to lose … Why? I don't understand. I don't know if it's UNICEF publicity, I don't know if it's the power of *señor* [Ángel María] Villar at UEFA, I don't know if it's because they're very nice, I don't know. I don't understand. Congratulations on a great football team. But congratulations also for all you have too, it must be very difficult to achieve. You've gained this power and the others have no chance. Against Chelsea, Drogba and Bosingwa were sanctioned. Against Inter, Motta didn't play the final. Against Arsenal, Wenger and Nasri were penalised.

'Today, I'm punished. I don't know why. I'm here just to pose a question that I hope one day will be answered. I was sent off with a red card and shouldn't even be here. There was a foul against us, a foul against Barça and suddenly, miraculously, Pepe is sent off, a team with 10 men, and space for them to solve problems that they'd not been able to solve before. The second game is in Barcelona: obviously, if we're talking simply in sporting terms, it's a very difficult mission. Today, we've seen that that's impossible. They have to get to the final – and they will reach the final. I can live my whole life with this question, but I hope one day to have an answer. Why? Why a team of this size, a great footballing team, needs something that is so obvious to everyone? Obrevo, De Bleeckere, Busacca, Frisk, Stark … I don't understand.

'Football should be played with the same rules for everyone. The same for everyone! Then the best man wins. Maybe today we'll draw 0–0 and in the second game Barcelona will win with merit, and we accept with fair play. But why now …? In a balanced game, that's going to finish 0–0 …? Why do what you have done? Only the referee can answer but he will not because he'll go home and doesn't have to answer to anyone about anything. And me, nothing … We worked a miracle last year and this year it's not been possible to have another miracle with 10 men.

'Madrid are eliminated from the final of the Champions League … We'll go to Barcelona with all the pride and respect we feel for our world of football, but sometimes it disgusts me a bit. I'm a bit disgusted to live in this world and make a living in this world, but it's our world … If by chance we score a goal and slightly open up the tie, they'll kill us again. Today has shown that we've no chance. And my question is: Why? Why not let the other teams play against them? If they're better they'll end up winning. Why is this? I don't understand …'

Mourinho brought his soliloquy to an abrupt end. A reporter then asked about the conservatism of his approach and the fact that this made victory less likely. With extraordinary disinhibition, Mourinho explained that the one thing he really wanted from a game was that it end goalless:

'My approach has different moments of organisation, depending on the game. It passes through not conceding goals, to thwarting the adversary, to playing compactly and deep as in the other two games we played [the league *clásico* at the Bernabéu and the cup final] … And then at a certain moment, we look for a change of organisation with the arrival of a fixed centre-forward, and at a more advanced stage, another change, playing a number 10 behind three attackers.

'It's the approach of a match that's 0–0, which looks set to finish 0–0, and then, in a moment of frustration for the opposition, you risk trying to win. You can lose or draw 0–0, which is the most logical. But you have a plan that the referee hasn't let you carry out. And I continue with the same question. Why? Why send off Pepe? Why? Why not give four penalties in a match against Chelsea …?'

The coach repeated his claims, with some variations, for about 10 minutes until he swept out of the room. Only he knows if his conviction was feigned or not. What is certain is that his complaints centred on insinuations of deliberate misjudgements from referees on a massive scale – and he knew very well how to spread these – and the certainty that UEFA had cheated them, and the Madrid directors and Pérez in particular. For weeks many of the directors encouraged the debate on the sending-off. To support their side of the argument, they supplied images to the media that supposedly showed that Pepe's studs had made no contact with Alves's leg.

Wolfgang Stark had simply rigorously applied FIFA Rule 12, which considers the showing of a straight red card in cases of serious foul play in the following terms: 'A player is guilty of serious foul play if he uses excessive force or brutality against an opponent when challenging for the ball in play. A tackle that endangers the safety of an opponent must be sanctioned as serious foul play.' The rule does not say that physical contact is a prerequisite for imposing the sanction.

Inspired by their coach, Madrid filed a misconduct complaint against Guardiola and eight of the Barcelona players to the Control and Disciplinary Committee of UEFA. The short statement argued that, following a 'preconceived tactic', Guardiola, and his players Alves, Pedro, Busquets, Piqué, Mascherano, Pinto, Valdés and Keita, 'persistently simulated aggression with the sole purpose of misleading the referee, which led to the manifestly unjust decision to send off Pepe'. The appeal was dismissed. On hearing of the rejection, Pérez broke down. According to a witness, he ignored his lawyers when they told him of the weakness of the evidence Madrid had provided. The president did not believe in legal arguments. He believed in his coach, and said, with considerable force, that the tape submitted to UEFA provided irrefutable evidence of both Barcelona's violations and Pepe's innocence:

'But the video is perfect! It proves everything! They should ban half the Barcelona team!'

Ronaldo ended the game enraged. He was just as annoyed with the referee as with his coach, whose tactical plan had left him so isolated that over the course of the entire game he was unable to get one shot on target from open play: just one free-kick against the wall and a shot that deflected off a defender. His frustration was compounded by Messi's goals; Messi had it all handed to him on a plate, in his view, by the attacking football from Barcelona that so benefited him. When Mourinho asked Ronaldo to face the press and denounce the conspiracy, he by and large followed the script:

'I don't understand. I don't understand why in all qualifying Champions League games Barça end up playing against 10 men. Arsenal, Chelsea, Inter … Every year the same thing. Mourinho is right. The people at Barcelona have a lot of power, and not just on the field – off it too. Barcelona scored their goals against us playing 10 men. Perhaps we didn't have a good game. But nothing was happening. Was 0–0 a bad result? 0–0 would have been a good result. We had a strategy. Kaká was warming up to come on for the final minutes. We were going to attack. Football is like that. Strategies. After a 0–0, in Barcelona they'd have to attack us and we could play them on the counter-attack … As an attacker I don't like to play that way, but I have to adapt to what the team asks from me.'

Sensitive to the more subtle signs of insubordination, Mourinho felt that with his last remark Ronaldo had betrayed him. When they met again in Valdebebas the following day neither greeted the other. Mutually offended by various little niggling disputes, they did not even look at one another. The squad's return to training meant a reawakening of their deep-rooted malaise against the coach. Casillas and Ramos headed the large group of players who claimed that approaching games with the aim of getting a 0–0 was 'a disgrace'. A tactical and aesthetic error. They were supported by Benzema, Özil, Higuaín, Ronaldo, Alonso, Arbeloa, Marcelo and Kaká. The Brazilian, who had felt marginalised for the previous three months, could not believe that Mourinho really saw him as the catalyst for defeating Barcelona.

'We are Real Madrid!' they repeated, as if the historical ideals of the club were being betrayed. What hurt them above all was that Mourinho's plan suggested he lacked faith in their potential. They felt slighted; play like the coach wants, and we'll only win by some fluke. That, or we'll lose as a small team loses. 'Playing that way, it's as if we're all useless,' they said. 'Mourinho only thinks of himself.'

Mourinho did not pick Ronaldo to face Real Zaragoza on Saturday 30 May. When, on the Friday, the striker found out he was not in the team he felt like he was being punished, and began banging the lockers and the walls. 'Son of a bitch,' he shouted. 'Son of a bitch.' He was beside himself. The coach, who felt betrayed by the statement that Ronaldo had made after the last *clásico*, had sidelined him, knowing that there was nothing that made him suffer more. When it came to taking advantage of a crisis to accrue more power, Mourinho had few rivals. The exemplary nature of correcting the principal star of the squad was the most influential message he could send out to his players. If he could send his top player to the dungeons, others would do well to take note of the consequences of defying his attempts to make everyone sing from the same hymn sheet.

Mourinho knew that there were grudges festering between Ronaldo and the Spanish players over the alleged favouritism enjoyed by the forward. Some interpreted Mourinho's dropping of Ronaldo as being the coach trying to curry favour with the Spanish sector. But the real difference between Ronaldo and the rest lay in the nature of Ronaldo's friendship with his agent. He only had to make a call to complain to Mendes and the agent interceded on his behalf – and no one was able to persuade Mourinho like Mendes. Ronaldo's call to

Mendes had a lasting effect. Ronaldo never suffered a similar punishment in the two years he remained under Mourinho's orders. Others were not so fortunate.

Easter Sunday came on 1 May. Upon reaching Valdebebas the players were summoned by Mourinho to the dressing room and all the support staff – kit-men, masseurs and medical staff – were asked to leave and close the door behind them, as they were suspected of leaking information to the press. Only the coach, his assistants, the players and Zinedine Zidane remained. The former French footballer had started working in a liaison role between management and the coaching staff, in the vacuum left by Jorge Valdano, who had been relieved by Mourinho of his former functions as a bridge between the offices of the club and the team. Mourinho began by saying that, without asking for it from the club, they had called him to announce their firmest support:

'The club supports me. The club has gone against UEFA because it's with me. But the videos that have been sent are nothing to do with me. That's an initiative of the club …'

Casillas listened, sitting on a bench to one side, looking down at his lap. Sour-faced, he followed Mourinho from the corner of his eye. The coach outlined his plan for the visit to the Camp Nou on Tuesday 3 May:

'We'll go out to play a calm game. To wait. We must defend very near the area with a low-block so the game ends 0–0. If it ends 0–0 we can say that the tie was decided by the referee in the first leg.'

The players exchanged looks of disbelief.

'At Barcelona we have three options: two impossible and one possible. The only possible option is that the game ends with a close result and we lose the tie. Of the two impossible choices, the first is that they thrash us. This must be avoided at all costs so we can blame the referees. This can never happen. The other impossible choice is to win the tie. If, in trying to preserve the 0–0 we end up going to the final by chance, then perfect. But the priority is to finish with a close score so that we can blame the referees. A 2–1, 1–0, a draw … this will be enough to say that we were robbed at the Bernabéu.'

Mourinho tried to convince his team that they should lose the tie in a calculated way. He invited them to turn the game into a dialectical argument – this would provide him with a propaganda weapon that, with his rhetorical powers, he could then wield to devastating effect. He continued, with nobody interrupting him:

'Real Madrid have hired the best lawyers in the world, and I have it from a good source that after the semi-finals they'll make it public that they are going to ban Alves for two games for play-acting and Busquets five games for racism, and the great Pep … because this one believes that he's great … they're going to give him two games. Maybe he'll get three for being the boss of the *teatreros* (play-actors), for encouraging all this theatre. I can assure you. That's why we need to get a close result. Because then I'll go in front of the press and say that the tie was lost at the Bernabéu and the media will agree with me that they robbed us. But if they give us a beating then we'll be left looking ridiculous in the eyes of world football, because the next day the media will say: "Where are the referees, Mourinho? Where are the referees, players of Madrid?"'

Mourinho was so engrossed in his own world that the players heard him make a slip in talking about himself, revealing that his real concern was his own personal prestige. He immediately amended what he had said to include 'players of Madrid'. Those who heard the speech and then reconstructed it described the situation as 'incredible' and 'amazing', but did not dare say anything at the time.

The reaction of the players was mixed. Some tried to show that they had been moved. Pepe, Di María, Alonso and Granero seemed convinced, Granero saying approvingly, 'How clever ...' There were also the sceptics and those who were indifferent, such as Adebayor, Carvalho, Lass and Khedira. A group remained that were outraged – Casillas, Ramos, Arbeloa, Higuaín and, above all, Ronaldo. They believed that Mourinho was prepared to chuck the tie out with the rubbish just so that he could justify 15 minutes of craziness in the press conference room at the Bernabéu. He hoped that Barça, on seeing them sitting so deep, would sign the armistice. But that was not enough. A mere act of collective obedience served no purpose. Mourinho wanted to convince his players that it was best for everyone to surrender, following his instructions, because in this way no one would be accountable. On the contrary, in the eyes of the fans they would be free of any responsibility because they would be presented as martyrs, their sacrifice serving to expose to the world the truth about Barcelona:

'This is the team of the beautiful game. We must fight to reveal exactly who they are. So that on a global scale everyone knows that the pretty boys of world football play dirty, which is what they do. There they are, Alves, Busquets ... How can we prove that they play dirty? By getting a close result ...'

Leaning forward, Casillas held the edge of the bench with his left hand as if to twist it off. He passed his right hand across his face while shaking his head. Not a single player questioned the coach. No one opened his mouth to ask for explanations, as if there were no doubts, as if everything were obvious and reasonable. Having finished his tactical-political speech, Mourinho turned to Ronaldo and questioned him in front of everyone:

'You, Cris! Come here so that I can tell you something. I'm going to say it to your face: you complain that we play defensively. But do you know why we play this way? For you. Because, as you don't want to defend or cover the wings, I have to have the team sitting deep. You get upset because I didn't bring you on in Bilbao, because when you come on you do your own thing. To achieve your own personal goals. And perhaps I'm to blame for that for allowing you to do it. But you concentrate on your game. Then you go to the media and, instead of doing what you have to do, you criticise us for being defensive. You know what you should have done? Criticise the referee. Think of me, think of the team!'

Ronaldo stirred and gesticulated, cursing in a strong Portuguese accent, attempting to cut Mourinho off. But he could not:

'I have to look after you because you're my brother's brother, and when someone is their brother's brother, that makes them a brother as well. But the other day instead of doing what I told you, you went and criticised my tactics. You criticised me! You don't respect your team-mates. You're watching them run. You're watching the way that Pepe and Lass are running, and you raise your hands to protest that the ball is not reaching you. You could be a better team-mate and, instead of raising your hands, go out into the press area and talk about the referee. Because I've invented this system for you, so that you're comfortable, and you don't have to run and you score goals. It's your fault that we play this way. If you concentrate on running in behind Alves you let him run away free. What is it? You think that Di María is less than you?'

Ronaldo was not to be discouraged and started yelling in Portuguese. He demanded that Mourinho tell him what the hell he had said, he accused him of misrepresentation, mixing up events that had no connection in order to manipulate things for his own convenience. The shouting grew louder, so that it became hard to hear who was saying quite what. Ronaldo, stunned, then blinded by anger; Mourinho colder, but still articulate:

'You, right now, don't love me. You'll talk badly about me. But I love you because you're my brother's brother. If you're not clear about that, I am. What my brother asks me to do, I do. I've given everything for you. Now you ought to do the same for me.'

The meeting came to a close after 40 minutes when Zidane, who had kept himself in the background, looking very serious, was invited by the coach to say what he thought. The Frenchman nonchalantly contradicted what he had just heard:

'You're very good players and you should try to beat Barcelona. We are Real Madrid and Real Madrid always go out to win.'

Mourinho threw Zidane an indignant look before leaving the dressing room. (A month went by before the Frenchman returned to Valdebebas, to hold a lengthy discussion with Mourinho. In the dressing room they believed he had been reprimanded for not supporting the coach's position.)

Ronaldo stayed in the dressing room bad-mouthing in Portuguese. He had been the only one who had dared to respond to Mourinho during the 40 minutes that he took to give his speech. 'How this son of a bitch has sold me out', they heard him shout.

Kaká was the only one to confess that he did not understand whose family was constantly being referred to by the coach. To find out he asked Higuaín, one of his close friends.

'Who is his brother?'

'The brother is Jorge Mendes,' Higuaín told him.

The players could not believe what they had just witnessed. 'This is shit!' they said. They agreed that if their careers lasted another 100 years they would struggle to ever experience anything even half as strange as this. Going out on to the field they questioned each other in whispers, trying to work out whether everyone had understood the same thing: 'They had to prepare to lose.' Then there was the open confession, with no scruples whatsoever, that the coach had plotted with Mendes, his 'brother'. They recalled that he dared to say that he had changed the tactical model to satisfy his 'brother' and agent. But now the needs had changed and this invited him to change the pieces on the board. 'He's given us Cristiano's head,' someone said. 'He wants to make new friends.'

Ronaldo went out on to the pitch, took a ball, and kicked it so hard that he sent it flying high out of the enclosure. Then he went to the physiotherapy room and had a massage.

Casillas confessed to a friend in the club that he had never felt so embarrassed. He could not get out of his head the image of his former coach, Bernd Schuster, who was fired in the winter of 2008 for publicly saying, on the eve of a *clásico*, that it was not possible to win at the Camp Nou.

Zidane contacted Pérez that same Sunday to tell him what had happened at the meeting. Club sources say that the president did not like what he heard. The senior players waited for a call from the president, thinking that Pérez would overrule the coach and ask them to try by all means possible to win the tie. The team travelled to Barcelona on 2 May without receiving any such order and stayed at the Hotel Juan Carlos I. Mourinho insisted that they should be concentrating on defending their goal. Nothing about planning a comeback.

He met with the president at the hotel but there was no change of plans. No one knows what Pérez said. Then it was time to go to the stadium. Uncertainty reigned. Casillas waited for a call, a signal, a message to force the issue. Compelled to show his hand, Pérez made the choice that would characterise what remained of his mandate: backing Mourinho to the end. The president had decided to use Mourinho as the figurehead of his project long before that trip to the Camp Nou. By the time the team took the team bus to the game, the die was cast. Mourinho, suspended by UEFA, decided to stay in the hotel and watch the match on TV.

For a long time afterwards, Madrid employees on this trip recalled Casillas's distress in the bus on the way to the stadium. No Mourinho, and Aitor Karanka silent in the front seat. The captain called his team-mates to the back, then told them to try to win the game. He asked them to respect the agreed tactics but to forget to take as many precautions and dare to attack Barça without inhibition, thereby going against the strict orders of Mourinho, someone with more power in the club than anyone in his position since Muñoz:

'Come on! We've got to go out to win. We have to respect the formation but our attitude has to be to try to win the tie,' Casillas shouted. 'It has to be seen that we're trying to win the game. They have to see that!'

Casillas said to his team-mates that they could tell the press what the coach had instructed them to say, but that on the pitch they should not surrender, adding that if they closed up shop they would look incompetent to the watching world. Huddled around him, everyone agreed.

Caught out by Madrid's sense of adventure at the start of the match, Barcelona failed to impose themselves on the game. But despite the creativity of players like Kaká, Higuaín, Ronaldo, Di María and Marcelo, Madrid's play failed to result in goals and their improvised tactics eventually faltered. Both teams failed to make the final ball count and the game finished 1–1. Manchester United – and ultimately the title of Champions of Europe – awaited Barcelona at Wembley.

UEFA did not fine Guardiola or any of his players. Quite the opposite. A Madrid director consulted Ángel María Villar, president of the Spanish Football Federation, on the chance of doing something about the appeal. Villar said that the best Madrid could do was to rid themselves of their coach. He warned that complaining was a mistake because UEFA thought that what Mourinho had implied was that their most prestigious competition – and their main source of income – was not clean. It was a head-on attack on the credibility of their organisation. The same competition that had enabled Mourinho to become a internationally known reference point in world football was now the subject of a complaint by the coach, with the formal backing of his club.

CHAPTER 8

REBELLION

'What a worthless, burnt-out coward I'd be called if I would submit to you and all your orders.'

HOMER, *The Iliad*, Book 1

One day during the 2010–11 season Madrid were staying in a hotel ahead of a match when some supporters gave Iker Casillas a photograph in which he was shown lifting the World Cup in Johannesburg. A team-mate came up to him to look at the image with admiration.

'How cool …'

'Six and a half kilos. It weighs six and a half kilos.'

Casillas mentioned the weight when talking about the solid-gold trophy that Silvio Gazzaniga had designed for FIFA and that he had held aloft as captain of the Spanish national team. Although, according to some, the weight of the trophy is eight kilos, the goal-keeper thought differently. For him it was six and a half kilos. When he remembered this moment, his team-mates saw how he got excited as only small boys and extremely happy men can. If there were two things that he felt deeply proud of, they were the 2010 World Cup in South Africa and the 2008 European Championships in Austria and Switzerland. To have represented one of the greatest national football teams of all time filled him with total satisfaction. The team-mates who helped him to achieve it occupied a special place in his heart. Especially Xavi Hernández, who had been his accomplice in the national team since the time they were both teenagers.

Casillas was not picked by Mourinho to play the last game of the 2010–11 season against Almería at the Bernabéu on 21 May. Mourinho, seemingly content with Casillas's work, had given him the day off. He was not in the dressing room when, after the referee blew the half-time whistle, his team-mates found Mourinho at his most challenging. They were winning 3–0, but, before they went back out on to the pitch and then went on their holidays, he wanted to send them off with a message that was both cryptic and threatening, according to certain witnesses:

'Let's be clear. You're the first to know … I'm going to tell you the truth … Apart from the fact that we've lost the league because the *titulares* [first-team regulars] surrendered, the year has been fucking shit. A disaster. Why? Because of the *titulares*. Because they haven't shown their faces. Between ourselves, let's not kid anybody. The *titulares* haven't been up to it. I'm sure that next year, with new recruits, we're going to win everything.'

One player tells of a dressing room full of pent-up physical violence. Another thought that the absence of Casillas had encouraged the coach to come out and say things in a tone that he would not have been bold enough to have used if the captain had been present. Ronaldo tapped his boots insistently on the floor. Ramos looked disapprovingly at Mourinho. Albiol puffed out his cheeks and blew. But nobody opened their mouth to interrupt the boss. Mourinho finished his team-talk with a brief coda in which he attributed the team's salvation in the public's eyes to the distraction that his campaign of systematic denouncements of the referees, the TV companies and UEFA had generated.

'It's a good job that, thanks to me, we've come out of this looking OK. Thanks to me, people haven't realised how bad the season has been.'

They went back out on to the pitch so motivated – or so afraid of losing their places ahead of the squad overhaul that had just been announced – that Almeria were to concede another five goals. It meant an 8–1 scoreline against a team that had already been relegated. Some fans celebrated as if this spectacle of humiliation had some sporting value, and the home team, with the backing of the crowd, went about their work with enthusiasm. But the magnitude of the result did nothing to diminish the sense of impending threat that accompanied them on their holidays. Many began to realise that the excuses that they had given Mourinho throughout the season came at a considerable price.

The 2010–11 season ended with Madrid winning the cup, and Barcelona the league and the Champions League. A modest return, but lauded by the club. Before the final match, Casillas and Karanka held press conferences to broadcast Mourinho's version of Madrid's year:

'I would give this season 8 out of 10.'

If there was one player who deserved his season to be rated at 8 out of 10 it was Casillas. But the captain has never stood out for his ability to sell himself. Introverted and not particularly hot-blooded, he lacked the gift of self-promotion. The more famous he became, the more uncomfortable the resulting social commitments made him. He liked the fact that he was still treated as if he were some kid from the suburb of Móstoles, but what he most longed for was the contact he had with the residents of Navalacruz, the village of his grandparents. In this small bastion of the Sierra Avila he was able to enjoy some isolation, in the company of people who believed that parish-life routines provide a person with everything they need. He lacked the ambition for power and the desire to control others that distinguish many great football leaders. Lazy when it came to official matters, he was someone who avoided disputes until there was no other alternative. He was 'Cachazudo': calm, easy-going, phlegmatic.

In the summer of 2011 Casillas celebrated his 30th birthday. He had made his début in the first team in 1999 and had stood out when Madrid won the Champions League, although he was still practically a youth-team player. He was more experienced than any of his teammates, and even though he found Mourinho unbearable he was prepared to travel along the same road with him for as long as that was what the club wanted. Mourinho had put Casillas up for the Ballon d'Or in 2010, knowing that it was to Casillas that he owed his continuity and his consolidation at the club. He was convinced that not even Pérez would have been able to justify backing Mourinho if he had not won the Copa del Rey, the cup secured by Casillas with some unforgettable saves.

The goalkeeping coach, Silvino Louro, said many times that he had never in his life seen a save like the one produced by Casillas to deny Iniesta in the final at the Mestalla. The Barcelona midfielder popped up in the number 10 position and hit a shot that looked to be curving perfectly into the far corner. But Casillas reacted incredibly quickly. His legs propelled him like two springs and his elastic body stretched, floating in mid-air as he reached for the ball, turning it away with the tips of his fingers for a corner. Mourinho admired the save so much he stressed its importance to Louro, Faria, Karanka and Chendo on the bench. They heard him say that the reason his time at Chamartín had not ended miserably in June 2011 was because of Iker's saves at the Mestalla. But the manager would never recognise this outside of his inner circle.

After a year of insisting that the club needed modernising urgently, the sacking of Jorge Valdano, his immediate superior in the organisation, had given Mourinho control of all the levers necessary to remodel the institution from its centre: the squad. The coach had dreamed all his life of such a scenario – counting on the support of a club with worldwide influence, working shoulder to shoulder with Jorge Mendes, financially backing him to pick up players in the global market, with control over who was brought into the club and who left, whose contracts were improved and whose renewed. It was the kind of control that would give him influence in the market, prestige in the media and an impressive image in the eyes of his players. Until then not even Pinto da Costa, the Porto president, nor Roman Abramovich, the owner of Chelsea, nor Massimo Moratti at Inter, had offered him such a wealth of resources. In the summer of 2011, after a career as first-team coach spanning 12 years, Mourinho reached the summit of his power.

Alarmed by what they had learned on the last day of the season, the Madrid players imagined a wave of intimidating new signings capable of challenging them for their places in the team. The dressing room never expected the list of new players that was eventually announced: Varane, Altintop, Sahin, Callejón, Coentrão, Pedro Mendes. Neither had it foreseen that the most expensive and most requested new recruit from that group would be Fabio Coentrão, a left-back signed to replace Marcelo, the best left-back on the planet, whose progression had seemed unstoppable.

Coentrão had been a winger for most of his career, but had not found recognition until he established himself at left-back at Benfica.

A tenacious player, strong and daring, he stood out less for his ability, more for his motivation. As soon as his enthusiasm waned he struggled to lift himself much above average. The supporters at La Romareda only vaguely remembered him for his spell at Real Zaragoza – where Benfica sent him on loan during the 2008–09 season – because he rarely played. Marcelino García Toral, his coach at the time, tried to get him back on track following several visits by the police to Coentrão's house after calls by neighbours complaining of noise in the early hours of the morning.

'He didn't take his football very seriously,' said Marcelino. 'He was 20 and lived alone with some friends whose appearance suggested they weren't perhaps the best influence on him. He never really got involved in games and maybe for that reason I let him go. As the years passed he transformed himself. At the time I didn't really look at him as a potential full-back. He wasn't lazy, and he was obedient, but he was soft, flimsy in the challenge, and didn't offer a great deal defensively. He was a forward player, a little winger.'

Madrid paid €30 million for Coentrão. The left-sided player became the fifth-most expensive signing of the summer, after Falcao to Atletico (€47 million), Agüero to Manchester City (€45 million), Pastore to PSG (€42 million) and Fàbregas to Barça (€34 million). Below him in the transfer rankings that summer were Nasri to Manchester City (€28 million), Alexis to Barcelona (€26 million), Mata to Chelsea (€26 million), Ibrahimović to Milan (€24 million) and Cazorla to Arsenal (€23 million).

Bayern were on the brink of signing Coentrão in 2010 for €15 million but Benfica did not close the deal. Jorge Mendes, according to Gestifute sources, offered Benfica the chance to wait a year when they would be able to sell him for double that. Benfica only took 50 per cent of the transfer. The other half was for the investment fund Benfica Stars, the private capital group that shared players' rights with the club.

At first, even though Mourinho said that Coentrão had not come to play as a left-back, Marcelo felt that a competitor had been signed. At 23, Marcelo Vieira was a Brazil international, had played for Madrid since the 2006–07 season, and enjoyed the friendship and respect of his team-mates. There are some players that have the kind of sensibility in their feet that most people only have in their hands. Maradona belonged to that category. At Madrid the only player with those juggler's qualities was Marcelo. Quick, skilful and brave, over the years he improved his level of defensive concentration. He was a marvellous footballer. Both Mourinho and Mendes saw it immediately.

Marcelo struck up a friendship with Pepe and Ronaldo, the three of them soon spending every day together. That is until they starting to propose to him that he put his affairs in the hands of Mendes. The Brazilian pretended not to pay too much attention until one day at the start of 2011, during a lunch in the presence of Mendes himself, they put the question to him directly: 'Are you going to sign with Jorge?' Marcelo explained that his agent had been with him since the beginning, was like a member of the family to him and that he did not want to leave him. From that point, according to the full-back, strange things started to happen. Pepe distanced himself. On one occasion, Mourinho criticised him in a press conference without mentioning him, saying that he preferred full-backs like Arbeloa because they never surprised him with moments of carelessness. And then he saw in a magazine that Ronaldo had said that he would be pleased if Madrid signed Coentrão.

For the Spanish contingent the influence of Mendes had become oppressive. The agent intervened in almost everything that happened at Madrid, either directly or indirectly, offering his mediation services or sharing work with other agents. One of his most regular partners was Reza Fazeli. The company director of the ISM agency based in

Düsseldorf, Fazeli represented Altintop, Sahin and Özil. According to sources at Gestifute, Fazeli tried to convince Özil that the best thing for him was to let Mendes become his advisor, moving on to his payroll. Persuaded that in Gestifute there were very well-defined hierarchies, and suspecting that, for example, he would be attended to with less care than Ronaldo, the German took a step that few footballers dared: he told Fazeli that he would be leaving him, that he was Mesut Özil and did not need any professional agent to promote him. Since then he has been represented by his father Mustafa.

Unpredictable with the players whom he brought in, Mourinho was ruthless with the footballers he no longer wanted. The list of those discarded included Drenthe, Gago, Canales and Pedro León. First of all he arranged one-to-one dates for them with José Ángel Sánchez so that he could tell them that the club would take care of the business of finding them new clubs that suited Madrid's interests. When Sánchez mentioned German, Italian and Turkish clubs the players believed he was acting in concert with Mendes, whose relationships in Germany and Turkey were well known. The players refused to sanction the deals and as a result were not taken on the pre-season tour, being left out of the squad and left to train alone at Valdebebas while their team-mates went to California. According to one interpretation of the sports labour law, their severance from the heart of the team was a footballer's equivalent of being expelled from the workplace. It was the first time in the history of Madrid that a coach had separated players from the team without having disciplinary reasons for doing so.

Lass was a case apart. His team-mates nicknamed him 'antisistema', as he combined an indomitable spirit with the defiant republicanism taught in the French schools he attended. Mourinho wanted to take him to Los Angeles because he appreciated him as a player; Lass refused to go, saying that he did not want to spend any more time under Mourinho's charge, and that he had warned him months earlier that he hoped he would be allowed to leave. When Mourinho continued to insist that he join up with the squad and did not stop calling him, Lass told him where to go with a string of insults, turned off his mobile, ordered his agent to do the same and disappeared for a few days, presumably to Paris.

Lass loved football. It is not known what he did during this time; the only thing he told his friends was that he did not get much sleep. He stayed up late to watch all the games of the Copa América that was being played in Argentina. He remained unreachable until one day he turned up at Valdebebas. It was midsummer and he found the training complex deserted; the only people around were some maintenance staff, and Pedro León and Drenthe doing laps of the training pitches without the ball. The balls, they said, were under lock and key by order of Mourinho.

Mourinho knows better than any coach that there is nothing that annoys a player more than being denied contact with the ball. Indeed, in his own training programmes there are no exercises that don't involve the ball. What he had done upset Lass so much that he called the club and told them exactly what he thought. His insistence was so great that the staff at Valdebebas eventually gave the balls to the players. What had happened was so unusual that the Sports Association of Spain sent an inspection team to the club to look into it.

If those who stayed behind had a miserable time, those who went on the trip to California did not fare much better. Madrid's preseason at the UCLA campus did not go smoothly. The support employees accompanying the team claimed the atmosphere was 'suffocating'. Mourinho was obsessed with the idea of starting the season by defeating Barcelona in the Super Cup and had brought his squad together a week before Guardiola's team came back from their holidays. He was convinced that if Madrid won the Super Cup he could renew the protest he had made in the semi-finals of the Champions League. His first step was announcing that if his players beat Barça they would thereby demonstrate to the world the truth of everything he had said about the conspiracy hatched by UEFA and its referees to destroy Madrid; and that if they were capable of beating the best club in Europe they would make it manifestly clear that nobody other than Madrid should have won the Champions League at Wembley.

Mourinho was constantly agitated. He did not like the pitches at the UCLA. He said that the colour of the grass was not right and ordered the pitches to be returfed, costing Madrid thousands of dollars. He did not like the food, either. At the beginning of the previous pre-season, relying on his famously critical palate, he had tasted each dish the chefs served then sacked the lot of them. He behaved as if he were a gourmet. The food seemed delicious to the players, but Mourinho found fault with everything and suggested changes to the way it was cooked.

He focused his attention on the hot-plates, on the grass, on the politics of agitation and propaganda, and finally on the captaincy. He began to seriously consider taking the captaincy away from Casillas and giving it to an outfield player, although doing so would go against the club's tradition that the armband should go to the most senior member of the team. Among his assistants, Mourinho defended his position with sporting arguments, saying that there were certain decisive moments when a goalkeeper could not act like an outfield player, such as communicating with the strikers or complaining to the referee. For the role of captain Mourinho first considered Ramos, Ronaldo and, above all, Pepe. Ramos was Pérez's favourite. Ronaldo treated the idea with contempt and refused the offer. Pepe was Mourinho's preferred choice because of his docility.

Neither Casillas nor Ramos had shown themselves to be very flexible in terms of taking on board Mourinho's suggestions, and the coach wanted someone who would act as his mouthpiece. Someone completely loyal, who would never question him. And, if possible, someone who was not a Spanish international. Since his arrival at Madrid he explained to his assistants that he did not trust those players who had just won the World Cup because he found them lacking in ambition and the requisite nervous tension. The commotion over the captaincy did not result in anything more than a growing climate of mistrust between Casillas and the coach, who began treating his goalkeeper with indifference, dealing instead with Alonso, Pepe and Ramos.

The journalist Santiago Segurola, match reporter for *El País* during the 1998 World Cup, coined the neologism '*trivote*' to define the concept Cesare Maldini had introduced to the Italian midfield. Dino Baggio, Di Biagio and Pesotto constituted the *trivote*. The only thing different from the double pivot first seen in Spain in the 50s with Maguregui and Mauri was the addition of a third defensive midfielder. The result was a stiffening of the midfield – one that lessened creativity, tending to leave no room for players who operated just behind the striker – and a narrowing of the formation, all serving a single purpose: defending deep in numbers and attacking on the break. The term '*trivote*' became part of everyday football-speak in Spain. The Madrid players used it every day to describe what Mourinho had implemented in April against Barcelona. In the summer of 2011, when they explained the tactics the manager had prepared at UCLA, they again referred to the *trivote*. The new version, it seemed, would feature Khedira, Alonso and Coentrão.

Mourinho was so keen to have a strong, athletic and flexible holding midfielder in his team that he could not stop thinking about Lass. Even though he knew that the Frenchman had disowned him, he did not stop sending him texts asking him to stay at Madrid. The player returned one of the messages in front of his friends, one of whom read the exchange and related it in the following terms:

'Get out of my life and leave me in peace …'

'You should know that I'm not going to sell you for less than €20 million. Get back into the pre-season and you'll play.'

'Let your mother go to the pre-season.'

'I'm going to send you to Castilla.' [Castilla are the club's second team, who play in the second division.]

'OK, well, I'll earn the €9 million that they owe me and wait in Castilla until I'm a free agent …'

'You won't be able to stand it in Castilla. After three months you'll return with me to compete …'

'I won't be able to stand it? You forget that at Chelsea I didn't play for so long that you had to transfer me to Arsenal. And I was 20 years old. Imagine what I am capable of doing now that I'm 26.'

Mourinho's bad mood accompanied him to the training ground. To his assistants he insisted that the squad were missing certain quali ties. In front of the players he appeared more weighed down, more demanding, more inflexible in his principles. The idea that the only important thing in football was to win, and that taking the greatest defensive precautions, with fewer concessions than ever to attacking licence and elaboration, formed the core of his sermons.

If in the summer of 2010 he practised on the basis of a 4-2-3-1 formation, 4-3-2-1 prevailed in 2011. To instruct his players in this new formation Mourinho forced natural wingers such as Di María and Coentrão to play as defensive midfielders, escorting Khedira and Alonso. During the friendlies he came up with *trivotes* and *pivotes* (two defensive midfielders) of all kinds: Khedira, Alonso and Coentrão; Coentrão, Alonso and Pepe; Alonso and Coentrão; Khedira and Coentrão; and Granero and Coentrão.

Mourinho's concern for picking Coentrão in any position other than at left-back, laid bare to the players his desire to justify a signing that had led to so many doubts. The fact that on the pre-season tour he had gone out of his way to show affection towards Pepe, Di Maria and Coentrao, did nothing to lessen suspicions. The majority of the squad believed that his favouritism towards these players was not based wholly on footballing reasons but also on his friendship with Jorge Mendes. These were not the only questions that arose among the squad. In the team-talks the players began to cast doubt on some of the technical observations of their manager.

The first leg of the Super Cup was played in the Bernabéu on 14 August 2011. Considering both sides' lack of preparation it turned out to be a great game. There were notable absentees in the team sent out by Guardiola. Barcelona started with Valdes, Alves, Mascherano, Abidal, Adriano, Thiago, Keita, Iniesta, Alexis, Messi and Villa. Madrid, who had had one more week of pre-season, were able to field their strongest side: Casillas, Ramos, Pepe, Carvalho, Marcelo, Di María, Khedira, Alonso, Benzema, Özil and Ronaldo.

A superb move involving Benzema and Özil gave Madrid a 1–0 lead after they had made an irrepressible start. The words that Mourinho had used in April remained the same in August. He had insisted on the word 'hard' to describe the way he wanted his players to go into challenges, reassuring them that Spanish referees did not dare give red cards to Madrid players. Sending them out to press using high-block for throw-ins and goal-kicks, he warned that if Barcelona played more than three passes then they had to get back quickly. As Barcelona were struggling to put even two passes together, Alonso and Khedira were able to move 20 yards forward, closer to the fully switched-on Madrid forward line. From the touchline Mourinho looked on with silent approval.

Before the game he had told his players, regardless of where on the pitch they won possession from Barcelona, to finish off their attacking move as quickly as possible. This hurried Madrid's play. No backward or sideways balls, and at the slightest hesitation the moves would be channelled to the wings and end in crosses. But Madrid's vertigo suddenly went with the 1–0. Realising he should make the most of the advantage, Mourinho ordered the retreat, and Madrid went from chaotic attacks to sitting deep and waiting. Goals from Villa and Messi were the consequence. Only a shot from Alonso on the hour brought the scores back level at 2–2. Mourinho's reaction was immediate. He put Coentrão on for Di María, forming what he had spent so much time practising in Los Angeles: the *trivote*. The measure at least served to protect Casillas's goal. But Madrid no longer had control of the game.

Every minute that Coentrão played in midfield revealed more and more of his ineptitude. If he did not receive the ball, he lost his position on the right wing; he was not able to lose his marker nor was he capable of making diagonal runs on goal. As a midfielder, and as part of the *trivote*, he had great difficulty making space for himself to receive the ball – or he was simply trying to hide every time that his team got possession of it – and the central defenders never found him in a position to give him the ball. Physically, he was best suited to the left wing. He was a willing marker, but what he was most happy doing was going past the full-back and crossing, or arriving in the area himself. He had vision and a good change of pace, but he was a long way from being able to replace Ronaldo in that position, at least not without anyone noticing the marked difference between the two.

* * *

The return leg on 17 August was probably the most dramatic *clásico* of all these years. In his eagerness to play Coentrão, and persuaded that the team lacked stability in other areas, Mourinho did exactly what he had managed to avoid doing during the seven friendlies in the pre-season: he put him at left-back, the only position in the team where he could play to a certain level. This was Marcelo's position; the Brazilian was dropped to the bench, humiliated, and spent the first half passing caustic comment on his boss. A substitute on the bench at the time summed up the feeling of an increasingly influential part of the dressing room with the following remark as he watched Pepe, Carvalho, Coentrão, Di María and Ronaldo:

'Five Jorge Mendes players on the pitch. What he wants to do is play an "eleven" made up of Mendes players!'

For the second half Mourinho reorganised his team to re-establish the *trivote*. He brought on Marcelo at left-back and moved Coentrão into midfield. The deciding goal, giving a 3–2 victory to Barcelona, started with a piece of skill from Messi in the zone that Coentrão should have been patrolling. Messi received the ball on the right side of midfield, played a pass out to Adriano and scored from the return pass. The Madrid players blamed Coentrão for the delay in closing down Messi and then for not cutting out the ball from Adriano.

Just before the end of the game, Marcelo, still annoyed at not having started, kicked Cesc Fàbregas in front of the bench. There were protests from everyone: Madrid called for action to be taken against the alleged play-acting of Fàbregas, and Barcelona wanted Marcelo to be punished for his violent play. In the middle of the melée, involving substitutes, employees and coaches from both clubs, Mourinho slipped into the Barcelona technical area. He was followed by his bodyguard, a young man, shaven-headed and well built, squeezed into a white shirt, who never left him before, during and immediately after games.

REBELLION

On seeing Guardiola's assistant Tito Vilanova with his back to him, the Madrid manager moved in from behind and poked his index finger into Vilanova's eye before quickly retreating. When Vilanova turned he could only stretch out his arm and slap Mourinho in the back of the neck. The bodyguard stepped in, preventing Vilanova from advancing any further. The next day, Madrid's lawyers sent videos of the incident to the Competition Committee in an attempt to show that the occupants of the Barcelona bench had provoked Madrid. In the video images it is difficult to distinguish anything out of the ordinary. The only judge, Alfredo Florez, a regular in the directors' box at the Bernabéu, gave Mourinho a two-match ban and Vilanova a one-match suspension. As far as Guardiola was concerned, the evidence showed that Madrid had positioned themselves carefully with respect to the regulating body of Spanish football.

Mourinho told his players that if Barça won the Super Cup they should not remain on the pitch for the presentation of the trophy, so they retired discreetly to the dressing room. Casillas got caught up in the collective hysteria, and told Fàbregas exactly what he thought about his 'simulation'. Xavi could not persuade him that he was wrong, and both captains argued until they had to be separated. There were no congratulations. It was a turning point for the captain. When Casillas saw the footage later on at home, not only did he discover that Fàbregas had in fact been hit hard by Marcelo. He also suspected that he himself had crossed the line into the ridiculous, and that he was compromising his prestige in a crusade that was neither his nor his club's, in a childish war that undermined the unity of the Spanish national side – those ties of complicity, those shared emotions, those friendships that had taken such a long time to forge. He felt his own identity as a player and as a person might be irreversibly stained if he did not act straight away.

Casillas decided to call Xavi and Puyol to apologise for what had happened over the last few months. He asked for their forgiveness, admitting that he had made a mistake, and he did it publicly so that all the supporters were aware of his position. An act of unprecedented grandeur, it took great courage. How many times has one of the game's giants apologised in front of the whole world? The initiative caught both Mourinho and Pérez by surprise. The coach saw it as a challenge to dressing-room unity and his principles. If until that point Casillas and Mourinho had maintained a civilised dialogue, from that moment on their relationship became one skirmish after another.

Pérez's, who as always had to manage a crisis with Mourinho in the middle of it, was ambivalent. He told his friends that Mourinho always did the opposite of whatever it was he asked him, and for that reason he had to be treated with extreme subtlety. As for the finger in the eye of Vilanova, he told the manager to do what he wanted but he recommended a public act of contrition. The response from Mourinho, one week after the events, was to issue a threat on Madrid's headed note paper. The statement, with messianic overtones, included a new term: '*pseudomadridistas*'. In this way, the manager was positioning himself as the Grand Inquisitor of Real Madrid, pointing the finger at those who confessed to be *Madridistas* but who did not share his way of working:

'I have a fantastic president, who is very intelligent and with whom I have a great friendship. I also have a director general who works 24 hours a day. Because of the way I feel, I believe that my motivation is enormous and my *Madridismo* is much larger than certain *pseudomadridistas*.

'I want to directly address myself towards the Madrid family to apologise to it, and only to it, for my attitude in the last game. Some are better adapted to the hypocrisy of football, they do it with their faces hidden, with their mouths covered and in the depth of the tunnels.

'I didn't learn to be a hypocrite. I didn't learn it and I don't want learn it.

'An embrace to everyone, and we'll see each other tomorrow in the Santiago Bernabéu.'

Madrid hosted Galatasaray for the Bernabéu Trophy on 24 August. More than an exhibition match and a friendly, this was a demonstration of extent of Mourinho's power. The stadium was covered in banners of support. In the ring of the highest stand of the Castellana side of the ground, directly in front of the directors' box, somebody had draped a significant banner: *'Mou, tu dedo nos señala el camino'* ('Mou, your finger shows us the way'). It was signed by the supporters' club of La Clásica, it was 100 feet long and had clearly been factory made. The club saw no reason to take it down.

In the 84th minute, Mourinho made a significant change: he took off Marcelo and put on Pedro Mendes. This young, right-sided central defender, an Under-21 with Portugal, had arrived on a free from Swiss team Servette to play for Castilla. His agent was Jorge Mendes and his new coach clearly thought highly of him, immediately inviting him to train with the first team. Mourinho then gave him his first-team debut in the Bernabéu Trophy and, finally, he included him in the club's Champions League squad. It was a lot of hype for an unknown player whose qualities did not make him stand out from any of the other young players at the club. His team-mates in Castilla did not take very long to nickname him *'El Enchufado'* ('The Connected One').

On the bench sat Casillas. The goalkeeper did not play so much as a minute in an exhibition match in which all his team-mates played a part. He knew he was being punished. Inside the dressing room he put on a calm face; he was ready to embark on a long journey. He told the team-mates closest to him that he could no longer bear the situation, that he had never believed in the non-football practices of the coach but even so, for the sake of the club, he had done his best to carry them out. In time, he confessed, he had come to realise that this role was not for him. He felt like an impostor. Mourinho, Casillas said, aside from being a bad person, had generated an intolerable division in the squad by creating what appeared to be a group of protected players connected to Jorge Mendes. He added that he knew that the manager had been outraged because he had tried to restore some harmony with Barcelona by calling Puyol and Xavi, but that they had not exchanged so much as a word about it. To conclude, he argued that it did not serve the club's interests to continue systematically reproducing what Mourinho called his 'communication strategy', and showed himself to be as decisive as former Spanish national team boss Camacho:

'I've got the balls not to do it!'

It is said in Valdebebas that it was Casillas who sought out Mourinho to clarify his position. He said he had to admit that they could not stand each other, that the feeling was one of mutual rejection, and that there was no need to pretend. Casillas told Mourinho that on the pitch he would give everything, but that off the pitch he wanted to avoid any complicity that went beyond what was absolutely necessary.

Mourinho was not able to hide his displeasure in the team-talk before the first game of the season, at La Romareda. Profoundly frustrated, the coach said that the unity of the group was the supreme value. He said that everyone had to go in the same direction, and he launched a coded message against Casillas and those who felt dislocated from the group, accusing them of undermining the general interests of the team. When he had finished, Casillas took him to one side and asked him exactly what he had meant by 'everyone going in the same direction', and if perhaps it did not rather consist in working for the particular interests of Mourinho. Because, he pointed out, what interested Madrid was one thing, and what interested its coach was another. Casillas also invited him not to use what they had talked about in private to discredit him later in front of his team-mates. He said this as if it were a threat, because he was still prepared to support his team-mates. The one who he would no longer speak up for was him: Mourinho and his many interests.

The contrast between the devotion shown by Mourinho for providing security to Di María and his disdain for Özil and Kaká – as well as his dedication to Coentrão, his indifference towards Marcelo, and his penchant for praising Pepe and criticising Ramos – led to a feeling of discrimination descending over a significant part of the squad. The trouble was not that Mourinho chose one group over the other. The trouble was that there seemed no way to reverse the footballing status quo. The players who supported Mourinho were invariably represented by Mendes, all lived near each other in the suburb of La Finca and ate together. They formed a solid core. And, unlike the others, they had easy access to information from Mourinho. They heard of his strategies directly or through Mendes, telling them what lay behind his decisions and comforting them when they were not playing. No one explained to Marcelo his overall role in the plan, let alone encouraged him when he was dropped to the bench. This dramatically contrasted with his treatment of Coentrão, whom the manager took out of the first team for six matches, claiming physical problems that were, according to Valdebebas employees, non-existent. Mourinho took him away to protect him from the press and the suspicions of his own team-mates; at the same time, he promised him that he could rest assured he would play in the big games when the season reached its climax.

In criminal law, rebellion is a crime against public order. In a football dressing room, a revolt is an attempt to force a change in the customs or the unwritten rules. There are coaches who listen to the players and avoid these conflicts, trying to establish common ground between the warring factions. During his first year in Madrid Mourinho did not listen. He talked so long and so vehemently, and accumulated so much power, that his players were scared to interrupt, hoping that, in exchange for silence and obedience, their coach would give them the security he had promised. When they began to suspect that they would not enjoy that security, and realising that the obedience and silence of all only meant more arbitrary powers being given the boss, the nuts of the Madrid machine began to loosen. The revolt began in September 2011, almost a year before Madrid won the league. For some employees of the club, and for many players, if the squad had not raised its voice, if it had not made demands, if it had not tried to limit the autocratic behaviour of the coach, winning the league would have been impossible. Nevertheless, Mourinho's virtue was that, like many other successful coaches, he had it in him to be able to listen and compromise. At least for a few months, Mourinho did not do everything he would have liked to have done. At the same time the team competed at a very high level.

It took only one spark, however, for the insubordination to explode. It was 18 September 2011, away to Levante, a ground that always tested the nerves of Mourinho and his players. Di María was lying on the ground, exaggerating the effects of a challenge, and Ballesteros leaned over him to say something when he was pushed off balance by Khedira falling down in front of the linesman. Ballesteros went down like a sack of rocks and Khedira was sent off. Real lost 1–0, and in the press conference after the match Mourinho blamed his German midfielder for the defeat.

Considered by his team-mates to be one of the manager's men, Sami Khedira knew very well how to distinguish between professional loyalty and being in league with someone. He was a serious individual. When the majority felt they had to laugh at the boss's jokes, the German remained unmoved. Although he did not make unnecessary concessions, he was inevitably obedient. Up until these last few months his impenetrable character cloaked any insecurities very well. On that trip to Valencia, however, he owned up to a concern that had haunted him since the pre-season, when he saw that the coach had toyed with the idea of putting Coentrão in his place.

Before the match, and in anticipation of the sort of tactics that Levante would deploy, Mourinho told his players to go up to the referee and encourage him to show cards to the opposition. He also told them to 'defend their team-mates' when they were under attack. What did 'defend' mean when the ball was not in play? Each interpreted this in their own way. Khedira had dutifully done what was asked of him. Seeing that Di María was getting bothered by Ballesteros, he defended him.

Mourinho's reaction came as a surprise to the squad. The coach had spent a year presenting himself as the champion and guardian of his players. He had assured them that he would allow himself to be exposed to public pressure in order to preserve them from external criticism, no matter what happened. Then suddenly, after a defeat, he publicly pointed the finger at one of his most loyal men to take away his own share of the blame. A sense of danger, of helplessness, became all too clear over the course of the next few days. The team was at breaking point. When Ramos demanded an explanation from the manager, in the next match against Racing Santander in the Sardinero on 21 September, three days after the trip to the east, he was dropped from the starting line-up by the coach. Madrid drew 0–0.

Toño, the Racing goalkeeper, did not have a save to make all night.

The match – Madrid's most anaemic of those three years – left Madrid a point behind Barcelona. A degree of anxiety was detected in Mourinho, followed by a gesture of utter helplessness in front of his players. According to two witnesses, the coach begged for an answer, as if he were completely unaware what the cause of the whole situation was:

'What's the matter with you all?'

'What's wrong with *you*?' they replied. 'Why are there some of us that you don't even talk to? Why do a lot of us not even exist as far as you're concerned? Why are the errors of some unforgivable and the errors of others ignored? We all want to be in this together.'

Having become accustomed to giving uninterrupted monologues over the course of the last year, Mourinho was startled that his subordinates were now speaking up. He was, however, prepared to listen to this, the first angry opposition he had encountered at the club. Casillas, Ramos, Arbeloa and Higuaín were the most vehement of those present. They laid before him the long list of grievances shared among the squad. Complaints about the favouritism with which he treated those in the group who were either directly or indirectly related to his agent were high on the agenda. They also asked him not to discuss his players' errors in public, as he had done with Khedira in Valencia. In the face of these protests, Mourinho offered up a 'scientific' justification of his behaviour:

'It's a psychological tactic. I do it to get more out of you.'

He told them he would stop systematically denouncing referees, and that never again would he ask his team not to attempt a comeback, as he had in his 1 May team-talk ahead of the return leg of the Champions League semi-final that they lost against Barça. The players said that from now on they would try to win every game, and would stop thinking about blaming referees or building off-the-pitch communication strategies:

'We're not going to go out and play a game just to prepare for a press conference where you can complain about referees.'

Pérez was so alarmed at what he saw taking place on the pitch that he had gone down to the dressing room to try to find out what was happening. Eventually, the president backed Ramos but also encouraged him – for the sake of a diplomatic outcome – to assume the role of mediator between the players and the manager that had previously been taken by Casillas. Ramos promised Mourinho he would give everything on the pitch if his coach put his faith in him. He assured him that he would be able to lead the team from the heart of the defence, where he could be more influential. From then on, Ramos played in the centre and returned to full-back only in cases of emergency.

A barbecue in Valdebebas put an end to the disagreements and inaugurated a new era. Everyone had their photos taken and toasted a new commitment to peace and unity. The atmosphere was festive, the players laughed enthusiastically in front of the camera and only the subdued look on the coach's face hinted that the harmony was perhaps not universal. Seated at a table in front of a few plates of left-over pork and beef, the man who a month ago had been at the height of his power and influence, realised he now had a problem.

Endowed with a keen sense of survival, Mourinho knew that he might just save his reputation if he could win some time. The players suspected that his capitulation was not genuine and had only been given because things had come to a head. 'When this crisis has passed, heads will roll,' mused one. Mourinho's concessions and compromises, guaranteed until December, formed a medium-term strategy to preserve 'their own', as the players referred to Mendes's men. There were still eight months to go before the end of the season and he needed to be more conciliatory if he wanted to win the league. He needed willing workers.

According to his colleagues, he very soon realised, however, that these measures would mean he could never fulfil the ambition of founding his own empire. The limits to his Spanish adventure were now becoming increasingly apparent. He had attempted to use the Super Cup and the pitched battle that marred it to proclaim the triumph of his own propaganda and establish Coentrão as a symbol of his infallibility – but the result had been a fiasco. The media not only failed to treat him as a 'living legend', they even began to discover his shortcomings. Not only was the signing of Coentrão presented as an incomprehensible error; everyone saw that the dressing room was coming apart in his hands, undermining the public's perception of his leadership abilities and his charismatic mystique.

In those weeks of September 2011 Mourinho began to convince himself that it would be best to find another club as he could no longer sign who he wanted to without being the object of constant suspicion. He let Jorge Mendes know, and Mendes headed to London, in search of offers and a better future.

CHAPTER 9

TRIUMPH

'How can the ability to lead depend on the ability to follow? You might as well say that the ability to float depends on the ability to sink.'

L. J. Peter and R. Hull, *The Peter Principle*

José Mourinho called his confidant and disciple, the fitness coach Rui Faria, and asked him to do him a favour. He had to call him on his mobile while he was giving a press conference, interrupting it so that everyone could hear the ringtone that he had just programmed into his smartphone. The call triggered the distant voice of Pavarotti singing 'Nessun dorma' in a pocket-sized *Turandot*.

The story circulated around the dressing room, lightening the mood. The boss's jokes – at first – were a source of amusement. For Mourinho, however, his antics were very serious. What impressed Aitor Karanka when he first met him was not Mourinho's passion for football but the overriding importance he placed on the image he projected to the media. Since first stepping foot in Valdebebas Mourinho began to send out a wide variety of signals, so that journalists would have both sophisticated and mythical elements with which to compose their portraits of him. What would they think when they discovered that he was not just a coach but a lover of *bel canto* and a former *habitué* of La Scala opera house in Milan?

Mourinho was raised in an environment that was more sporting than intellectual. His grandfather had been president of Vitória de Setúbal, the club par excellence of his homeland, and his father Félix a professional goalkeeper and coach. He himself tried – unsuccessfully – to embark on a career as a player, first for Os Belenenses and then for Rio Ave, where his father was manager, but not even enjoying this support helped him succeed. The frustration he faced on realising his footballing dreams would not work out fed his desire to excel in other areas, as well as his scorn for the intelligence of the average player, his underestimation of the whimsical and playful nature of football, and his overestimation of the science that supported it.

Besides being the founder of the so-called 'science of human move-ment', the versatile Professor Manuel Sérgio was the biggest academic influence on Mourinho. His classes at the Higher Institute of Physical Education in Lisbon in the mid-1980s made a deep impression on the future coach.

Sérgio convinced him that technical football knowledge was not as important as a broad knowledge of the human sciences, public speak-ing, psychology, pedagogy and dialectics. Sérgio also persuaded him that he was gifted. The old master would say, 'The genius of Mourinho goes far beyond just football.'

In keeping with his mentor's judgement, Mourinho wanted his colleagues not to think of him as simply a legendary figure in the world of football. That was not enough. He was utterly convinced that he possessed an extraordinary intellect, something he tried to let Karanka know every time he spoke with him about his discoveries in the fields of motivation, group management, methodology, training and tactics. From the long list of issues that inflamed his boastful imagination one was held above all others: it was what he called the 'high-pressure triangle'. What his players called the '*trivote*'.

Mourinho took advantage of time spent in hotels on the eve of games to pontificate about the 'high-pressure triangle' in meetings with his assistants. For hours Karanka, Morais, Faria and Campos listened to him reflect on what was essentially a 4-3-2-1 formation as if it were the secret workings of a miracle weapon whose devastating effect would leave Spanish football stunned and mark the history of the game for ever. On paper the invention could work with any midfielders, but in practice players with certain qualities were needed. Fate had put four such men at Mourinho's disposal: Alonso, Lass, Pepe and Khedira.

Pepe was in many ways the prototype in the role but, because he was the player most loyal to Mourinho and was needed in the centre of defence, he became the back-up option. Alonso was not a great athlete but made up for it with his passing ability; Lass possessed all the qualities that were necessary to play within the 'triangle'; and Khedira was a 1,500-metre runner with stamina second to none in the squad. His ability to cover so much ground was essential if Mourinho's plan were to be properly executed.

On the lookout for pieces that fitted perfectly into the system he wanted to play, Mourinho signed Khedira after studying the player's performance on the pitch for Germany. According to FIFA statistics from the 2010 World Cup, the midfielder had the best figures of the tournament. With 78.5 kilometres run in seven games, he was fourth in the list of players who had covered the most distances, after Xavi (80 km), Schweinsteiger (79.8 km) and Pereira (78.6 km). But what the coach most admired about him was what FIFA called 'intensive activity time'. In this Khedira was number one. The German put in high-intensity work over the course of 58 minutes, as against 57 from Xavi, 56 from Alonso and 54 from Schweinsteiger.

Finally, there was Lass. The Frenchman was Mourinho's perfect idea of what a central midfielder should be, and he considered him to be the most complete midfielder in his squad. He was fascinated by the speed with which he was capable of winning back the ball, his man-marking instinct and the tenacity he showed when harassing those he marked. Lass was the coach's defensive-midfielder 'fetish', but the two men had fallen out. To the perceived unpaid dues of his time at Chelsea, Lass added the resentment he felt towards Mourinho for having preferred Khedira to him for most of his first season. Mourinho thought the Spanish public were not yet ready for his three-midfielder system and, until he won the trophies that would allow him to do whatever he wanted, he chose to give a free rein to Khedira because he was a player signed by Florentino Pérez. All of this went against Lass's natural desire to play every minute of every match and, upset by his relegation to the bench, in January 2011 he agreed with Jorge Valdano that he should be sold in the summer. But Valdano was sacked himself, and Mourinho liked the player so much that he asked that he only be sold if his €20 million buy-out clause were met. As nobody was willing to do that, he was kept – against his will. Mourinho was willing to overlook all his 'insolent' behaviour just so he could put him in his side, telling him to train at his own pace and that he would make the team. Mourinho promised him that he would play the big games, and Lass accepted through gritted teeth.

Madrid's play on the pitch was a compromise, the result of an unstable equilibrium. The internal tensions at the club that had to be tolerated by Mourinho during the 2011–12 season were no greater than the pressures he put his players under. The attempted mutiny and the subsequent pact after the game in Santander reflected the different aspirations of the coach and most of the squad. Both sides pushed to protect interests that often clashed. The players protected their contracts. What interested Mourinho was the safeguarding of his image as a successful coach and a bastion of power, cemented over the last year with the help of Jorge Mendes.

In a club like Madrid, the amount spent on first-team players' contracts is unsustainable without winning silverware. Players knew that they would be facing what was commonly known as a 'cleaning' of the dressing room if they did not win the league or the Champions League very soon. The last league had been won in 2008, and Casillas and Ramos both understood the urgency of at least winning this domestic competition to give the dressing room some breathing space from the persistent feeling of disappointment felt by the club's fans. Since 2011, as well as the 'cleaning', staff at the club recognised a new source of professional instability. If the lack of trophies threatened many players' future at the club, the interests of Mendes were no less of a threat. Many players sensed the Mourinho's desire to fill the squad with his own men, resulting in more than a few casualties. They noted the importance of commercial and political motivations rather than sporting ones, and saw the arrival of Coentrão as an advance warning: the ferret pushing them out of the cave. Mourinho was suspicious enough to perceive the danger and, under the cloak of the prevailing institutional silence, the scene was being set for an inevitable conflict. As one employee of the club said, 'If Mourinho continues next year he'll have to change half the squad.'

Those who know him from earlier stages in his career say that Mourinho's pattern of behaviour has changed. At Porto, Inter and Chelsea he put sporting success before any other consideration. At Madrid, with a host of titles already on his CV, he seemed more concerned to win in his own way, to put a distinctive stamp on things. He set out to promote those players that he had signed in the transfer market and to implement his tactical principles, believing that this was the only way his brand image would be visible should the club win anything. Winning was not enough. He had already experienced that. He wanted his triumphs to go hand-in-hand with his own particular style and be achieved with his favourite sons. He therefore made it his priority that both Coentrão and Di María prospered.

In the dressing room a theory circulated: Di María and Coentrão were players who lacked time and judgement on the pitch and, anxious to please the boss, did nothing more than run and collide into opponents. Conscious of their rejection by the rest of the dressing room, Mourinho acted furtively until November and put his protected ones to one side so as to give some playing time to Kaká and Marcelo.

No player in the Madrid squad possessed the same mix of prestigious titles, both individual and team, as Kaká. Winner of the 2002 World Cup, the 2007 Champions League and the Ballon d'Or of the same year, his move to Madrid in the summer of 2009 was accompanied by the usual fanfare. Pérez signed him from Milan for €65 million in response to prolonged petitioning from the club. The desire to see him performing at his best immediately accelerated his fall. With expectations sky high, he had to prove his value, and he played for months with an injury to his pubis. He failed to shake this off over the course of the first year, there being times when the pain was so severe that he could not walk. As the months passed he decided against an operation so as not to miss the 2010 World Cup in South Africa. His fitness steadily deteriorated and during the tournament he suffered a serious knee injury. His recuperation took almost a year but by the summer of 2011, when he felt almost fit again, his teammates saw that he was training like never before. Mourinho, however, had already passed sentence. At 29 he considered the footballer to be finished. Rui Faria repeated his sentence among friends: 'Kaká is to Madrid what Shevchenko was to Chelsea.'

Against all expectations, the games that Kaká played during the 2011–12 season showed that he was still a splendid player. His understanding with Marcelo made him a potent force. The combination of the two Brazilians – each of them able to play in the space between the forward line and the midfield – with Benzema and Özil gave Madrid an alternative to the counter-attacking football that had been their strength in the previous season. At the heart of the team, Ramos and Alonso changed the way Madrid played. Between the two of them they improvised new ways of bringing the ball out from the back, enabling the line of defence to move forward and giving the play new clarity. This transformation meant Madrid could open up defences with elegant, sweeping moves, and in week 10 of the season they were top of the table, three points clear of Barcelona. The supporters and the dressing room were happy. But the coach was restless. He watched the team playing and no longer felt that it was his own. In public, at least, he made an effort to make it seem as if everything had been pre-planned:

'We've worked on organised attacks,' he said in a press conference on 21 October. 'We started this in the United States but it was in China where we worked exclusively on attacking movement and occupying space. We're improving individual movement a great deal, as befits a team that plays with organised attacks.'

When the players heard what the boss was saying they could not believe it. None of them could remember having worked on anything different during the pre-season in Los Angeles and much less between the friendlies in Tianjin and Canton in the summer of 2011. One of the players made fun of the situation, inventing the 'Peking Manual', an imaginary dossier that the coach neither knew of nor had ever applied to teach his players the art of static attack. The expression caught on. The mere mention of the Peking Manual sent the players into fits of laughter. In the coming months, on the many occasions when they lacked creativity and were unable to create chances against teams that defended deep, they usually recalled that press conference.

'Mou,' they would mumble under their breath, 'take out the Peking Manual!'

On 19 November 2011, in the 13th week of the season, Mourinho dared to unveil his secret weapon against Valencia. The Mestalla would be the final testing ground. At last, after the failed experiment in the semi-final of the Champions League at the Bernabéu, he would once again insist on three defensive central midfielders. The chosen team was Casillas, Arbeloa, Pepe, Ramos, Marcelo, Lass, Alonso, Khedira, Özil, Benzema and Ronaldo.

That night Mourinho felt happy. He had carefully studied Barcelona's visit to the Mestalla, the 2–2 draw forewarning him about the transitions in Valencia's attacks, their ability to hit the space behind Barcelona's defence, making the most of Banega's shooting, and their ability to go past defenders with the runs of Mathieu and Pablo. His conclusion was that Madrid should pull their defence further back to deny Valencia's forwards any space behind, and at the same time press all over the pitch. Usually, when a team tries to press in this way they move their line forward in one co-ordinated movement that takes them gradually further away from their area, squeezing up, like a piston in a hydraulic press. The operation runs the fundamental risk that the opposition can attack the space that opens up behind such an advanced defence. But Mourinho firmly believed that he had a formula that now did away with this risk, enabling his team to close that space behind the defence but still press high up the pitch with what he called his 'high-pressure triangle'.

On the tactics board this system was not designed to gain Madrid a great deal of possession. Mourinho thought that if a team reduced the amount of possession they had they also reduced the possibilities of making a mistake in possession, passing the risk of error on to the opposition. Madrid would sit back and wait, provoke an error from Valencia by pressing in low-block, and would then hit them on the counter-attack at maximum speed without squeezing the pitch and keeping the defensive line close to Casillas. They would try to finish their move as quickly as possible, getting the ball far away from their own goal and trying to prevent Valencia from anticipating them in midfield. If they lost the ball, ideally this should be close to the opposition's area, where Khedira and Lass would press the Valencia players to force another error so they regained the ball and could mount another attack.

Ramos and Pepe set the defensive line close to the area. When the team started their moves, the two centre-halves would weigh anchor. Alonso, the deepest point of the triangle, held his position. The highest points – Lass and Khedira – began to move forward step by step, covering the space generally occupied by three or four players, but trying not to get involved in the development of the move, at least not unless the ball rebounded into their paths. Then they would react by trying to penetrate the area or shoot from outside the box. Alonso gave possession out to the wings, looking for Özil, Marcelo and Ronaldo, or would bypass the midfield completely and pass directly to Benzema, who, backing into the opposition's central defenders tried to force them back. Lass and Khedira joined in the moves until Valencia won the ball back, when they immediately began the high pressing, trying to stop Albelda and Tino Costa from playing their first passes. Di María closed off the right flank and Özil helped the midfielders press, with Benzema pursuing the central defenders. The objective was to provoke another mistake as Valencia came out with the ball, and hit them on the counter-attack again. If Valencia were able to string three passes together then everyone had to retreat to the original position in front of the defence.

If results are the best measure of things, the operation was a success: Madrid won the game 2–3. Valencia wore themselves out trying to string passes together, unable to give continuity to their play, and were exposed on the counter-attacks. The Madrid players did not know to what extent they should attribute this to the actions of Alonso, Khedira and Lass, or simply to the absence of Éver Banega, Valencia's best passer of the ball. According to the statistics, the *trivote* did not seem to have given Madrid much advantage. Analysing the games they have played since the 2010–11 season with this system, the results are inconclusive. With the *trivote* they conceded on average a goal a game, and with just two defensive midfielders they conceded 1.4 goals a game. With the *trivote*, however, the opposition seemed to get closer to Madrid's goal, with an average of 12 chances, and only 10.6 without the *trivote*. But the number of goals scored dropped dramatically: 1.4 goals per game with three holding midfielders, compared with 2.3 with just two.

Although Mourinho wanted to establish his 'triangle' as the team's standard system, there were two things that prevented him from doing so. First, the majority of his players did not believe in it. The most sceptical group was headed by the Spanish contingent, but also included Higuaín, Özil, Benzema and Ronaldo. Second, a large part of both the media and the supporters saw it as a step back to the conservative approach promoted by many during the post-war period. In an attempt to preserve his plan, the manager sought to dampen dissent. After the game at Mestalla on 22 November he gave a press conference in which he defended the worth of his idea:

'We have to invent another term because I don't think "*trivote*" reflects well on how the team has played. The team has played with these three players, but the team has been very offensive. We have pressed very high up the pitch with the three of them. Lass and Khedira both ended up in goal-scoring positions. Khedira even scored, albeit in an offside position. Both players played very high up the pitch and for this reason "*trivote*", which has such defensive connotations, deserves to be identified another way. This triangle was a "very high-pressure triangle".

As usual, the preparations for the visit of Barcelona, set for 10 December, dominated life at Valdebebas. On a propaganda level – and in light of the fact that they topped the league by six points – Mourinho ordered everyone to hold fire; whatever they heard, whatever the provocation, his players were forbidden from talking about anything that had any connection to Barcelona. Nor could they discuss referees, nor match scheduling – 'nothing about nothing'. The explanation was simple: there was no need to rouse the enemy.

As for the way the team were going to play, Mourinho was worried about the feeling of honour felt by the Spanish players, the belief that whoever gave up possession was some sort of a coward. To rebuff this perceived prejudice he gave a series of team-talks in the weeks leading up to the game that were designed to instil in his players the idea that courage was just as intrinsic in those who defended in their own half. In one of these talks he said the following:

'If you, in a certain moment of the season, seeing the qualities of the opposition, see that you have to be more defensive, this doesn't mean that you're the more cowardly, nor the more brave. What it means is that you're the more intelligent. Because in the end he who is more defensive can end up doing more damage; in that sense he who is more defensive is more offensive.'

At this moment, Mourinho's relationship with Ramos and Casillas was going through its most bitter period. The Madrid players looked at the front pages of *AS* and *Marca* every morning, and if they saw that Casillas and Ramos were making the headlines they could predict the mood of the boss: 'cold, with rain probable'. Of the two, Ramos tried to be the more communicative. Casillas ignored

Mourinho and could barely stand Silvino Louro, the goalkeeping coach. His team-mates saw how angry he had been made by the prospect of receiving Barcelona from the vantage point of a trench.

'The thing is, at the Bernabéu you don't have to be afraid of anybody,' he said.

For the first time since 2001–02 Casillas went two games in the Champions League without featuring in the starting line-up. For the last two matches of the group stages Mourinho had replaced him with Adán. The captain knew that they were trying to make life difficult for him.

The week before the 10 December *clásico* Mourinho trained with a 4-3-2-1 formation, Alonso, Khedira, Lass and Özil all featuring in the team. An injury picked up by Arbeloa had enabled him to put Coentrão at right-back. Mourinho announced the line-up at the hotel on the evening of the match: Casillas, Coentrão, Pepe, Ramos, Marcelo, Özil, Alonso, Lass, Di María, Ronaldo, and Benzema, with Khedira being sacrificed. Everyone was given precise instructions, the most complex, as always, being given to Özil, the player he doubted the most.

Instead of organising the team to play around the German, Özil was an integral part of the machinery set up to force the opposition into making errors, as if he were merely a substitute for Khedira. The list of demands placed on him proved overwhelming: if Barcelona started a move from the back, the midfielder had to support Benzema in pressing their central defenders; if they channelled the play to the wings he was told to close down the advancing full-backs, working with Ronaldo and Di María, according to which area of the pitch he found himself in; if Barcelona were still pressing forward, he was to place himself between Lass and Alonso, who in turn were under orders not to lose their position and form a defensive block of six men in front of Casillas.

Benzema made it 1–0 in the first minute and Madrid retreated in an attempt to reproduce what had happened at the Mestalla. But Özil was not Khedira and Barça were not Valencia – Piqué, Busquets, Xavi, Iniesta and Fàbregas did not squander possession so easily. The more they moved the ball around, the more tired Madrid became, and in the second half Madrid became exhausted. As on other occasions, Guardiola's team ended up imposing themselves and won the game 1–3.

At the end, in response to somebody asking him why he had not deployed his 'high-pressure triangle', Mourinho suggested that his plan had not worked because Özil had been unable to perform the job normally done by Khedira:

'I decided against it because we were playing at home, we wanted to win, because we wanted to be more offensive and because I thought that Özil could give me a very good performance playing at home.'

Tensions grew once more. The finger Mourinho pointed at Özil was also a message to the group – led by the Spanish players – that most backed the German from within the squad. The Spanish, for their part, picked out Coentrão as being at fault for all the Barcelona goals. They said that for Barça's first goal he forgot to push up, playing Alexis onside; for their second his clearance only got as far as the edge of the box, turning into an assist for the opposition; for Barça's third, that he allowed himself to be tricked by Fàbregas. Above all, however, they blamed him for Barça's first, when Messi accelerated away from the centre-circle, skipping his way over 30 yards of *trivote* territory with ease. The Argentinian burst past Özil, bypassed Alonso and, hand-brake applied and head up to see what best to do next, with Lass arriving late, the ball reached Alexis, who was being played onside by Coentrão. The best efforts of Pepe to see off pending disaster were futile.

The defeat marked one of the most depressing periods in the relationship between Mourinho and his players. After Christmas, Madrid played Málaga in the cup and let in two goals from set-pieces in the first half. At half-time in the dressing room an indignant Mourinho for the first time threatened to use the media against them.

'I'm going to give names to the press,' he said.

Casillas's team-mates used to criticise the captain for being too phlegmatic. It was precisely when a problem needed his intervention that he tried not to get involved, and far less express any anger. That night, however, they say that Casillas went for the manager. He was fed up with Mourinho for breaking what he considered to be a ground-rule of their relationship, upset that Mourinho – behind his back – appeared to be blaming him for one of the goals. A little later Mourinho entered the press room to give the first of a long series of observations that, as well as being critical, contained an element of hostility against his own team.

'In the second half the team wanted to clean up the mess it made in the first half … At half-time I said to the players it's a shame that I cannot make 11 changes because, if I could, then I'd have changed the entire team. I was very clear with them so that they understood exactly that I didn't want to point the finger at any one individual. Far from it! A break [for Christmas] is always a break. There are people who interpret it as holidays – a time when they can relax, enjoy themselves, travel, go to eat at their father's house, at the house of their uncle, their aunt, their grandmother. And they don't stop eating and drinking during Christmas. And perhaps they come back here a little bit different.'

Mourinho had never shied away from scathing criticism. But in none of his previous clubs had he been so cruel in public towards his own players. Now the disapproving outbursts included not only his technical comments but also his contempt for the professional integrity of his players. That demonstration of vitriol against Pedro León, something many saw as an isolated incident, began to become the custom from 2012, Mourinho now a coach whose frustration was palpable. The New Year Málaga diatribe was not spontaneous. Like almost everything he did it was calculated, a product of his obsession.

At the turn of the year he did what he tended to do when he found himself in a difficult situation; he called his agent to come up with an escape plan to get away from the blaze that would soon envelope them. At Gestifute the two of them started to spread stories about what really bothered Mourinho. First, that the relationship he had with the squad was intolerable; second, that the club had not given him all the power he wanted, denying him control of the youth system; third, that his way of playing did not make the supporters happy and that the Bernabéu would end up getting on top of him. With his mind set on a way out of the club, an order of preference was established: Manchester United, followed by Chelsea and Manchester City, then Tottenham and even Arsenal, taking into account the fact that Mourinho's wife would rather live in London. As a point of principle, they made it clear that he would accept any offer from United or Chelsea to leave Madrid. If either of those two clubs did not open the way for him he would study other offers, should the situation at Madrid deteriorate and he did not win a trophy.

Mendes started talks with Manchester City and with Chelsea. Roman Abramovich, owner of the London club, recognised that he needed someone to put things back in order after the team's disastrous spell under André Villas-Boas. He also made it clear that his priorities were Guardiola, Joachim Löw and Guus Hiddink. When the rumour began to circulate that Chelsea wanted Guardiola, Mourinho became so anxious that for several weeks he was on the phone to his agent at all hours. Mendes tried to distract him, saying that it was an invention of the press. But he knew the truth. Abramovich had offered Guardiola €15 million net per season. Guardiola remained silent and, as Abramovich needed to close the signing with a degree of urgency, Mendes played the 'ultimatum' card. According to sources at Gestifute, he let Chelsea understand that if they did not make him a firm offer before 25 February then Mourinho would be staying at Madrid. The date passed and Chelsea said that they did not want to take such an important step at a time when they were still in the Champions League. Their win over Napoli had put them in the quarter-finals and they preferred to wait.

For the first time in his career Mourinho was managing a squad full of world champions. He said it himself: it was the most talented group of players he had ever had. It was a new experience for him to have taken over a team that, rather than underachieving, had recently won four league and two Champions League titles. Ever since he had been head coach at Benfica in 2000, his players had generally believed in his work, at least for the first year and a half. But in Madrid a significant part of the dressing room resented him personally and professionally from the first season. The players felt that he did not repay the loyalty that he demanded from them. They had given everything, they said, and in return they were increasingly marginalised by his desire to form a team within a team, composed of a few protected individuals.

Mourinho saw himself as trapped in the confines of Valdebebas, uncomfortable in an environment in which neither all the public nor all the press accepted him; where players, many of whom he considered traitors, ignored, feared or failed to appreciate him. He felt intolerably controlled, lacking the power to freely develop his ideas. The most popular story among the longest-serving employees at

Valdebebas was that the manager was not used to working with a club that had members, where transparency was so great. With every day that passed he felt that his legendary image was crumbling around him.

The atmosphere was dire when the players met ahead of the first leg of the semi-final of the Copa del Rey at the Bernabéu on 18 January. Facing Barcelona once again, all the same old dilemmas were thrown up for Mourinho, and his team-talks began to peter out in the face of his players' growing scepticism. When he brought them together for the penultimate meeting and announced the line-up, many shook their heads: he'd selected Casillas, Altintop, Ramos, Carvalho, Coentrão, Pepe, Alonso, Lass, Higuaín, Ronaldo and Benzema.

With Arbeloa, Di María and Khedira injured, the coach was forced to improvise to save his *trivote*, reaffirming his principles and infuriating the Spanish contingent. The unexpected relegation to the bench of Marcelo and Özil, together with his decision to pick Coentrão, were a declaration of intent against his internal detractors. The response from Casillas at the end of the meeting was raucous:

'Where are we going with this? *Madre mía*! All over again!'

Madrid's strategy was the same as in previous *clásicos*, prompting questions about the coach's tactical competence. Ronaldo put them ahead after 11 minutes and then they waited in their own half to see if they could hit Barcelona on the counter-attack. With plenty of the pitch to play in, Barça ended up breaking through and staging a comeback with goals from Puyol and Abidal. The 1–2 final score was greeted by whistling from the home fans. For the first time the public started to suspect that Mourinho's strategy was getting the team nowhere. The image of Pepe stamping on Messi while he was on the ground was seen worldwide via TV and internet. This time, in the dressing room, Mourinho at first showed no signs of life. Affected by the whistles from the stands, he instinctively returned to the propaganda battleground, persuading Zinedine Zidane, nominally the first-team director, to come out in his defence. The legendary status of Zidane should have served to help put the fires out. The interview that he gave *Diario AS* was published on 20 January and shocked the dressing room. The Frenchman, who very rarely commented in public, exalted Mourinho in such a way that the players were given the impression that he felt they were completely irrelevant.

'I don't understand everything that has been said about the system employed by Mourinho against Barcelona,' he said. 'You can put whatever system you like up against this team, but right now they're a rung above the rest … At the break Madrid were 1–0 up. Then came the error for Puyol's goal from the set-piece … What upsets me is to have to listen to these attacks on the team's system. I challenge all the coaches of the world to identify the system that should be used to beat Barça … You reach a point where the only beautiful thing in the game is victory … I don't understand certain people in the press who criticise Mourinho's Madrid when, deep down, they're only motivated by personal grudges. How can people say that we should change the coach? Are we crazy? We're lucky enough to have Mourinho, the coach who makes things evolve and who is building a stronger Madrid … Mourinho is creating the conditions that will enable the team to be successful. Look at the statistics of the team since he took over the reins. They're incredible. And he's the person responsible for these performances.'

Zidane suggested that the squad was nothing without the magic hand of the leader. For days after the *clásico* Mourinho barely even spoke to his assistants. He limited himself to attending training sessions, sporting a defiant air, and not saying a word about Barça until the day before the return leg. Then, rather than his usual habit of giving a series of team-talks to his players, he condensed everything into one laconic speech. He delivered this with a bureaucratic coldness, although there was a slightly ironic tone when he said, 'You have to press, when on the pitch you see that you have to press.'

Some players ended up thinking that he wanted them to lose – and, if possible, for them to lose big – so that the humiliation taught them a lesson. 'He wants us to crash,' said one. In that sense, they believed he wanted to show them they had been wrong in thinking that they could play Barcelona on their own terms as equals. As Zidane had said, echoing Mourinho, Barcelona were a 'rung above the rest'. The line-up, with the exception of Coentrão, was what most of them wanted: Casillas, Arbeloa, Pepe, Ramos, Coentrão, Lass, Alonso, Kaká, Özil, Ronaldo and Higuaín.

For the first time in years Madrid played better football than Barcelona. Their domination was impressive and was reflected in the number of chances both sides had. It seemed that the two teams had switched roles. The ball belonged to the whites. Özil, Ronaldo and Higuaín tested the Barcelona goalkeeper five times in the first half. With the help of the crossbar Pinto kept everything out. Barça only had two shots on target and scored with them both before the break. When Pedro made it 1–0, Mourinho joked so loudly that the substitutes heard him clearly:

'You're the clever ones. Didn't you want to play on the attack? Well, there you have it.'

Mourinho waited for the team in the dressing room with his back to the wall. He flashed half a smile as he looked at the faces around him. But the players went back out on to the pitch without him having given them a single order or any idea how they might come back into the match.

Aware that they had only made the team because Di María was injured, Özil and Kaká passed the game like two shipwreck survivors swimming towards a desert island, so that Higuaín, Ramos, Casillas, Arbeloa and Alonso had to do all they could to help them get into the game. Around the German and the Brazilian a creative complicity was generated that spread throughout the team, with Ronaldo and Benzema scoring the goals that earned the draw on the night. Madrid were at 2–2, with 20 minutes to go until the final whistle. The knock-out could still have had another twist. The emotion was as intense in the stadium as it was non-existent in the visitors' dugout, where Mourinho was unmoved by both of his team's goals.

Madrid did not reach the final of the Copa del Rey but the game lifted the morale of the dressing room, fed up with having to accept a fatalistic sense of total inferiority. Even Arbeloa, after the return leg, bragged at how he had been able to take on Barça playing football. In the midst of such euphoria, Özil settled some scores and gave an interview in which he said something that the coach perceived as a potential threat:

'When Kaká and I play together we've never lost.'

The two attacking midfielders had played together in nine games; Madrid had won seven of them and drawn two. But the return of Di María always interrupted their partnership. Against Málaga on 18 March, these two friends – two of the most gifted footballers on the planet – found themselves starting together for the last time that season. In the next campaign they would line up alongside each other in just two games, against Rayo Vallecano and Celta Vigo in the league: two wins, with four goals scored and none conceded. Kaká tolerated being marginalised because he earned more than €9 million net per season. But prolonged spells out of the team – and his advancing years – ultimately destroyed his enthusiasm for the game. By the summer of 2013 Rui Faria's verdict coincided with the truth: Kaká was a shadow of the player he had previously been.

Mourinho was now behaving in an openly authoritarian manner. He accused the Spanish players of leaks to the press, and over the following weeks came across as reclusive and haughty. The theory doing the rounds in the dressing room was one that suggested that he wanted to move to another club, denouncing the indiscipline and disloyalty of the squad to justify his failure at Madrid. Karanka suggested that the situation was insupportable for his boss and that he had said that he would leave in the summer.

Pérez met with Madrid's senior players, pleading for group cohesion for sake of the supporters. 'Offer a sense of unity,' he would say, 'whatever it takes.' The president implored them to give this impression to the supporters. They had to think of the supporters because Mourinho never did, and if one day he left they would still be answerable to them. Casillas and Ramos made it known to Pérez that Mourinho was not a clean, fair, good guy, and that he had other interests close to his heart in addition to Madrid's. Pérez said nothing.

In a private meeting the players agreed that they should not give the coach any grounds for accusing them of treachery, proposing that in all of their statements to the media they should stress their support for Mourinho.

But inside the club, scandal was the norm. Mourinho, who avoided Casillas as much as he could, did not miss any opportunity to make accusing comments against his captain to everyone from the president to the directors, the director general, the team delegate, the sporting director, his assistants and the team doctors. Everyone received a little bit of the antagonism that he felt towards Casillas. There was a feeling that Mourinho saw him as a grass, a mole, a traitor, an egoist, and that all that was missing was for Mourinho to scrawl his stock verdict all over the walls: 'He thinks he's the boss of the club.'

Casillas got to hear the gossip but his reaction was measured. He believed that a mutiny would really complete Mourinho's plan for him, serving to explain to the world why he had not been able to make the team win things playing good football. Instead of giving him what he wanted he looked the other way. But insiders at the club say that when Pérez called Casillas to ask him what he thought of Mourinho, the captain said that the sooner the coach left the club the better it would be for everyone, that he did it no good at all, that he was very destructive and that he did not deserve to represent Madrid. Casillas told his team-mates that the president told him that these things happen in football and that he had to put up with them for the sake of the supporters.

This internal turbulence did nothing, however, to dent Madrid's league form. The league in general was showing signs of a decline in standards and it was difficult for them to find any resistance anywhere. Casillas, Ramos, Alonso and Ronaldo were the principal motivators in the dressing room. They not only refused to accept that four years could pass without winning the league; no one could contemplate losing their positions in the first team – or even on the subs' bench – at the end of the season. The squad wanted to stop living under a cloud of suspicion in front of the fans, and the desire to lift this cloud led to an inspired run of results. The team won the title in this part of the season. Between the defeat in the *clásico* in the 16th week of the season and the draw with Málaga in the 28th, Madrid won 11 consecutive matches. After the league *clásico* Madrid and Barça were level on points in the table, but by week 27 the difference was 10 points in Madrid's favour. When the hard work seemed to have been largely done, however, problems arose.

In the 27th week of the season Madrid played their most difficult game in weeks in La Liga at the Benito Villarmarín in Seville. An injury to referee Eduardo Iturralde González meant that he was replaced by a rookie substitute, which made for a chaotic night. Alonso and Ramos got away with handballs in the area, and Ronaldo scored Madrid's third and decisive goal with Khedira in an offside position. The referee missed it all and the players went down the tunnel laughing, having secured what had looked like an impossible victory, with Ramos showing off the reddened arm that had blocked Jefferson Montero's shot in the box.

Madrid's refereeing delegate Carlos Megía Dávila went to see Mourinho in Valdebebas when the squad got back from Seville. In his capacity as a retired referee, Megía Dávila had good contacts within the governing bodies of his old guild. At Madrid he enjoyed a position that involved being an analyst and link between the club and the refereeing establishment. Employees at Valdebebas saw him arguing with Mourinho, both seeming very agitated, like two men on either side of a council office complaints' window.

Whatever the message from Megía Dávila, Mourinho was left simmering with anger, and the 1–1 draw in Málaga in the following game did nothing to calm his nerves. In talks with his assistants he began to spread the idea that referees would steal the title from Madrid, and his assistants, in turn, passed this on to the Portuguese players, especially Pepe and Ronaldo. The desperate desire to ensure a result in the next game, and the belief that he knew how to do it, prompted Mourinho to use the *trivote*. In Villarreal on 21 March he lined up Casillas, Arbeloa, Pepe, Ramos, Marcelo, Lass, Alonso, Khedira, Özil, Benzema and Ronaldo.

Madrid took the lead in the 62nd minute with a goal from Ronaldo. Then they deliberately split the team into two parts. The coach indicated that at the back they would form a block of seven players and that they would play the ball directly forward to Özil, Ronaldo and Benzema, who had to stay forward to receive the long passes. Villarreal set up camp in their own half and made it impossible for Madrid to fashion another goal. When, in the 83rd minute, Senna equalised from a direct free-kick, Mourinho exploded. He protested so vehemently to the referee that he was sent off. Özil and Ramos followed him, both for red cards after the referee blew the final whistle. At the end of the game Pepe and Ronaldo, together with Rui Faria, Karanka and Silvino Louro, barged their way down the tunnel in a group. José Manuel Llanez, the Villarreal vice president, said that they were like a 'herd of bulls', insulting and provoking everything that moved. Llaneza remembered the war-cry: 'They have robbed us!' In the stampede, Ronaldo found himself with Villarreal's president, Fernando Roig. The director claimed that the forward said to him, 'This is a shit ground and you're a shit president.'

The game against Villarreal finally brought the *trivote* to a noisy end, at least in its purest form, the mechanism suffering a sort of implosion. Lass, the most irreplaceable part in its make-up, had come on and kicked so many people that his team-mates believed he wanted to get into trouble. The referee showed him a yellow card and, feeling that the player was trying to get himself sent off, Mourinho took him off after 29 minutes, replacing him with Callejón. The Frenchman went straight to the shower, changed, put on his head-phones and listened to some hip-hop. He looked so proud of himself that the coach was left dumbfounded.

Nobody could say that Lass's behaviour took his boss by surprise. Here was a player who was so obsessed with the game that he could not bear sitting on the subs' bench. Nor was he capable of remaining indifferent towards a coach who on the one hand flattered him and on the other denied him any time on the pitch. He did not want to play for Mourinho for another season, something he had by now repeated time and again for almost a year. He challenged Mourinho to fire him on the grounds that he thought of himself as a captive. One day in February, upset because he was not in the side, he found his way into Mourinho's office and railed at him while his boss remained silent:

'You're a traitor. Forget about me. You live your life and I'll live mine. I've told you a thousand times, I'm sick of you.'

For a month between February and March Lass did not return to the first-team squad. Officially, the club claimed that he was injured. The reality was that he detested his coach, but Mourinho appreciated him as a player to such an extent that, until very late in the season, he did all he could to avoid losing him. The other players saw the situation as peculiarly comic.

'We all knew that he loved him,' said one of them, 'and that because he loved him he would end up playing him sooner or later. Most people love the model Gisele Bündchen – but he loves Lass Diarra, and he will end up forgiving him because of that love. It was unrequited, but unflinching.'

The romance finally came to an end at Villarreal. Although Mourinho was tempted to give him back his first-team place at the start of the following season, in September 2012 Lass signed for Anzhi and went to live in Moscow, doubling his wages.

After having been sent off, Mourinho bounded around the El Madrigal dressing room in the animated state that always accompanied his dismissal. The idea of Barça being just six points behind put him on edge. He called his players together to tell them that it was obvious that referees were stealing the league from them, begging that the players come out and denounce them to journalists. Headed by Casillas and Ramos, the majority of the squad refused. Not even Pepe – nor Ronaldo – agreed to go against their colleagues. A disgruntled Mourinho looked for an alternative, asking Zidane to say on TV that referees were conspiring in favour of Barcelona. The first-team director knew he had upset the players by aligning himself with similar positions in the past and turned down the idea. Mourinho took this as a betrayal. Appearing a beaten man, he announced that it was best for him not to talk to anyone. It was the beginning of what some called the 'law of silence', the principal consequence of which was the disappearance of Zidane from Mourinho's immediate group.

Next, Mourinho briefed Karanka to go around saying that Zidane was the latest name on the list of those who had been disloyal. Meanwhile, the Frenchman confessed to a friend that the further away you kept from Mourinho the better, since he had not met anyone more devious in the 30 years he had worked in professional football.

Mourinho called the squad together on the way back from Villarreal and tried to explain why he thought he had to vilify referees. Those attending the meeting suggest that, just as he was starting to say that he knew there was a conspiracy against Madrid, Casillas interrupted him.

The goalkeeper said, 'Look, everyone here can do what they want. We're all old enough so anyone who wants to bad-mouth referees can do so, and anyone who doesn't want to doesn't have to. What I think is, instead of thinking about which referees we've got, we should forget the stories and concentrate on the matches, because this is very complicated. If we're going to concentrate on the stories we're going to get distracted. It would be a mistake. If we keep talking about referees then we're going to lose the league – that's for sure.'

Any analysis of the refereeing of the games involving La Liga's big two between 2010 and 2013 would invite the conclusion that Mourinho's paranoia – if he really had any – was unfounded. This is especially true for the 2011–12 season. In this campaign Madrid had five players sent off, one more than Barça. In everything else they enjoyed the more favourable decisions. Madrid were awarded a single penalty against them for every 13 in their favour, while Barça were given one against them for every 11 in their favour. In that season Madrid benefited from the sending off of 14 opposition players as against the eight that were sent off playing against Barça. In total, between the 2010–11 and 2012–13 seasons Madrid were given 34 penalties and Barcelona 21, despite the fact that, statistically, the Catalan team enjoyed far more possession in their opponents' half.

The players were well aware of these numbers. What is more, they had decided a long time ago that they were not going to get involved in the boss's battles, particularly when he was fighting them in Villarreal. It was at this point that many thought that Mourinho had finally been completely laid bare following his outburst against a team that were about to go down. Later on, Rui Faria and Karanka admitted that what he really feared was being thought of as the manager who lost the league after having enjoyed a ten-point lead. With the pending trip to the Camp Nou, the possibility of a Barcelona league comeback made him suspect that his players had abandoned him and that they could even intentionally lose the game in order to destroy him. His reaction was to refuse to give press conferences for the remainder of the league season.

The major concern of the players was now no longer the link between Mourinho and Jorge Mendes, their relationship with the media, propaganda, referees or their own contracts. All of these had retreated into the background. Everything was secondary to the most pressing issue, winning the league. This alone would redeem them, return their workplace to a state of peace, put them in a better position in front of the boss and regain the respect of the fans, and guarantee them a good price in the market for a future transfer. But all this depended on them solving one problem: how to play the game in tight spaces.

After two years, Mourinho had failed to come up with any solutions to make the team more creative at times when they needed to attack their opponent's goal without much space in front of them. The difficulty of controlling games when they had control of the ball but were faced with teams that packed the area led various players to hold a meeting after the Villarreal match. The first players to speak were Alonso, Ramos, Casillas, Arbeloa and Higuaín. They agreed that since the coach could not help them in this particular matter, then they should themselves devise a remedy. They planned to squeeze the pitch more and ignore the order that the forwards had to remain up front, never dropping deeper to offer themselves in midfield. They also contemplated the idea of the central striker getting into wider areas to generate more space.

Although the team had problems developing their play, they counted on a universally accepted remedy. It was called Cristiano Ronaldo and he had just turned 27 years old – a magical number for goalscorers, the age at which Romario, Van Basten and Henry clocked up their career-best goal tallies for a single season. With four games left to go before the end of the campaign, on the eve of travelling to the Camp Nou, Ronaldo had scored 41 goals in 33 matches. His statistics were unbelievable. Since the times of the legendary Puskas and Di Stéfano there had been nobody capable of beating or even matching their goal returns. Although he did not possess the vision, the timing or the range of passing of these two giants of the game, he surpassed them in terms of finishing. What he could not manage with subtlety he resolved with a missile strike. He had been decisive in almost all the difficult games. In Málaga (3 goals), in Valencia (2), against Atlético at the Bernabeu (3) and the Calderón (3), against Sevilla at the Sánchez Pizjuán (2), against Athletic Bilbao (2), against Betis in Seville (2) and in the Sadar against Osasuna (3). When he failed to score, Madrid suffered. Of the 11 games in which Ronaldo went goalless, his team lost two and drew three. If Ronaldo responded in the right way, having to play the game in tight spaces could be forgotten. It was enough, as at the Calderón or the Sadar, for him just to fire a rocket from outside the area.

Events sucked the two contenders into the funnel of the Camp Nou. On Saturday 21 April Madrid faced Barça, hoping to settle the league. The sun had warmed up the afternoon as if it were summer and a warm breeze was blowing when the two teams took to the field. With just four games left, Madrid led the table with four points. Lass had been banished for insubordination, so Mourinho picked his least experimental midfield in a team featuring Casillas, Arbeloa, Pepe, Ramos, Coentrão, Khedira, Alonso, Di María, Özil, Ronaldo and Benzema. More innovative was Guardiola, who left Pedro on the bench, lining up with Valdés, Puyol, Mascherano, Adriano, Alves, Busquets, Xavi, Thiago, Tello, Messi and Iniesta.

This was Casillas's 15th game in the Camp Nou. He knew the dressing room, the tunnel, the music all off by heart. The Barça hymn was about to begin when the captain shouted as loudly as he could for the players to go out on to the pitch. His voice was so loud it could be heard from both benches.

'*Señores*,' he said. 'We're going to forget about the controversies. We're going to forget about the referees. And we're going to put all our energy into playing football. We can do it! We can do it!'

It was a vociferous call to play the game in the way Madrid once used to. After two years of confusion, the message was crystal clear. Mourinho, who was well within earshot, pretended he had not heard.

In the event, Madrid played one of their least vigorous *clásicos* in a long time. Under the direction of Ramos, an increasingly influential leader, they carried out the basic idea of pressing deep in their own half and then counter-attacking. On previous occasions such tactics had proved to be woefully inadequate, but this time Barça did not play to their usual standard. The Madrid players commented that Messi was like someone playing within themselves because they are carrying a muscle injury – he walked, looked around and brooded.

Was he saving himself? If so, for what? Something in the home side was not quite right. As the game went on, it became apparent that Guardiola and Messi had had an argument, perhaps even completely rupturing their relationship. Messi no longer wanted to play under the Catalan and Guardiola knew that his own time at Barcelona was up.

Barcelona started to fall apart from the inside, and Madrid were ready to take advantage – with Ronaldo at his peak.

A fan's vision tends to be less sharp than a professional footballer's. The supporters in the stands – or those watching the game on TV – often get the sense that something dramatic is happening but do not know what. On the pitch players see the small details with such clarity that they can distinguish the banal from the extraordinary. That afternoon in the Camp Nou the Madrid players were left in no doubt about one thing: the magical touch of Mesut Özil.

It is not just fans who build players into legends. On certain occasions the players themselves admire a fellow professional to the point of worship. From that day in Barcelona the members of the Madrid dressing room gave one player this legendary status; a player who was just 23 and who, with all the pressure of the situation, was able to do something that very rarely comes off, even in training. A touch worthy of a champion.

It happened in the 72nd minute. Barça had just drawn level at 1–1 through Alexis, the goal confirming that the home side had regained their rhythm and poise. Bit by bit the *Azulgrana* were taking control of Madrid territory with their passing and fluid movement, making the Madrid players expect that another defeat was just around the corner, another league title squandered. But then the unexpected took place.

Three minutes after Alexis scored, Özil received the ball on the right-hand side of the Barcelona half. For a left-footed player getting the correct body shape to play a pass from the right is usually difficult because the effect of the foot on the ball tends to send it towards goal. But the German magician acted with a cold but completely correct impulse, even though it went against the nature of the mechanics of the human body. He controlled the ball, then with his next touch, as if he were cutting something with a knife, he sent the ball forward, giving it a little bit of swerve, using the top of the foot to impart just the right amount of speed.

The 40-yard pass was perfectly weighted. The ball flew low and at pace but because of the screw-back Özil applied, instead of running through to Valdés it slowed down just behind Mascherano, who could not turn in time, and too far away from the goalkeeper. Then Ronaldo appeared like a bullet.

He confessed to his team-mates that when he received such a perfect pass he was at first stunned, then anxious.

'I was nervous. I knew that if I didn't get my first touch right the chance would be gone,' he said.

Ronaldo did not fail. Controlling the pass with the outside of his right foot, he found his range, took two steps forward, dropped his hip and drove his foot through the ball. It gained height halfway through its trajectory, clearing the outstretched hand of Valdés. It was the most important goal of Ronaldo's career in Spain, and meant that Madrid were all but champions.

When the game finished Madrid's dressing room was soon full of excited players. From the showers a bellow could be heard that shook the walls, an almost superhuman noise, in a voice not dissimilar to Higuaín's:

'Are we going to talk about referees now?'

Everyone broke down in hysterics. Mourinho's Madrid had just completed their first clear victory in a *clásico*. The statistics reflected the mountain the team had just climbed: two wins, one in the cup final and the other in this league game, set against four draws and five defeats.

Madrid competed in their three last games with a renewed vigour, finishing the season with two records. They picked up more points than any team had done before with 100 and they scored a record number of goals with 115. Never before in the league had three players from the same team reached 20 goals: Benzema on 20, Higuaín with 22 and Ronaldo's extraordinary 44.

Celebrations in Madrid started with a lunch at which the Spanish players discovered that Mourinho had raised Di María's salary in January, with back pay. The Argentinian, despite having had a very bitty season, jumped up the pay scale to the extent that with his €4 million net salary he was now on the same level as Alonso, Ramos and Higuaín, all of whom had won silverware, including two leagues in 2006 and 2007 – and in the case of the two Spanish players, a World Cup. Players contracted to Jorge Mendes, it was observed, renewed their contracts with greater speed than any others. Since 2010, everyone apart from Coentrão had received a pay rise thanks to Mourinho's insistence. It all reminded the dressing room that favouritism would continue if the coach stayed.

The celebration in the Plaza de Cibeles acted as a release. Casillas climbed up the statue of the goddess after whom the square is named and draped the club flag across her; when he clambered down he embraced Ronaldo before the vast crowd, signifying the beginning of a close friendship. As for Mourinho, he spent the open-top bus journey taking photos with his assistants while holding up seven fingers, one hand open and the other with two fingers raised in victory: his seven league titles, two in Portugal, two in England, two in Italy and one in Spain …

After the party at the Bernabéu the entourage headed for the official dinner. They had spent several hours laughing together and at this point most did not care who they were with. But not Lass. The Frenchman asked if Mourinho would be present. When it was confirmed to him that the coach would be attending he said he would rather go home.

CHAPTER 10

SADNESS

'And this is because injustice creates divisions and hatred and fighting, and justice imparts harmony and friendship; is that not true, Thrasymachus?'

Plato, The Republic, Book 1

The Glasgow Hilton is a hotel for businessmen. It is located in the tallest tower in the centre of the city, silhouetted against a grey skyline. The 20-storey structure, rising above the nearby M8 motorway, dripped with rain in the early hours of 16 May 2002. In a poorly lit room on one of the top floors, what looked to the untrained eye like the annual convention of a kitchen-appliance multinational was taking place. It was actually the celebratory dinner of Real Madrid, who had just been proclaimed champions of Europe and were celebrating the *novena*, their ninth European Cup, in an event presided over by Florentino Pérez.

'We have won the *novena* and next year we will go for the *décima*, and then the *undécima* and the *duodécima*,' said the president, in reference to the 10th, 11th and 12th European Cups surely soon to follow.

The team's victory, winning the final 2–1 against Bayer Leverkusen, had been swallowed up by institutional protocol. Before the salmon pie, the sirloin steak with potatoes and the ice cream were served, Pérez gave a speech that at the time amazed some of the players because of the casual way in which he spoke about what they had just achieved.

Steve McManaman recalled the evening at the Hilton in his auto-biography *Macca*, like someone remembering a glass of tap water they once had. 'With Real Madrid,' wrote the former England inter-national, 'you have to make the most of celebrating on the pitch because it's never a great laugh afterwards. They don't so much party as mark an occasion. You go from twenty or thirty people, the team and support staff, going ballistic celebrating, spraying champagne everywhere, to a three-course banquet at the Hilton with hundreds and hundreds of unfamiliar faces, TV cameras and press everywhere. There's nothing personal about it. I'd won my second European Cup winner's medal, but I didn't have a wild time. We had a very formal, sit-down meal and speeches. My dad and all our mates were out drinking until dawn, having a fantastic time, but I was on best behav-iour at the official banquet.'

The random nature of football conditions the industry that surrounds it in the most profound way. Perhaps, following the logic of other types of industries, Pérez saw the accumulation of European Cups as something normal. He did not know at the time that after Glasgow, in the eight seasons in which he presided over Madrid until 2013, there would be no celebrations for winning the tournament or even for reaching the final. Nor did he imagine that his theory that European competitions could be dominated by the club's spending power – nobody was able to match him in the market place – would turn out to be so difficult in practice.

In the decade that followed the Glasgow final Madrid's signings broke all transfer records in the history of football. Their investment in new players approached the €1,000 million mark. Of all the champions of Europe in this period, only Chelsea (€950 million) came close to that figure. Barcelona (€600), Inter (€590), Manchester United (€550), Bayern (€400), Milan (€400) and Porto (€300) did not need that much money to win the remaining trophies.

The '10th' Champions League went from being an almost tangible reality in the imagination of Madrid supporters to becoming a utopian dream. But 10 years after the dinner at the Hilton the feeling among supporters was that they were not far from another European title. The progression of the team during the 2011–12 tournament was as comfortable as the apparent weakness of their opponents suggested. Olympique Lyon, Ajax, Dinamo Zagreb, CSKA and APOEL offered little resistance in Madrid's march to the semi-finals. There, Bayern Munich, who were second in the Bundesliga, awaited them. Bayern's total revenues, according to Deloitte, were €321 million in the previous season. In the same year Madrid had earned €480 million, and were now leading the league with two Ballon d'Or winners, a handful of world champions and a coach with a very successful record in UEFA competitions. Renewed optimism swept through both the board of directors and the supporters.

Two questions dominated Madrid's trip to Munich: first, would Mourinho have the courage to replace Marcelo, the best left-back in the world, with Fabio Coentrão, who almost all his team-mates thought was the worst player in the squad? Second, would he play with a *trivote*?

The probability of the *trivote* returning increased the moment that Lass, who had been out for a long time, was named in the squad list. But when the team met up at the Westin Grand Hotel in Munich on 16 April Mourinho had already decided that the insubordination of the French midfielder was exceptionally serious. In order to defend his own authority as coach – and as Lass seemed perfectly able to get himself sent off on purpose to hurt him – he chose to give up his midfield fetish. This made Lass for the time being a mere tourist in Munich and meant the 'high-pressure triangle', in its most celebrated version at least, was ruled out. But nothing deterred Mourinho from implementing the same ideas with appropriate modifications: in place of Lass he could play Özil, Di María or even Marcelo.

The team-talk helped answer the first of these two questions: Coentrão would play. The team would be Casillas, Arbeloa, Pepe, Ramos, Coentrão, Khedira, Alonso, Di María, Özil, Ronaldo and Benzema. The plan was to lean towards a 4-2-3-1 formation, with the line-up favouring the more subtle members of the squad, although many of Mourinho's instructions were more in keeping with the *trivote*.

Until then, when preparing the 4-2-3-1 Mourinho had asked his line of three attacking midfielders formed by Di María, Özil and Ronaldo to drop deep and offer themselves to the rest of the team so the ball could be played out from the back. Against most opponents he did not object to building from the back. In Munich the instruction was to play direct, missing out the midfield with long, diagonal passes to Di María or Ronaldo, or even longer passes to Benzema, all taking the load off Özil. The German midfielder was told to venture forward, watch for the second ball, without taking the risk of dropping deep to join in the passing moves. Mourinho told his team they should only come out on the charge if they provoked an error from Bayern. Worried about losing the ball in midfield and suffering on the counter-attack at the hands of Robben and Ribéry, he had decided to play as if the midfield did not exist.

The two teams had finished their warm-ups in the Allianz Arena when Kaká crossed paths with his friend Marcelo in the tunnel. The two embraced.

'What?' Kaká said. 'You're not playing today but you'll play in the Bernabéu to save the tie? Don't get your hopes up, though. You won't be playing in the final!'

Kaká laughed. Marcelo, a compulsive joker, incapable until then of confronting a set-back without a smile, looked very serious. He shrugged his shoulders and looked down at the ground, as if he were trying to overcome his dejection. Kaká grabbed him round the shoulders and tried to cheer him up.

'Really, it's very unfair. You gifted us the knockout at APOEL. If we've got this far without any problems it's been thanks to you.'

The game was deadlocked. Both teams were keen not to give away any space and to deny their opponents time on the ball. They were still finding their way when Ribéry controlled a rebound from a corner and scored through a forest of standing legs. The 1–0 scoreline alarmed Mourinho, who changed the formation on 20 minutes from 4-2-3-1 to 4-3-2-1. Di María left the wing to switch to the right of Alonso, while Özil moved to the far right. An improvised *trivote*, it provoked a barrage of long-balls that spoiled the game. When Özil scored, following a counter-attack by Ronaldo and Benzema, it was in Madrid's only attack on goal. In his attempt to close the match down at 1–1 Mourinho ordered a complete withdrawal from Bayern's half, as well as adding some brawn to the midfield by replacing Di María with Granero, Benzema with Higuaín and Özil with Marcelo. The Brazilian took up his position on the left of the *trivote* with so much frustration and so little enthusiasm that he seemed to be making every effort to get himself sent off. The kick he gave Müller should have been a red card. But referee Howard Webb missed it.

A feint and a change of direction from Lahm on the edge of the area sent Coentrão to the ground in the 90th minute. The German crossed the ball with the outside of his right foot and no one got in front of Mario Gómez, who stabbed the ball home. It was the winner on the night, making it 2–1. And it was the goal that would completely transform the tie.

After Webb blew the final whistle, the revolt that had been organised in the visitors' dressing room had only one theme: the stubbornness of the manager to 'make his mark', as the players said, even if it meant harming his own team's chances. Arbeloa, Higuaín, Lass, Callejón, Casillas and Ramos were among the most forceful of those who spoke. They did not question the conservatism of Mourinho's approach nor the changes he made, which they also judged to have been wrong, with anything like the vehemence that they criticised his decision of who to play down the left. They said Coentrão was a problem; he was no better defensively than Marcelo and offered nothing going forward; they regretted that by insisting on his place in the starting line-up Mourinho had jeopardised everyone else's hard work. They said that lately the impression had been given that the squad was there merely to serve Coentrão's promotion. Now getting quite angry, they reeled off his errors: in Moscow he gave away a useless foul that enabled CSKA to draw 1–1, in Cyprus the team did not function properly until he was replaced by Marcelo, and against Barça at the Bernabéu in both the league and cup he made significant errors in marking Fàbregas, Iniesta and Messi that prevented his team winning the game.

To point to the failings of Coentrão was, if possible, even more relevant than usual. For a counter-attacking team like Madrid, according to the majority of the players, there was a massive difference between taking a 1–1 or a 2–1 into the home leg. The 2–1 meant that Bayern could go to the Bernabéu, sit back and wait for Madrid to attack them. It was exactly what they did not want after two years of being coached on defending deep and playing quick counter-attacking football themselves. They had lost the ability to play in compressed spaces and take the initiative in matches.

'Now we're not going to have any space,' they said. 'We get choked by teams who stick everyone in the area. It happened against Sporting. So how's it not going to happen against Bayern?' Their feeling of impotence was reflected in a remark that was repeated more than once: 'It's all Mourinho's fault.'

The *décima* that was so very attainable in the eyes of the media close to the club was now transformed into an odyssey in the corridors of the home dressing room.

'When are we ever going to have such a good draw?' they asked themselves. 'When are we ever going to have the return leg at home again in so many ties?' The players believed that in Munich the coach had compromised a historic opportunity.

In the return leg Madrid played with the same formation and the same men as in Munich, except for Marcelo, who, as Kaká had predicted, came in for Coentrão. Bayern took to the field with Neuer, Lahm, Boateng, Badstuber, Alaba, Schweinsteiger, Luiz Gustavo, Robben, Kroos, Ribéry and Mario Gómez.

Mourinho told his players to press in medium-block, never taking the defensive line any further than 20 yards from the edge of the area. Madrid made a thunderous start. Alonso released Di María with some probing passes, Khedira pushed forward in search of the second ball and Neuer did not take long to make his first save. Another run and cross from Di María ended with Alaba handling the ball in the box, and Ronaldo scoring the resulting penalty. Before the quarter-hour he was put through by Özil and beat Neuer to make it 2–0. Bayern were not to be intimidated. Robben missed with only Casillas to beat and Khedira cleared a shot from Ribéry. It was enough to make Mourinho come into the technical area, shouting and gesticulating for his players to drop deeper. The team sat back in low-block. Anti-climax. Bayern exploited the new situation by taking control of the middle of the pitch with Schweinsteiger and Kroos.

Madrid were in full retreat mode when Pepe brought down Gómez in the area after 27 minutes, with Robben scoring the equaliser from the penalty spot.

The half-time team-talk would for ever stay in the minds of the players. Mourinho took to the floor and addressed his audience. According to witnesses the message was the one that had been ruminating for months.

'*Señores*,' he said, 'we must be intelligent ...'

The use of the word 'intelligent' in the euphemistic language of the manager amounted to requesting that the players renounce their childish scruples. They had to leave to one side the ball, their vanity and their pride. To explain what he wanted he said that the game had become complicated; they had to keep pressing in low-block in order to conserve energy because they were deep into a long season and their energy levels were low. As if the instruction were based on a detailed half-time study of each of his players' fitness, he told them to stop pressing at goal-kicks and throw-ins because it was wasted energy. 'We'll wait for them a bit,' he said. 'We'll float.' But if they won the ball back they could allow themselves to counter-attack without losing their shape at the back.

The talk had an immediate effect. Until that point the game had belonged to the players. Now it passed into the hands of the coach. For some players the instructions might have served a purpose, but this was a dressing room containing some of the best players in the world. On hearing that it was best to surrender both the ball and most of the pitch to the opposition they became demoralised.

This change on the pitch silenced much of Madrid's support from the stands. As the team became more and more reclusive, the home fans quietened down. Meanwhile, the Bayern supporters could be heard for the first time. The decrease in the volume coming from the home fans made Mourinho furious and he showed his frustration to his assistants by pointing to the stands. Every time that Bayern got anywhere near Casillas's area, he vented his frustration:

'These supporters are an embarrassment.'

Madrid bled until the end, when penalties sealed their fate. Casillas saved from Alaba and Mario Gómez, but Ronaldo, Kaká and Ramos missed their spot-kicks. Madrid's elimination, as far as the players were concerned, was in large part the fault of Mourinho, who had made more bad decisions than good. The players worked out how many times their manager had complicated matches for them since 2011, coming up with the four most significant examples: the Super Cup, the semi-final of the Copa del Rey against Barça and then these two games against Bayern.

The displeasure was both profound and universal. Mourinho did not want to stay at Madrid. In March he began conversations with Manchester City through his agent Jorge Mendes but the City option evaporated when they were proclaimed Premier League champions. As far as Chelsea were concerned, he reached an agreement with Roman Abramovich. But there was an unexpected twist. The London club, under the stewardship of Roberto Di Matteo, lifted the Champions League trophy in Munich on 19 May. The triumph persuaded both Mourinho and Abramovich that it would be best to undo the agreement. It seemed politically costly to the Russian to sack the man who had just won the most important trophy in the club's history. For Mourinho, taking over a club in transition from one generation of players to another did not appeal, especially with little to gain and with expectations higher than ever. Such a commitment went completely against the challenges he usually took on.

It seemed as if Pérez and Mourinho had enjoyed a magical communion in the spring of 2010. But two years later this magic was gone. Not even the party to celebrate the winning of the league provoked anything more than cold pragmatism between the two men. Publicly, they preached indissoluble unity but when on their own and in private, surrounded by their respective entourages, they contemplated futures in which neither man needed the other. They both understood very well that the exorbitant amounts of money paid out had not been satisfactorily repaid with sporting success.

In spite of the fantasy that surrounded Madrid, mixed up with the fanaticism, Mourinho's communications strategies, and the constant generation of excitement and anticipation, the two principal actors appreciated that this was not a movie being played out on the big screen; this was harsh football reality. The destruction of Barça's exemplary image in the media and on the pitch was as much an unfulfilled target as winning the Champions League. As the summer of 2012 advanced, Pérez and Mourinho showed signs of caution, even of complete resignation.

On 22 May 2012, after exhausting his search for a route back to England, Mourinho renewed his Madrid contract, prolonging his link to the club until 2016. The news surprised the majority of his players as they prepared for the European Championships in Poland and Ukraine. The trophy remained in Spanish hands, with Casillas, Alonso and Ramos being three of the team's most important players. The internationals rejoined the squad in Madrid on 28 July, then flew out for the pre-season in Los Angeles. There they found a mysteriously transformed Mourinho.

The coach seemed to have subtly distanced himself from his Portuguese players. Coentrão, Pepe and Ronaldo – the players with whom he talked most during the team meet-ups before matches – did not now attract him as much as the recently crowned European champions. The retention of the title had lent an aura of success – and personal appeal – to Casillas, Ramos, Alonso and their peers that Spanish players had never previously enjoyed. Mourinho shared a joke or exchanged opinions with them at every opportunity. He wanted to be on the right side of Ramos:

'Sergio! Where did you go on holiday? You look very tanned ...'

Footballers tend to be jealous. Pepe, Coentrão and Ronaldo were indignant – and incredulous – at hearing such pleasantries; these players, beaten by Spain in the semi-finals, now felt displaced. The Spanish, whose mistrust of Mourinho if anything increased amid the new niceties, were convinced that if they had lost to Portugal in Donetsk their situation would have remained suffocating. Even Arbeloa, who in public appeared to be a *Mourinhista*, compared Mourinho's intentions during the tournament to the planning of a military coup. Everyone knew that the sporting prestige of the winner would translate into power and that Mourinho had crossed his fingers for a Portuguese victory. Had they won, Gestifute, the company that co-ordinated his representation, took it as a given that the manager would have wanted to sign Meireles and Bosingwa that same summer, both players being represented by Mendes. The plan was to augment the Portuguese colony, the club within a club. But, after the Euros, conditions were no longer favourable. It was against this backdrop that when Mourinho saw Ramos he winked:

'I like your haircut. Is there a stylist in the family?'

Casillas tried to avoid the boss. Every time he was interviewed he tried to make it clear that he belonged to a quite different school. He repeated this as if it were a formula, even though what he was being asked had nothing to do with such an answer. He would then be riled to see that some publications, when they edited his answers, cut out that particular part.

'I possess the values taught to me by Hierro, Raúl, Redondo, Roberto Carlos, Guardiola, Abelardo or Luís Enrique,' he'd say. The inclusion of Guardiola was no coincidence, and Mourinho was furious when he heard it.

SADNESS

The summer passed peacefully in between all the frivolities, the political conjecture and subliminal messages, but when it seemed that behind one triviality there was nothing more than another triviality, a fire storm started, one that was to grow to an enormous size and create all sorts of unwanted repercussions.

Ronaldo was reserved from the first day back at work. He avoided everyone, not just the Spanish. He even distanced himself from Pepe, who had previously been his shield, and passed the hours in the company of Coentrão. The kid was irritated. One day in the United States a fan threw a ball at him for him to sign; he refused to do so because it hit him or because he had got out of bed the wrong side, and sent it back by blasting it into the crowd. The rest of the squad thought his irritation was a result of his failure to win the Ballon d'Or. A Spanish team-mate believed that his desire for the trophy was more than an obsession; it was like 'a sickness'. But no one knew for certain because he had been silent for almost a month, scarcely holding a conversation with anyone.

In the last week of August 2012 Madrid beat Barcelona in the Super Cup on away goals. The first leg ended 3–2, and it was 2–1 in the return fixture. This was Barça's first tournament with Tito Vilanova in charge, the man whom Mourinho had assaulted the previous year having become Guardiola's successor in the dugout. The effect of the change seemed to be immediately obvious with Barça's tactical misjudgements during the Super Cup. They displayed a surprising mix of indolence and dislocation in defence, and had not seemed so vulnerable since 2008.

The league kicked off at the Bernabéu on 19 September with a 1–1 draw against a Valencia side of no great substance. It was a poor game. At the end, Mourinho stormed into the dressing room and launched into his first tirade of the season. Even though he had developed a childish devotion to his Spanish players over the summer, old habits were hard to kick. He said that some players had still not come back from their holidays and that he had observed a lack of hunger on the pitch. His aggressive manner was nothing special; what was new was the disinterest with which most of the players listened to his diatribe. For most of them it was as if he did not exist. They showered, changed and went home.

The only player who seemed to be affected, and not by the words of the coach, was Ronaldo. He had not overcome his melancholy. Jorge Mendes never stopped talking about the Ballon d'Or every time they spoke together. Ronaldo, who found in the protective influence of his agent a substitute for the father he had lost as a boy, had suggested that he would only have a chance of shifting Messi from the throne he had occupied since 2009 by winning the Euros. With the tournament lost and gone, so were all of his chances of winning the individual award. He felt frustrated, something he needed to get over, but the ruling member of his entourage did nothing to help him. Mendes dedicated a large part of his energy to designing new grand projects that centred on distinctive publicity campaigns for his top player. He wanted to be considered as the number one agent because he represented the world's number ones.

With the aim of making these projects a reality, Mendes became Diego Maradona's agent, and in 2010 he was the force behind the creation of a parallel world football gala called the Globe Soccer Awards, to be celebrated in Dubai. He would attend this celebration as master of ceremonies with his team, introducing various awards tailor-made for himself and his players. Mendes is the only person who has won the award for 'best agent' – the first of its kind – coming top in 2010, 2011 and 2012.

SADNESS

If the existence of Messi frustrated Ronaldo's dream, the strength of the Spanish national team took Ronaldo even further away from the Ballon d'Or prize he sought. The evening held in Dubai has the lavish setting of the Persian Gulf in its favour, but it is FIFA who are associated with the prestige of the golden ball. For many years Mourinho and his agent had repeated to Ronaldo that the Argentinian footballer was the one he had to beat. They called him 'El Enano' ('The Dwarf') and entertained themselves discussing his shortcomings. The coach assured Ronaldo that it was the political power of Barcelona that kept Messi on the throne, and that it could not last for ever. At some stage in the summer of 2012 Ronaldo realised that fantasy and reality do not always coincide, and that what the people who had always believed in him had told him might not be the truth.

Ronaldo's troubles explained his dark mood in training. Missing the frenetic spark of his best days, he had not scored in the first two weeks of the season, which marked a major dip for him. In the second match, Madrid lost in Getafe and were already five points behind Barcelona. The dressing room was like a blast furnace. The group of players headed by Madrid's senior players turned their back on Mourinho again. They held that the team would never make up the gap in the table, although they insisted that this was not down to any lack of competitiveness. Winning the title – such a necessity last season – had not taken away their edge. One league title was certainly not enough, hardly satisfying their thirst for glory. Teams don't exhaust themselves because of the trophies they have won but because of a breakdown in unity and togetherness. The majority of the players, for one reason or another, confessed to being unable to respond to a coach in whom they had lost belief.

Ronaldo put his best marine blue suit and navy and charcoal tie on to go to the UEFA gala in Monte Carlo on 30 August. He was nominated alongside Messi and Iniesta for the European Footballer of the Year Award 2011–12. The cameras recorded his disappointment when Michel Platini, president of UEFA, announced that Iniesta was the winner. But what really upset him was seeing the other two nominees accompanied by the Barcelona president Sandro Rosell, while he was accompanied only by Emilio Butragueño. It was not a question of the individuals concerned, but of etiquette and protocol. The player thought he deserved better. He was going through a difficult time and he found himself somewhat abandoned.

The Monte Carlo gala threw up a first. Never before had Messi and Ronaldo shared second place and, what is more, with the same number of votes. Perhaps they understood that, despite all their differences, they had finally coincided in something. Making the most of the situation, Iniesta, who had an excellent relationship with Ronaldo, moved the player closer to Messi. They spoke. Almost certainly about football and for their shared admiration for the winner. There is a Spanish phrase '*el roce hace el cariño*', meaning that constant friction ends up giving way to affection, and the two enjoyed each other's company. Jorge Mendes, Ronaldo's agent, was there to watch over his friend and player, and, as the day went on, he started chatting with Rosell, apparently as if the two were old friends.

Madrid beat Granada 3–0 on 2 September. After scoring two goals, Ronaldo showered, changed and, donning his black baseball cap, appeared before the press in what appeared to be another innocuous media appearance. That was until someone asked him why he had not celebrated his two goals.

'It could be that I'm a bit sad,' he replied. 'It's the only reason. I don't celebrate goals when I'm not happy. And it's not for the UEFA award. That's the least of my concerns. There are things that are more important than that. It's something professional. The people in the club know why.'

Casillas and Ramos pushed for a meeting with their team-mates to ask Ronaldo if he had a problem that they could help resolve, and seeing that it was something that had nothing to do with them they offered him their support. Rumours began to circulate in the dressing room about the cause of their top scorer's woes. The most widely accepted story was that he had sought out Pérez in a meeting and had made it clear to the president that he did not want to stay at Madrid, under the current conditions, without receiving greater backing from the institution, the supporters and his team-mates. In time his fellow players came to realise that Ronaldo held nothing against them and that his relationship with Mourinho was as irrelevant as always. The person who had been upsetting him was the president.

Ronaldo told his friends that on returning from Monte Carlo he had contacted Pérez to tell him of his frustrations for the somewhat offhand treatment he had received at the hands of the club since 2009. It was a brief encounter. Ronaldo suggested that if the club did not want him then they should listen to offers from other teams that did. In response, the president said that he could go, as long as his sale earned the club enough money to pay for Messi's buy-out clause.

Everything that made Ronaldo stand out as a player he owed to his own self-respect. His tenacity came from his vanity, his ability to overcome obstacles from his ambition, the feverish desire to compete and to work meticulously on his physique, all this acted as a shield to protect him against external challenges. The man had a touch of naivety about him, too, and this was also part of his great strength. He believed in himself to the point of accepting his own legend – and he loved football because it served as a reaffirmation. In the stadium he could repeat to the world: I am Cristiano. Pérez's words, whatever they were, must have opened up a crack in that shield, confirming to him the truth of all the whispers he had heard about the low esteem in which he was held at the club. For some reason, perhaps because he had been signed by Pérez's predecessor Ramón Calderón, the president had not been able to hide his lack of tact and affection. Ronaldo would never forget this.

Wishful thinking takes root very easily in football. For months there was a feeling around Madrid that the season was going to lead to something big. It suited very few people to believe that anything else should come to pass and the overwhelming majority of supporters had faith in the team's recovery. But by the end of the second week in September, with eight months remaining before the end of the season, Pérez found himself on the edge of the abyss. He was about to lose the confidence of his principal player. His team were about to slip out of the title race, with his coach already mummified in a sarcophagus of constant and irreparable conflict with the senior players and indeed most of the squad.

Barça started playing almost as badly in the league as Madrid. They won comfortably against Real Sociedad (5–1), but struggled to beat Osasuna (0–1; Messi did not score until the 76th minute), they struggled to beat Valencia (1–0) and did not kill the game against Getafe until the last quarter of an hour (1–4). They were lucky to reach the fifth weekend of the season with 12 points. Madrid only had four points after a draw against Valencia (1–1), a defeat in Getafe (2–1), the win over Granada (3–0) and a defeat to Sevilla (1–0).

In some respects everything ended on 15 September just after 10 p.m. local time. Piotr Trochowski converted a Rakitić corner and put Sevilla 1–0 up in the first minute of a game that froze from that moment on. It was the fourth week of the season and Madrid were unable to respond to a set-piece goal, despite having 90 minutes in which to do so. For the players it was proof that their age-old problem of playing against closed-up opposition had not disappeared. But in the press conference after the game Mourinho only focused on what had taken place in the first minute, springing to his own defence and emphasising his professionalism while noting what seemed to be the inexplicable dereliction of duty by his players:

'We cannot train any more or any better on set-pieces. Every player knows his position and his mission. Those who have individual responsibilities know who their opponents are and who's in their zone, and what zone they have to occupy. We have the graphics in our own dressing room … My problem is that my team at this moment are not there … I'm worried that since the start of the season we competed in the Super Cup but have not done so in anything else.'

It was not just that he was criticising his players in public. It was that he denounced their lack of professionalism and lack of interest. After his tirade at Getafe the manager had set sail on his own ship. The communication strategies of 2010 that he exhibited to the squad as a sophisticated defence policy had, two years down the line, become a weapon that he would turn on them.

No one knew better than Mourinho that the only reason for renewing his contract until 2016 was financial. The president might have thought that it would make him more committed but Mourinho never believed he could continue in the role unless he was able to dismiss half the squad. That was impossible. The transfer of Ramos and Casillas, two of the pillars of the World Cup and European Championships team, was not even worth thinking about. Mourinho saw calamity around every corner, with Madrid itself seeming like a monstrous trap. Embarrassed by a sense of impending failure and afraid of destroying his prestige, propaganda was his last recourse: in order to maintain the idea of his own innocence in the public's eyes, he insistently repeated that his players had given up, something that he had expected to happen when the league began. Now he would use his devious techniques as much as he could over the following nine months.

Concerned after the defeat to Sevilla, the Madrid senior players asked for a meeting. It was attended by Casillas, Ramos and Higuaín. The most impetuous of the three was Ramos, but all of them confronted Mourinho face-to-face. They berated the coach for trying to discredit his players as part of a method whose ultimate goal was to avoid publicly assuming any sort of responsibility himself – 'like I said before and like I will say again,' Casillas added. The players said that they had often swallowed their complaints, reminding him of the tie with Bayern:

'In Munich we lost the game because – among other things – you played Coentrão, and nobody criticised you for it … And in the second leg, when Bayern were dead, you told the team to sit back … And no player said that we were going to miss out on the final because of you.'

Mourinho did not respond. He stayed silent and dismissed his players. On 18 September, in that season's first Champions League game, he gave his reply. Manchester City visited the Bernabéu and in the home team line-up there was no Ramos. Instead, Varane played, an 18-year-old centre-back who had barely seen more than a few minutes' action over the previous 12 months. Casillas was sure that he played that day because the coach did not trust Adán, the reserve goalkeeper. Despite City's error-strewn play, Madrid almost lost the game. After 86 minutes Kolarov gave City a 1–2 lead. A minute later Benzema equalised, and Ronaldo scored in the 90th minute to make it 3–2, avoiding what could become a very difficult group stage.

Madrid's advance through the Champions League group stages and beyond was rough from start to finish, much like the relationship between Ronaldo and Pérez from the gala in Monte Carlo onwards. The president admitted to his advisors that it had been a mistake not to go to Monaco. He was informed that too many ties were established between Mendes, Rosell, Messi and Ronaldo, and he was even told that Messi and Ronaldo had got along. He did not buy that. What he did admit to was that had he been present he would have cushioned the pernicious effect of all this on his team's star. Monte Carlo laid the foundation of Ronaldo's sense of abandonment. It also moved Pérez to worry seriously about making the offer that he had retracted since 2011.

Between 2011 and the start of the summer of 2012 Madrid had improved the contracts of Di María, Carvalho, Pepe and Mourinho, four of the six men represented by Jorge Mendes at the club, the other two being Coentrão and Ronaldo. If Di María's took a year and a half to renew, Ronaldo's deal had not been touched in the three years that he had marked him as the most prolific scorer in the history of the club with his 202 goals in 199 matches. The first person who struggled to believe the indifference with which his extraordinary performances were greeted was Ronaldo himself. Madrid could never get their money back on their investment in Pepe, Di María and Carvalho. As for Mourinho, the renewal of his contract was a financial burden for the club rather than the coach. With Ronaldo it was different. His market value in 2013 was well over the £80 million that Madrid had paid for him in 2009.

Rumours that Ronaldo and Messi were becoming increasingly friendly made Pérez stay ever more alert. There was one fact that troubled him more than any other. The Barcelona president was invited to give a lecture to the World Soccer Awards, the gala that Mendes co-ordinated. At the closing dinner, Capello, Mourinho and Maradona, among other guests, saw Mendes and Rosell break off from the group to go and chat in private. An acquaintance of Pérez who attended the meeting assured him that they had one topic of mutual interest: Ronaldo.

At first, Pérez completely ruled out the idea that Messi and Ronaldo could appear in the same team, given the degree of personal rivalry between them. Over time, however, he began to think that maybe it *was* possible, taking the idea so seriously that he proposed going to the FIFA Ballon d'Or gala to keep a very close eye on his star player. And so it was that the president could be found on 7 January 2013 in a secluded corner of the lobby of the Kongresshaus in Zurich watching Messi give a TV interview. Suddenly, Ronaldo appeared from the other side of the room. Then came what the president had feared. Messi called Ronaldo over and the two of them warmly embraced. Pérez told his friends that he was extremely upset, sensing the approaching danger and imagining exactly what was going to happen. Ronaldo would be free in January 2015 and then any club, including Barcelona, could move to sign him without first negotiating with Madrid. Friends say that the president imagined with horror the attacking line-up, player by player. On the left, where he loved to play, Ronaldo. In the middle, Messi. On the right, Neymar. An unforgettable forward line, a return to the *galácticos* concept in an alien city. Something to be avoided at all costs.

Obsessed with eliminating all risks, Pérez even ended up considering selling Ronaldo to another club in the summer. Imagining that Ronaldo might did not want to renew his contract, he set the balls rolling for his officials to scour the market in search of offers for the player. A price of €150 million looked possible – to whoever could afford him. But Barcelona were of course ruled out as a buyer.

The months from 30 August to the season's end saw a role-reversal. Ronaldo regained his calm and the club's directors were now the impatient ones. The club asked him three times to sit down and discuss his contract. Ronaldo ignored all of these invitations, saying publicly that he wanted to see out his current contract – in other words, until the end of the deal in 2015. At Gestifute, the company looking after Ronaldo, they assured him that if he went on a free he would be much richer and urged him not to accept Pérez's conditions.

In the spring he was offered a deal that guaranteed him €60 million. In May that rose to €80 million. But he just had to wait until January 2015, when he would be 29 and had clubs willing to pay that amount as a bonus, in addition to a salary that would be better than what he was on at Madrid.

From January onwards, and in the absence of any response from their star player, Madrid had made a late bid to sign Neymar. Their courting of the Brazilian ended when his transfer to Barcelona was made public on 26 May, compounding the growing sense of anxiety in Pérez's presidential office at the construction firm ACS. He apologised to his circle of close advisors for having missed the opportunity of renewing Ronaldo's contract in 2011, when the player was still interested. Then, they would have been able to raise his basic salary of €9 million to €11 million net, far less than it would eventually cost them in September 2013 when it became a matter of urgency.

Ronaldo went on holiday at the season's end without having passed through Pérez's office. It was Jorge Mendes who received the offer of a renewal of his contract. This consisted of an extension until 2017, with the option of a further year, and a salary of €14 million a year. With the recently introduced tax laws this would see Real Madrid pay Ronaldo an annual total of around €30 million, making him the best-paid player in the western world. But before Ronaldo responded he wanted to enjoy his holidays. Why worry when time is on your side? What did it matter that Pérez wanted to start things moving now when the initiative was with Mendes, his agent, his friend and the real winner in all these games.

CHAPTER 11

UNREAL

'All entrepreneurs claim to be realists. But the reality is that there is a strong sense of denial in many companies that prevents them from taking the right decisions. Why don't people face reality? (…) And if you don't then you cannot keep your company at the cutting edge.'

LARRY BOSSIDY and RAM CHARAN,
Execution: The Discipline of Getting Things Done

The warm, humid air of the Calblanque spilled serenely down towards the sea. Lying on a deckchair on the terrace, warming himself in the afternoon sun like a lizard, was Jürgen Klöpp.

'The best thing about working in Spain would be the climate, that's for sure,' he said, smiling.

The Borussia Dortmund coach struggled to find any other advantages. In January 2013 he had taken his team to Murcia for the duration of the Bundesliga mid-winter break, as the air on the coast was balmy and clear. Klöpp said that he was concerned about the impoverishment of La Liga and the huge financial inequality between clubs. He had read that in polls he was the fans' first choice to be the next Madrid coach; their support pleased him, but he made it clear he was happy in Dortmund for one fundamental reason:

'Dortmund is exactly what a football club should be. We're delighted that it carries on being a club and not a business where they say, "Today one thing, and tomorrow another." We want to work as a team over a longer period of time. I've been here for four years and my contract runs out in 2016. That excites me because it means I can develop new things. I see players aged 10 or 13 years of age, and I know that in four years' time I'll be coaching them.'

The influence of the wildly successful English Premier League had led to a wave of reforms being made across most clubs on the continent. Players now trained in isolated environments far from the supporters, who were increasingly treated as 'consumers'. Marketing technocrats, inspired by business models that held the old order in disdain, gained new and wider powers at these clubs. They spoke of professionalism, about 'the industry' and of science. The fact that Mourinho behaved more like a chief executive of a multinational than a coach was indicative of the spread of this tendency.

Dortmund had seen this obsession for the administrative 'future' during the previous managerial regime and had suffered when their debt bubble finally burst. Since 2008 they had reverted to being a more straightforward institution, with their legendary Westfalenstadion rising up from the middle of a wood close to the Rheinlanddamm. Less than 100 yards on the other side of the avenue are the club offices. The structure of the club is simple. Ninety per cent of shares in the club belong to its members. There is a council, split into four parts led by four people all with something in common. The president Hans-Joachim Watzke, the sporting director Michael Zorc, the youth academy director Lars Ricken and the coach Jürgen Klopp are all former players. Watzke boasts of having muddied his knees in the fourth division before becoming the man holding the Dortmund purse strings.

Dortmund's income stood at €189 million for the 2011–12 season, according to Deloitte. The same report put Madrid at the top of the revenue list, the first team to go past the €500 million mark, making as much as €513 million at the close of 2012. This money was spent on the squad. Between 2008 and 2012 Madrid invested close to €550 million on signing players, while Dortmund had spent €80 million, €10 million less than Madrid had spent on Ronaldo alone. The gap was also well demonstrated by what the two coaches had achieved just prior to joining their new clubs: Klopp came to Dortmund after getting Mainz 05 promoted in 2008, while Mourinho had just won the Champions League with Inter when he signed for Madrid.

The evening of 24 October 2012 in Dortmund was cool and damp, and the pitch was playing fast after all the drizzle. In the 34th minute Pepe, under pressure from Reus and Lewandowski, lost possession. From the centre-circle Kehl lofted the ball back in behind Pepe; Lewandowski ran on to it, shooting past Casillas to open the scoring. Dortmund won the game 2–1 in this, the first group match between the two sides. Mourinho, dressed appropriately in black, appeared at the post-match press conference to mourn the fact that he had warned his players of their fate in the pre-match team-talk:

'I said to the players that this would be the game of the lost ball. Possession given up by Madrid, counter-attack from Borussia. The ball given away by Borussia, counter-attack from Madrid. I didn't see any other way for the teams to score goals. It would either be from set-plays or on the break.'

The Portuguese coach went on to say that Dortmund were a mirror-image of his team. But instead of praising this meeting of two like-minded teams, there was a surprising note of frustration in his description of the game:

'It was evenly contested. What little space there was only appeared on the break. If we'd scored first we'd have closed up as much as they did when it was 2–1. They scored and closed the game down – and we had no chance of finding any space. There was nothing. Counter-attack. Only counter-attack.'

Mourinho puffed out his cheeks then slowly exhaled, as if blowing out his exasperation, his powerlessness. His players remembered the Peking Manual. They commented that they had suffered the same old fate, only instead of it being at the hands of Celta Vigo or Betis, this time it had been against players of the very highest quality. Their opponents had surrendered the ball and much of the pitch, and Madrid had been obliged to mount static attacks, just as their opponents wanted. Forced to move the ball about in an attempt to disorientate Dortmund, they managed only to disorientate themselves as this was something that they had not practised on the training ground. What is more, without the injured Marcelo and with Alonso being patrolled by the attentive Götze, they had no one who could get the ball moving easily from one half of the pitch to the other, either with a cross-field run or a pass.

'Mourinho doesn't offer us any ideas for how we should move when we have possession,' the players repeated among themselves. 'Pre-match simulations can't always be translated to the real thing. We don't find the space because we all move into the same areas and get in each other's way.'

The Spanish internationals pointed out the difference between Mourinho and coaches such as Luis Aragonés, who, despite having made his name with a counter-attacking team, knew how to work on the more elaborate forms of attack necessary against teams that defended deep. Aragonés had coached the Spanish national team in the 2008 Euros with a tenacity and an ability that surprised even Xavi Hernández, the master of positional play. Arbeloa, Ramos and Alonso recalled that even though they won the first game of the Euros against Russia in Innsbruck 4–1, they found that Aragonés was less than pleased in the dressing room because they had played so many long balls:

'I'm happy with the result but not with the football we played,' he said, 'because you cannot play like that. That's not the style that we've decided to use. If you get the ball down and play out from the back more, then you're going to be champions.'

Aragonés believed that there were things that went above and beyond his method. As far as he was concerned, a 4–1 win was not enough, even though his team had played a style of football that had long been associated with him. He understood that ultimate success did not have to be linked to any personal brand of football. But Mourinho raised his own flag above all other considerations, and anyway had more faith in goading his players' competitive nature than in any one particular style of play.

'The good player is the one who thinks about winning,' he proclaimed.

Mourinho had a great number of attributes but, as his own players observed, he was incapable of being flexible in certain situations. The passing of time had reinforced his conviction in the methods he preached, and doubts were not permitted. The series of four games that Madrid played against Dortmund between October 2012 and 2013, two in the group stage and two in the semi-finals, exposed his unusual approach. The message he gave his players before the first game at the Westfalenstadion encapsulated his approach to football: 'This will be the game of the lost ball.'

'Don't lose the ball' was Mourinho's order of the day, a four-word summary of his strategy. And so, to ensure that they did not lose the ball, the central defenders were told that they must avoid coming out of the area in possession, as Pepe had tried to do with a pass to the central midfielders. Instead, he should have played a longer pass, bypassing the lines of pressure established by the opposition. This message, repeated with such insistence during Mourinho's three years at Madrid, ended up in the collective conscience of the team. The team associated short passing moves with problems and long balls forward with convenient solutions; one-touch football created fear, but the long ball brought calm.

'This match will be the match of the lost ball' should be seen as part of a code: 1. The game is won by the team who commits fewer errors; 2. Football favours whoever provokes more errors in the opposition; 3. Away from home, instead of trying to be superior to the opposition, it's better to encourage their mistakes; 4. Whoever has the ball is more likely to make a mistake; 5. Whoever renounces possession reduces the possibility of making a mistake; 6. Whoever has the ball has fear; 7. Whoever does not have it is thereby stronger. The doctrine was the exact opposite of the one that had helped Spain become double European and World Champions, and was the opposite of what was being practised by the majority of teams in La Liga. It also went against what many of the Madrid players believed in.

Arbeloa, Casillas, Ramos, Alonso, Higuaín, Benzema, Özil and Marcelo all asked themselves the same question after the defeat in Germany: apart from the Copa del Rey, which is played on a neutral ground, how many games had Madrid won away from the Bernabéu with Mourinho? The list of matches against potent rivals away from home was a brief one: in the 2010–11 season, the San Siro (2–2) and the Camp Nou (5–0 and 1–1); in the 2011–12 season, the Camp Nou (3–2, 2–2 and 1–2) and Munich (2–1); and in the 2012–13 season, until Christmas, the Camp Nou (2–2 and 3–2), Dortmund (2–1) and Manchester City (1–1). Eleven games in total and only one victory. For the most expensive group of players on the planet it raised some major issues, at the very least.

Jürgen Klopp had realised that Madrid showed signs of rigidity when forced to have the ball. He worked out that the direct football played by Mourinho's team could be neutralised by employing exactly the same tactics, telling his players that they should let Madrid have possession and the space on the pitch to force them to take the initiative. At the end of the night the statistics offered up one bit of information that generally reflects well on the footballing health of a team, but which created a considerable problem for Madrid: they had 56 per cent of possession.

'Madrid,' said Klopp, 'had more possession – but that's not a bad thing. It's only bad if the opposition has more of the ball and has the better idea of what to do with it. I think on the day of the 2–1 we had the better idea because we knew who'd have more problems if they dominated possession. We knew where they would send their passes, how they would look for Ronaldo. Our plan was to cover Alonso because if he plays as he wants to it's impossible to defend against Madrid. But if you block him you force Pepe to have the ball. And, of course, that's quite a different thing.'

Mourinho said that Dortmund had played like Madrid, but that was an oversimplification. Both teams were highly effective at counter-attacking and both sides placed a lot of emphasis on pressing. But thereafter there were differences. Klopp concentrates much of his work on the first pass out of defence. The centre-backs Subotić and Hummels, the midfielders Kehl and Gündoğan, and the full-backs Piszczek and Schmelzer offer plenty of movement to help the ball come out from defence. And the ball usually remains on the ground. Dortmund would not hit a long ball, except for when it was really needed. Klopp was so concerned with the pass from the back that his players had to perfect the technique involved. The coach even made the club spend €2 million on a capsule called the 'footbonaut', where players were subjected to mechanical training procedures that improved passing and control to a volume and speed that took them beyond the limits of conventional training. The players who struggled most with the technique, such as Kehl or Subotić, would have to spend extra hours in the capsule, not to improve their long balls but to perfect the 10-yard pass.

As far as pressure was concerned, the German coach designed a model that converted this into a vehicle of attack. Klopp's coaching of pressing was based on what he called 'impulse'. With enough training the players learned to recognise tell-tale signs in the opposition's movement, so that they could choose exactly the right moment to start pressing any given player, normally a central defender or a midfielder. Klopp gave the name 'impulse' to this collective intuition. The manager coached it in such a way that it became a game for the players, as much in an attacking sense as a defensive one.

The analogy that Klopp used to explain the synchronised move ment of the 'impulse' was a pack of wolves. These predators instinctively know how to sniff out the most vulnerable individual of the herd and, from various directions, pursue them as a single pack. When practising 'impulse', they ensured that the claws of the system dislodged the opposition's central defenders and, as soon as possession had been regained, the move would be finished in or around the area by three or four players. Defenders tended to freeze, knowing that any foul would result in a penalty. In this way Dortmund became the team who scored most goals from shots inside the area in the Bundesliga.

Before the return leg in the Bernabéu on 6 November the Dortmund squad picked out their ideal target. Pepe was to be the weak link. They called him the 'pressing victim'.

At the end of January 2013 there was still something about Mourinho that surprised Klopp. When remembering the matches against Madrid, one question arose about his colleague. Considering he managed the team with the biggest budget in the world, why did Mourinho not sign better defenders?

The commitment to Arbeloa instead of Carvajal, to Pepe and Carvalho instead of Ramos, and to Coentrão instead of Marcelo was something that anyone unfamiliar with Mourinho's strategies would struggle to understand. In footballing terms it made no sense, unless it was thought that defenders should never participate in the preparation of an attacking move. When adding other criteria, however, such as psychology, using intimidation as a means of persuasion, and building a shield of loyal players who might not be at the highest technical level, the reasons behind Mourinho's selections become more understandable.

On 3 December an extraordinary episode took place in a press conference given by Mourinho. After two and a half years in his position as the most powerful sporting figure at Madrid since the death of Santiago Bernabéu in 1978, Mourinho came up with the best definition to date for his style of play:

'We need to play every game with the same amount of concentration, with the same personality, the same ambition. We need to be at the limits of our potential and with the objective of winning clearly in our minds, even when we have difficulties. We lack emotional continuity. That is the first thing. Then the football questions come on their own. We have a perfectly designed style, but sometimes when we're not mentally right it makes us lose that identity. In order to have continuity of identity the emotional aspect is very important.'

The previous week Mourinho had given up on the league, after the 1–0 defeat against Betis. Madrid were 11 points behind Barça. In the 2012–13 season the questions would come thick and fast, but there were other puzzles where the lack of solutions worried fans. How had the team that had won the league while breaking records and scoring so many goals disappeared so fast? What were they playing at, after their model had been so rigorously monitored for two and a half years? The speed, the strength, the goals, the competitiveness already existed. So what were the positive things that the manager had brought to the club?

Reluctant to talk about football when there was nothing concrete at stake – and far less to give details about his most intimate football convictions – suddenly on 3 December, during those few seconds, Mourinho had suggested something completely taboo. The model did not exist. The rage, the ambition, the fear that each player projected; the storm of energy, channelled to a particular goal – that all existed. But when all of these were extinguished the team had nothing left beyond a collection of individual wills and a few obedient people waiting for orders.

What most exasperated Mourinho in the autumn of 2012 was the discovery that his players were no longer afraid of him. He would have preferred to be surrounded by enemies who hated him. But they treated him like anyone else. They ignored him. And the less they responded to him, the more anxious he became. He was restless when watching games from the bench. One of his most quoted comments was when, testing his team's mental state, he said something that would usually be anaethema to him: 'Go out and enjoy yourselves!'

Speaking at a conference on chaos, the philosopher Jorge Wagensberg, scientific director of La Caixa, warned that shamans are 'masters of chaos' and that primitive societies need these individuals for evolutionary reasons. Wagensberg found some logic in the behavior of Mourinho:

'If not for crisis we would all be just bacteria,' said the philosopher. 'Uncertainty is the engine of innovation. The chaos forces you to decide between persisting or disappearing. Nothing ever comes from balance and tranquillity. The second law of thermodynamics says that when a system is isolated thermal death occurs. Canned sardines are in a state of perfect equilibrium. Living beings flee that balance. Since the environment sometimes fails to cause sufficient doses of uncertainty, the shaman offers the solution by instilling fear.'

The second law of thermodynamics also warns that the amount of chaos in the universe tends to increase over time. In other words, destiny is irreversible, dark and quiet. No matter how rabid their grappling, shamans are ultimately consumed by the cosmos's own chaos.

The players could no longer stand to live in this state of continual upheaval without the compensation of enjoying the game. But Mourinho had failed to explain in his 3 December speech how to maintain this continual upheaval. The misunderstanding was mutual, leading to all sorts of assumptions or simply to bad faith. The manager told his aides that he believed the players were capable of bringing forth his destruction by no longer performing at their best on the pitch. Disoriented, he began calling José Ángel Sánchez and Pérez, warning them of this while at the same time asking for more power. He made it known to Pérez that if he did not get what he wanted, then he would leave the club.

The list Mourinho presented to the president in mid-November 2012 was half ultimatum, half desideratum. His first demand was that senior players should be reprimanded, with the warning that Casillas and Ramos now possessed intolerable levels of power. He complained that Casillas had belittled him by publicly saying that he was inspired by Guardiola and that the club had not officially corrected him. He highlighted similar incidents in relation to Ramos, calling him subversive. The club as an institution, in his opinion, had to apply exemplary punishment to those who dared to question his authority.

His second demand was for the signing of a goalkeeper to compete with Casillas. He clarified that it should not just be a regular goalkeeper but a young one, about 24 or 25, who was an international in a world-class team. Casillas, he added, was getting older.

Next he demanded that Madrid hire a spokesman, someone respected by everyone connected to the club, such as a former player with an untainted record. This person should say whatever he was asked to say by Mourinho and, if necessary, publicly criticise the players.

The fourth requirement was that the club get rid of those players whose names he had included in a list, and that it was the institution that took care of this so any comeback in the media was not directed at him. Of the names included in the list there were five that circulated through the offices of the club: Higuaín, Albiol, Kaká, Marcelo and Özil.

Pérez responded that if he won the Champions League then he would give him what he wanted, but that without the credit afforded him by a Champions League title he did not feel he could bow down to Mourinho's demands. He repeated that Madrid belonged to its members and that he would need their backing for such measures. At the moment such backing seemed unlikely because support for the manager had declined since 2010. Put a Champions League trophy on the table and, in the new presidential cycle that was due to start in 2013, the landscape would change. As far as Mourinho's request for a spokesman was concerned, the president promised to search for someone who fitted the profile requested.

As the weeks went by Pérez told his manager that he had not found anyone suitable. Those consulted rejected the idea, not wishing to lose credibility as Karanka had done. On hearing this explanation Mourinho flew into a rage, saying he could not believe that there were people who thought representing him or Madrid would be to the detriment of their own image.

Madrid's defeat against Betis in the league on 24 November

followed the pattern of matches that took Madrid down a familiar footballing cul-de-sac. Betis took the lead with a goal from Beñat on 16 minutes and then shut up shop. Being given most of the pitch and virtually all of the ball, Madrid suffocated. The game ended 1–0 and Pepe Mel, the Betis coach, repeated what Klopp had said, by now the worst-kept secret in Spanish football: 'We tried to make sure Madrid had the ball because that way they harm themselves.'

What Mel suggested was confirmed by the Madrid players, who recognised that they had been found out. In the press room of the Benito Villamarín Mourinho accused his players of a lack of ambition:

'When I see a guy like Štěpánek, who's 34 and plays Davis Cup games three days in a row, and who dies to win and give victory to his country, don't tell me that guys who are 23, 24, 25 and 26 cannot play on a Wednesday and a Saturday. Sport's about the head and the heart, too, not only the legs. When you want it, when you want it a lot, you can be dead but you come back to life … But it's all my fault, because that's the law of football. When we win, we all win – and some more than others. And when we lose, the coach loses. So it's my fault.'

While Mourinho delivered his accusations, in the dressing room the rumour spread that Pérez had called Casillas to ask him – for the benefit of the fans and the club – to come out in front of the press and denounce the referee.

'There were a few things that the referee didn't get right,' Casillas said before the cameras. 'Perhaps the referee hurt us on these occasions. The manager does have to feel better supported by us. We're on the pitch and it's true, there were certain key moments that changed the game. There was a goal ruled out for an offside that never was, there was a handball that was not spotted and the Betis players were time-wasting. Sometimes we have to come out and show how upset we are by these type of incidents.'

The team and the officials set off for the airport when the players discovered that Mourinho had criticised them in front of the press for negligence and laziness. Casillas felt betrayed. The next day he addressed the coach in front of his team-mates:

'Who were you referring to when you said that when we lose, it's you who loses, and when we win, some win more than others? So that's fine, is it? I've gone out and criticised the referee for the good of the club even though I don't believe the referee was a determining factor; last season against Betis the referee did not give a penalty against us. And then afterwards I find out that you've said this against the players. I bit my tongue in public for the good of the institution. Why don't you do the same? And if you have something to say to someone then say it to their face.'

While Casillas told him off like a schoolmaster reprimanding a rude child, the manager smiled, turned and walked away, eventually saying:

'I wasn't talking about anyone specifically. I was talking in general ...'

Pérez was afraid of being out of all competitions before Christmas. The road to the distant horizon, with a possible presidential election campaign in June, was a bleak one. In his search for solutions he began to look into how viable it would be for the manager to stay. Saturday night into Sunday morning was spent making calls to Madrid employees, directors, advisors and personal friends, trying to find an answer to these unknowns.

He wanted to know if people thought winning the Champions League with Mourinho was possible. Those closest to the first team told him that the relationship between the players and the manager was broken and that mistrust had now reached extremes. It was beyond repair. In its current condition, they advised him, winning major honours was impossible.

Zinedine Zidane and Antonio García Ferreras, the two advisors the president listened to most, usually had completely contrasting opinions. But they coincided in one thing: neither now worked for the club. Zidane was Mourinho's assistant for almost all of the 2011–12 season, until the Frenchman could no longer put up with him. Before withdrawing to one side he advised the president that with Mourinho the club was heading for a sterile crisis. The footballing and human analysis that Zidane presented was so clear that everything he predicted came to pass. 'It's happening as Zizou said it would,' repeated the president. 'It's happening just as Zizou said.'

In November 2012 Zidane warned Pérez that, if the team did not quickly react, the sooner he sacked Mourinho the more likely it would be for the squad to win something. He also said that Pérez needed to hurry because the players were suffering psychologically and that the spent energy would take its toll. Asked who would be the ideal coach to snap them out of their trance at least until June, Zidane proposed Marcello Lippi, winner of the World Cup with Italy in 2006.

Ferreras was the director of communications at Madrid between 2004 and 2006, before leaving to run La Sexta, one of the main TV stations in Spain. His friendship with José Luis Rodríguez Zapatero, prime minister of Spain between 2004 and 2012, had turned him into an extremely influential man. But it was his friendship with Pérez that gave weight to what he said in some of the most important decisions made at Madrid. Pérez respected what he said to the point where many in Pérez's inner circle considered the journalist to be the president's most valued advisor. They say he listened to him more than to his own directors and that in sporting matters he gave greater credit to what he had to say than his director of football Miguel Pardeza or his old sporting director Jorge Valdano. On this occasion, he put his opinions before those of Zidane.

Ferreras convinced Pérez that he should worry less about the players than about his own political future. What would happen if the team won nothing with Lippi? It was best to remain inextricably linked to Mourinho until the end because his banner carried Mourinho's name. If he sacked him his own position at the club would be weakened and only winning *la décima* or the league would save him. Ferreras's position was also laid out in his column in *Marca*, published on 3 May 2013:

'Some might celebrate and take pleasure in his departure, but for Madrid Mourinho has been a blessing. His management techniques, his strength, his raging against defeat, his rebellious and daring pronouncements have been key to ending the domination of the greatest Barcelona team in history. He arrived when the wounds of that famous 2–6 defeat had still not healed. He arrived when Messi and Guardiola were still floating around the world on a magic carpet. Florentino Pérez came back. He signed Ronaldo, he revolutionised the squad, he regenerated the club, and finally a year later he put in place the appropriate commander-in-chief. From then on everything changed. Of course, there are a lot of people who hate him. And many do so because they hate Madrid or they cannot boss the club around from the inside. The rest of us love him.'

On the morning of 15 December, Pérez declared his total support for his coach at an event to celebrate the awarding of badges of honour to the club's oldest members.

'We have built a dream team,' he said. 'A spectacular side that's home to some of the best players in the world, and full of the effort and talent that will help us meet all challenges. We have the best coach in the world, one with an incredible record and who always demands the best. He has had to endure some of the most disproportionate and unjust attacks on himself and his dignity as a person.

From here, José Mourinho, my recognition, my faith in your work and my affection.'

Far from pacifying him, Pérez's support seemed to further embolden him. On the afternoon of 15 December the manager and Silvino Louro tried to intimidate a journalist from Radio Marca before confessing that the dressing room at Madrid had been corrupted by the presence of three *ovejas negras* (black sheep). Three conspirators who needed to be purged. The following day *Marca* published something that Mourinho has never denied: that the manager had claimed that there were three 'black sheep' working against him. The players read the story in the hotel before the game against Espanyol, coming to an immediate conclusion: the boss had leaked an accusation that he would never have dared to make in public, that he had been betrayed by his players. It was a familiar refrain; all that was new was the method of dissemination.

Those who collaborated with Pérez in the administration of the club let the president know that they were now certain that the majority of the players were prepared not to win matches in order to destroy Mourinho. These same sources claim that to avoid disaster, the president made a pact with Mourinho on a communications policy that would distract the players. Both saw it as beneficial to let slip the idea that they had agreed that at the end of the season there would be an amicable parting of the ways. The news was released via newspapers and TV channels with long-established traditions of independence and objectivity. Pérez and Mourinho believed that this way the players would believe that the manager was not staying and the rebels would get back to concentrating on the business of winning with all their energy. During these months several club employees were told that Mourinho would be leaving in June in the hope that the news would reach the dressing room. Pérez met with Ramos and Casillas in January, asking them to ignore the manager's outbursts and attempt to 'manage themselves' in a bid to win both the cup and the Champions League. He repeated that the supporters were watching and that they should do it for them. He also offered them more money. If they won the Champions League he said he would raise their bonuses by 50 per cent to close to €700,000 each. They coldly replied that they would do everything possible but that there were certain footballing questions that only a coach could resolve, and that Mourinho seemed to be more concerned with himself than with the team.

On 19 December Barcelona announced that at the age of 43 Tito Vilanova had suffered a relapse of cancer of the parotid gland and would require months of treatment in the United States that would keep him away from the squad. The Catalan club did not look for a substitute for their manager. Control of the dressing room was left in the hands of the players. The power vacuum was filled by Xavi, Puyol, Piqué, Fàbregas and Messi. The nature of the crisis lacked a precedent in modern football; it was unique and Barça suffered a depression in a number of respects, a gradual sinking that Madrid could exploit. But not only did Madrid fail to take advantage of the new situation; the internal conflict at the club became even greater.

On 22 December, days after leaking to the press that he was fighting against the 'black sheep' of the dressing room, Mourinho left Casillas on the bench. Madrid played against Málaga at La Rosaleda and the goalkeeper was Adán. None of the players believed the technical reasons for the decision. For several of his team-mates, Antonio Adán, the 26-year-old second-team goalkeeper who had never played regularly in the first division, was not good enough to be put between the posts at a big club. Mourinho told Adán that he was taking Casillas's place three days before the game, asking him to keep it secret. Casillas suspected something but, until he sat in the dugout, he was not sure what. His withdrawal from the team was a devastating message for the rest of the squad.

Every nation has its sacred footballing pyramid, the very pinnacle usually being reserved for those heroes who have lifted the World Cup. Generally these players were great leaders, flawless sporting figures who are protected because they form the emotional heritage of the followers of the national game. England elevates Bobby Moore; Brazil, Pelé; Argentina, Maradona; Uruguay, Obdulio Varela; Italy, Dino Zoff; France, Deschamps; and Germany, Franz Beckenbauer. In Spain the idol placed at the national summit is called Iker Casillas. The destruction of this hero, with all his symbolic weight, represented a supreme temptation for a man like Mourinho, obsessed by propagating the notion that he was the supreme legislator. The true champion. The only one who knew the way. The unquestioned leader.

That the move was made days after a complaint about the presence of 'black sheep' cast the dark shadow of propaganda over the club once more. Casillas did not complain publicly because he believed that if he did so he would have to contradict the coach, putting himself in the role of mutineer. He thought that was exactly what Mourinho expected him to do, and in a previous meeting with the other players he had warned them not to respond publicly to the Mourinho's provocations. Quite the opposite, in fact; the dressing room had already established that the best they could do was to project the idea of harmony and loyalty.

Pérez did not come to Casillas's defence. It was not the president's custom to support his senior players when they ran up against his project. Pérez would certainly defend dressing-room leaders when they were defending his strategy against the group, but his symbol was now Mourinho. Players who put the interests of the squad first were usually removed in the long term. Men of character – Redondo, Hierro, Raúl, Figo and finally Casillas, Ramos and Ronaldo – never had an easy life with Pérez. The squad was gradually running out of such defiant leaders.

Madrid lost 3–2 in Málaga. In the next game of the season, against Real Sociedad on 6 January, Casillas was again left on the bench. But Adán was sent off in the eighth minute for fouling Xabi Prieto in the area, conceding a penalty. The captain regained his position. Madrid won 4–3, having been made to fight to the last in a difficult match played in hostile conditions. The Bernabéu loudly jeered Mourinho. Never before in his career had the coach been the object of such derision and, troubled by it, he sought the help of Rui Faria. The fitness trainer was the perfect intermediary between the coach and Ronaldo, the player considering him a trusted friend and counsellor. Mourinho encouraged this relationship because it saved him having to deal directly with a player whose character he found somewhat difficult to deal with; moreover, he felt that having to personally approach such a popular and independent player diminished his authority. That night at half-time, Faria asked Ronaldo to show his boss a gesture of support, as a personal request. When the attacker scored his second he went to the bench and, by way of dedicating his goal to Mourniho, hugged the coach. Mourinho looked straight ahead, unconcerned.

Madrid hosted Celta Vigo in the cup on 9 January. Once again Mourinho received whistles from the crowd, and once again he mobilised Faria – together with Mendes – to encourage Ronaldo to offer a show of support. Casillas made a stunning save from a ferocious shot from Augustus, but the manager looked distressed and pale. Ronaldo buried Celta with three goals that helped settle the match 4–0. Before the end of the game Mendes sent messages to all those he represented to encourage them to give statements to the press in defence of the coach. In the dressing room the players saw Mourinho urging Faria to tell Ronaldo to ask the crowd not to whistle him. Mourinho also spoke to Mendes by phone from the dressing room. One player said that Mendes also spoke to Ronaldo, asking him to make an appeal to the fans. When he went in front of the cameras the question about the whistling was inevitable.

'Enough!' said Ronaldo. 'The coach is doing his best. I've asked the fans to show their support because we have to win something together. They've already shown what they think. The players on the pitch can sense it when the supporters complain about the coach and we've got to be together.'

Ronaldo did not take part in this campaign out of respect for Mourinho, but for Mendes. He did so reluctantly as he knew that he could hurt Casillas's feelings; what he said confirmed the conspiracy theory and restored Mourinho's standing.

Ronaldo was not prepared for the way Mourinho criticised him from the touchline during the first leg of the quarter-finals of the cup against Valencia on 15 January. Mourinho spent the game yelling at him, as if that night he was not doing anything right. The whole team saw Mourinho's annoyance, his gestures being unusually emphatic and aggressive. After the match, which ended with a 2–0 win, there seemed to be no reason to reprimand anybody. But the manager had already prepared what he was going to say to Ronaldo, whom he accused of ignoring his defensive duties. Ronaldo was not going to tolerate this. His team-mates saw his wounded pride and his reaction was savage. It was not easy to stop him when he launched himself against Mourinho, muscles tense, flushed with anger, drowning him with insults. In the end, Arbeloa and Khedira were able to protect Mourinho from being attacked by physically restraining Ronaldo as he tried to make his way through the crowd of bodies.

In the dressing room they called them 'montajes', small pieces of carefully choreographed theatre. The players said that such scenes were contrived so that they could be leaked to the press by Mourinho to prove he was a fair coach who did not show favouritism by distinguishing between those represented by Mendes and the rest. The list of those targeted was long, including Coentrão, penalised for violating disciplinary rules, and Di María for being greedy and selfish. Pepe and Coentrão were also left standing for turning up late for the bus at one team meeting. Nobody in the dressing room was convinced by any of these incidents. Di María even confessed, bitterly, that Mourinho had warned him in advance that he would be criticised in public just to set an example. Mourinho asked for his complicity as a favour owed. As a Mendes man, Ronaldo also had to be involved. But Mourinho never forewarned him, as he knew he would not play along with the game. This explains Ronaldo's reaction to his rollicking in the quarter-finals of the cup, and why things ended badly.

Gestifute employees knew the strategy. They said that during their autumn tour, when looking for deals for Mourinho with Premier League clubs, Mendes's business partners warned him that he should temper the divisive image that Mourinho projected in Madrid. English clubs were cautious, having heard rumours of Mourinho's influence, the way he introduced players from his own agent's portfolio or those shared with other agents, and then managing the squad in such a way as to create divisions within the club. The suspicion that he practised this sort of opportunist behaviour was widespread at City, United and Chelsea, making it difficult to strike deals. One of Mendes's trusted aides in Portugal told him that what most caught their attention was Mourinho's decision to give Pedro Mendes, the inexperienced, mediocre young defender, his début in the Champions League against Ajax. Alerted to the warnings, Mendes invited his friend to come up with a plan to show that the suspicions had no foundation. The *montajes* were the result.

In late January 2013 the breakdown in the Madrid dressing room was rivalled only by the deterioration of the mood in Barcelona's. Guardiola and Vilanova had always said that Mourinho would do their motivational work for them very effectively. The fact that Guardiola would be toasted with Cava after winning the Champions League in 2011 says much for the impetus which Mourinho had given players such as Messi, Xavi, Busquets and Alves.

Casillas's team-mates in the Spanish national squad told him that by 2010 complacency had begun to spread through Barcelona. Mourinho's strategies of agitation, far from accelerating this, actually delayed it. In 2012 several players tried to make him see this but Mourinho replied wryly: 'Very good! You're all so smart.'

Casillas, Ramos, Higuaín, Marcelo, Khedira, Arbeloa, Carvalho, Kaká, Özil and Benzema were sure of this in 2013. 'If we'd spared them the psychological warfare Barça would have disintegrated by themselves,' said one Spanish international. When they had to face Barça in the cup and the league between 30 January and 2 March, most of the squad had decided to manage themselves. They proposed not to criticise referees, match schedules or the opposition. There was to be no more systematic violence or protests on the pitch towards the referee. They had to put an end to the unsportsmanlike gestures and the stupidity of not greeting a team-mate in the Spanish national squad because of what the boss said. Everyone in the group agreed apart from Arbeloa, who understood what his colleagues were about but who wanted to take care of his relationship with the powers that be to save his contract with the club.

Alonso also did things his own way, as mysterious as usual. Signed by Valdano, the Basque midfielder was not the sort of player that Mourinho usually went for, what with Alonso's history, affiliations and physical conditioning. Mourinho considered him too slow for the job. In the players' meeting in Santander in 2011, Alonso was one of the most fervent critics of Mourinho's tactical approach. Over time, however, he stopped going to meals with his Spanish team-mates and would approach Mourinho to chat with him and to agree with him, although it had nothing to do with what he had said elsewhere. When Mourinho proposed targeting Casillas he enjoyed Alonso's silent understanding. When the players were told to touch Messi's face because, it was said, the Argentinian was infuriated by it, Alonso was right behind Arbeloa in the queue to offer to do so. 'But what are you doing?' Piqué asked him. If his vision, his tactical intelligence and his ability to organise the team with this passing were not entirely convincing, his demonstration of extreme loyalty convinced Mourinho that Alonso was an ally in his crusade.

Madrid's players had two different approaches. Some, like Varane, Arbeloa, Essien, Alonso, Khedira, Di María and Coentrão, played exactly in accord with Mourinho's wishes. Others, like Ramos, Higuaín, Özil, Benzema and Ronaldo, introduced their own personal touches. Against Mourinho's wishes, attackers would sometimes drop deep to receive the ball in midfield or move out to the flanks to open up space and create opportunities. The presence of Ramos in central defence completely changed the way the team played. In the three *clásicos* of 2013 he pushed the defensive line up towards the centre-circle with an unusual calm and mastery of the situation. Pushed back into their own half, the pressure exerted by Madrid on Barcelona was unbearable, and Messi was kept away from the area where he was most dangerous. The manager did not agree with such a high line of pressure but he consented to it because the effects were stunning. Lacking the direction of Vilanova, who was receiving intensive treatment in New York, Barcelona were defeated in the cup (1–1 and 1–3) and in the league (2–1), and Real Madrid enjoyed their happiest month of the season.

An accidental kick from Arbeloa broke Casillas's left hand during the fourth round of the cup at the Mestalla on 23 January. He would need two months to recover so Madrid signed Diego López as his replacement. The incident meant Ramos became first-team captain.

Voted best defender in the 2012 Euros, the former Sevilla player, about to turn 27, was finally where he had dreamed of being all his life. There are some players who find fulfilment by giving assists, others achieve nirvana by scoring goals or concentrating on dribbling, and a few enjoy organising. For Ramos, the most exciting, the most distinguished, the most glorious gift the profession has to offer is the opportunity to take charge of a team. He was one of the best full-backs in the world, although he could sometimes lose his position or play irresponsibly like an individual rather than a team-player. As a centre-back, he was unbeatable. The responsibility made him stronger. He was comfortable making decisions and delighted in directing his team-mates around the pitch. He did so with his voice but also with whistles, perfect for abbreviating instructions and for being instantly recognisable in the heat of battle. Ramos, a lover of flamenco, and of singing and dancing, had come up with various short musical codes. Each note meant an order on the pitch and his team-mates knew them all by heart. Pressing, retreating, squeezing and covering, calls for assistance and the order to push out were all conducted by a medley of whistles.

The 1–0 defeat in Granada on 2 February in the 22nd league match of the season was another storm cloud, disrupting the period of relative calm, and a setback to Pérez's advisors, who had come out in the media with message that things had changed: 'The Madrid of 100 points is back!'

Pérez spoke with Ramos in Granada. The president asked him why Madrid had lost and Ramos answered with his usual candour. He said the team were lucky to win the league in 2012, because their relationship with the manager was already very difficult and achieving something so great in such a difficult atmosphere was truly exceptional. He explained that players noticed that when Mourinho felt strong he took the opportunity to help 'his own' and disregarded the rest. Ramos also said that Mourinho's repeated complaints about their lack of professionalism had damaged the squad more than anything. To expect the team to give everything for this man went against the natural order of things. According to some board members Ramos's comments did not please Pérez one bit.

The victory over Barça in the cup on 24 February made Pérez glad to have kept Mourinho. Having solved the issue of continuity, his grand survival plan was to play with all the chips, to seduce both players and coach equally. He told the squad to manage itself, saying that Mourinho was not so important, at the same time as offering Mourinho more power in return for winning the Champions League. The directors closest to Pérez say that what he was really trying to do was to gain time to win Madrid's tenth European Cup, to keep Mourinho, letting him get rid of whoever he wanted to within good reason and without too great political consequences, and give him total control in the transfer market. Mourinho's blacklist had become increasingly full: Casillas, Ramos, Higuaín, Marcelo, Özil and Benzema were all marked, although Pérez hoped to save Ramos, Benzema and Özil.

The president was willing to stick with Mourinho in spite of everything. Without knowing that they were taking part in a poll, Peréz sent staff members to ask the players how they felt. When asked if the manager should continue in the 2013–14 season, of the 22 members of the team only seven responded positively. Of the 15 who said no, one was Ronaldo, and six added that if Mourinho remained they should be allowed to leave on friendly terms. Özil and Ramos were in this latter group. Meanwhile, the opinion of the supporters varied according to results. To those fans who said they wanted the manager, one other question was asked: why? Between 70 and 80 per cent indicated that it was because when the team lost, he was able to excuse it by pointing to external causes.

The passage to the quarter-finals of the Champions League was overwhelming for Madrid. If the 1–1 first-leg score against Manchester United at the Bernabéu gave the English team the nice cushion of an away goal, the 1–0 scoreline that followed Ramos's own goal at Old Trafford in the 48th minute after a mistake from Varane gave the impression of settling the tie. But it did not happen that way because of a peculiar incident. In the 57th minute Nani lifted his boot in an attempt to control the ball, not having seen Arbeloa arrive from the side, and the Spaniard felt the full force of the attacker's studs. Cüneyt Çakir, the Turkish referee, decided it was dangerous play and sent Nani off. It was the only contentious decision that he made on a night when he could have been much more draconian. Madrid's superiority lasted ten minutes, and in the time it took Ferguson and United to get over the Nani decision, first Modrić and then Ronaldo scored, making it 1–2. Madrid ran the last quarter of an hour down, clearing balls out of their own penalty area. Mourinho has never been so generous to an opponent as he was in the press conference afterwards.

'The best team lost tonight,' he said.

Pérez felt a great sense of relief. It reaffirmed the sense that he had made the right decision when he convened the board to announce a decision made months earlier: he wanted Mourinho to see out his contract until 2016. In his speech he admitted that if he could go back in time three years he might not repeat the signing of Mourinho. He added that he was also not completely convinced by the team's play. But he justified the contradiction by asking his peers what they would have done had they been in the same boat:

'I understood that if he was successful, we would be successful, too; and if he failed, we would also fail.'

The president's certainty in front of the board contrasted with the poisoned atmosphere on the trip to Istanbul, where Madrid were playing in the quarter-finals against Galatasaray. A club employee noted with surprise that even Coentrão, very much one of 'theirs', shunned Mourinho. The tension, discussions and blame between the players and their coach had given way to a deathly indifference. Only José Mario, Mourinho's son, seemed completely at ease with his father on the bus and in training, while Karanka, Louro, Rui Faria and Di María took turns to entertain him. The delegation stayed at the Kempinski Hotel in the Ciragan Palace, once a seat of the Ottoman sultans. With a splendid view over the Bosphorus, the cheapest room in the hotel cost €800 a night. Someone saw Pérez and Mourinho exchange a few words.

'I cannot continue here with this squad, you know,' said the coach. To which Pérez responded with his characteristic poker face.

Casillas's recovery posed a fresh question for the coaching staff, so Mourinho called a meeting in early April. Rui Faria, Karanka and Louro, among others, were all in attendance. One of those present tells how the manager stated that they had two options. The first was to put Casillas in the team for the semi-finals of the Champions League. If they ended up winnng the final at Wembley no one would remember the goalkeeper, and if they lost, in Mourinho's words, 'all the shit would be for him'. The second option was to stick with Diego López. At this point Mourinho winked at Rui Faria and told them that if they won without Casillas it would be perfect, and if they lost it didn't matter anyway. The public could say what they wanted, but there was nothing to worry about 'as we already have what we have'. He repeated the words: 'As we already have what we have …' The formal offer from Chelsea was the 'what we have'. There was nothing signed, but Roman Abramovich's word was sufficient. The emergency exit was clear.

Mendes had received the offer from Chelsea in the last week of March. The negotiations had taken more than three months to come up with a final document. The receipt of the contractual papers in Gestifute, however, left a bittersweet aftertaste. The joy of having a contract ready for his signature contrasted with Mourinho's annoyance on noting that between those clauses that had been mutually agreed Abramovich had imposed clear limits on his autonomy as a manager. The small reduction in base salary from what he earned in Madrid (about €10 million net) was not as upsetting to Mourinho and Mendes as the Russian owner's attempt to limit Mourinho's role to the coaching of the team. The contract stipulated that the technical structure of the club would remain intact, particularly with respect to who was responsible for deciding which players the club would buy. Mourinho could let it be known who he would like to sell, and if he needed a player he could say in what position and with what characteristics. But the decision on who would or would not be signed would continue to be a matter for the club and its owner.

Abramovich did not forget that between 2004 and 2007 Mourinho had tried to fill the team with players linked to Mendes and his friends. He did this with such devotion that he marginalised men such as Arjen Robben and Shevchenko, signed on the initiative of Abramovich. According to sources at Chelsea, the club's owner had studied Mourinho at Madrid and had watched how he sidelined a Ballon d'Or winner like Kaká because he stood in the way of his strategic plans. To avoid this, he vetoed Mourinho's access to the market. This limitation seemed like a forewarning to Mendes. Upset, the agent and his client decided not to sign the contract and continued negotiating, waiting for circumstances to strengthen their position. They calculated that if Madrid won the Champions League Mourinho could claim more power from Chelsea.

The draw meant that Madrid would play once again play Dortmund in the Champions League, this time in the semi-finals. The first leg was set for 24 April at the Westfalenstadion. It was a beautiful morning when, in the modest NH hotel where the Spanish journalists were staying alongside the main railway station, Pérez appeared with a group of directors. They had spent the night there, they said. The president was in a jubilant mood. He had not stopped receiving jokes on his mobile phone about the 4–0 scoreline from Bayern's win over Barça in Munich the previous night. The journalists who gathered round were encouraged when they saw that he was available for a relaxed chat for the first time in years. Sitting in the dining room after breakfast, they listened to the president in amazement.

Pérez said the team had only played well in four matches that season, although blame for this should not to be placed at the coach's door. Mourinho had done everything right and it had been the players' fault. They believed, he said, that having won the league in 2012 everything had already been achieved and they barely raised their game to win the Super Cup. Mourinho had been right to shake the group up, looking for a reaction, not picking Casillas, Özil, Ramos and others in order to provoke them to compete. He wanted to give them a warning. But they did not respond. Ronaldo's melancholy state did not help, in the opinion of the president, to save those two months of apathy with which the team began the season.

In conclusion Pérez said that footballers were generally capricious and frivolous people. Sometimes they were confused by the power that the money and the fame gave them. In this regard, he noted that Mourinho's squad was much more difficult to manage because it consisted of a selection of the best players in the world. Borussia Dortmund, however, was 'a team of children' trained 'by a child's coach'. Pérez's had complete confidence in reaching the final.

In the midday heat, the historic centre of Dortmund was filled with Madrid supporters, particularly the *Biergarten* in the Marienplatz. The loudest fans sang '*Pepe, mátalo! Pepe, mátalo! Pepe, máta-looooooo!*', meaning 'Pepe, kill him!'

His violent approach had made Pepe a cult figure among the most fanatical fans at the Bernabéu. This group, known as the Ultras Sur, worshipped Mourinho. Mourinho, in turn, had a natural inclination towards Pepe. The central defender was one of the few men at his disposal who had placed all his attributes on the altar of obedience to the coach.

Before the games against Manchester United Mourinho was asked if Ronaldo was the best player he had ever managed in his career. In response he explained why he appreciated other players more:

'Cristiano is the most fantastic player I've coached. But I always say I've been very lucky because I've had people who've given everything for me. That's why Cristiano doesn't have a privileged position in my heart in relation to others.'

Pepe was one of those 'others'. He was famous for killing and dying metaphorically, although sometimes bordering on the literal. He had come back as a substitute after an ankle operation, but on 24 April he was picked by Mourinho to occupy the centre of defence alongside Raphaël Varane. His commitment to Varane, a 20-year-old French international whose performances had been extraordinary, inspired mistrust in the dressing room because since the start of the season Mendes had shown great interest in representing him. Varane's father and agent held conversations at Christmas, and an agreement was eventually settled. The manager believed that the defence was of vital importance and wanted to put it in the hands of people whom he trusted. Ramos did not belong to that select group.

Ramos moved to right-back, Coentrão started on the left, Alonso, Khedira and Modrić made up the midfield, and Ronaldo and Higuaín played up front. Once again Özil played on the right wing, from where he would have less influence. The squad thought that Özil would be on the bench but he played because Di María's wife had given birth and the Argentinian had only arrived in Germany that day.

The team-talk did not command the attention of the players as would have been expected before a Champions League semi-final. Since the morning the Radisson Hotel had become a hive of hurried meetings, curses, calls to mobiles and hectic exchanges of information. The players were exasperated when some of the journalists who had been present at the NH told them what Pérez had said – that the president considered them the main culprits for losing the league and yet believed their coach had done everything right. Ronaldo, Higuaín and Ozil paced around furiously until an hour before the game. They formed Madrid's forward line and it was to them that Mourinho directed the key part of his speech. He stressed to them that if they could score one goal then the job would be done.

Lewandowski opened the scoring. Dortmund controlled the game confidently, defending and attacking with admirable order. But before the break, after a loose pass from Hummels to Weidenfeller, Ronaldo equalised to make it 1–1. Mourinho waited for the team in the dressing room and gave them precise orders. Above all, he said, they had already achieved the most important thing, which was to score a goal. To defend this treasure he called for maximum concentration, putting everything into defensive awareness, a closing of the lines between defence and midfield, and midfield and attack, and a reduced pressing of the ball.

Deep in their own half, Madrid became the victims of what Klopp called 'impulse'. In the face of co-ordinated pressure and a massed advance of Dortmund's attackers, marking became a nightmare. Moments before Dortmund went 2–1 up, Madrid were defending in their half and had eight players, as well as Diego López, inside their area. Dortmund attacked with six men, three in the area and three chasing the rebounds on the edge of the box. Blaszczykowski and Piszeck doubled up on Coentrão five yards from the byline; from the cross the ball rebounded to Reus and he played in Lewandowski, who nipped in front of Varane and scored. The central defender had tried to bring down the Pole but stopped himself to avoid conceding a penalty.

Pepe, strictly respecting the orders of Mourinho, took the line of defence so far back that Dortmund's every attacking move became a defensive nightmare. Any foul could be a penalty or a free kick very close to the edge of the area. Dortmund's third goal was much like their second, only the German team were this time even more uninhibited. Blaszczykowski rampaged down the right and crossed from the byline, Varane cleared with a header to the other side of the penalty area, where Schmelzer appeared, who sent the ball back to the centre of the box. This time Lewandowski had got ahead of Alonso and Pepe, and shot past López. When the goal went in there were seven Madrid players in their own area, plus the goalkeeper. Dortmund had put five men in the area and two on the edge of the box.

The more Madrid retreated, the more it allowed Dortmund to advance and the more vulnerable they became. The 3–1 scoreline forced the team to change tactics. Mourinho replaced Modrić with Di María in the 68th minute to try to move Özil into his more natural position. But it was too late. They had lost control and there was no way to regain it. Dortmund's fourth again came from the side of the pitch defended by Coentrão. Götze crossed, Alonso pushed Reus, the referee gave a penalty and Lewandowski scored.

The players considered the game to be a display of incompetence from Mourinho. He saw it the other way around. He bitterly told his friends that since he had started coaching Madrid they had made him suffer the two worst defeats of his career: the Camp Nou 5–0 and now the 4–1 against Dortmund. He had never conceded so many goals. He attributed it to the culture of the club that he now regretted ever having managed, and in particular to his players, as expressed in his dark monologue at the press conference he gave before the second leg:

'My team only plays within the laws. We're in one sense so pure, so innocent and so naive, that Lewandowski has scored four goals against us and we've not fouled him once … This could be the biggest game in ten years for Madrid, but I thought the same thing in Dortmund and we played as if it were a friendly.'

When Ramos was asked what he thought of his coach's idea of how to stop Lewandowski, his reply seemed to be challenging Mourinho:

'Maybe you can stop him higher up the pitch, because conceding fouls on the edge of the area is not advisable.'

Pepe was punished by being dropped, in a switch that anticipated Mourinho's defensive rules being broken. Ramos regained his place and raised the defensive line further up the pitch. He had a superb match. He managed the team from the back, made his team-mates play, superbly marshalled Lewandowski, conceded only two fouls, picked up a yellow card and scored a goal. He was the leader he could not be in the Westfalenstadion. But 2–0 was not enough to reach the final.

Mourinho's time at Madrid concluded without him being able to clearly impose his teams on any of the stronger sides in the Champions League. The four games against a young Dortmund side in the 2012–13 season highlighted his poor results, falling so far short of expectations: two defeats, one draw and a win.

In May Mourinho reached an agreement with Abramovich to join Chelsea. As he had not signed the settlement with Madrid, and because his current contract required him to compensate the club to the tune of €20 million in the event of its unilateral termination, Chelsea proposed paying him a bonus if he managed to leave Madrid without complying with the penalty. To achieve this he devised a strategy of provocations that, in his opinion, would destroy any residual esteem towards him from the club's members, forcing Pérez to let him go because it would be politically impossible to retain him. In Gestifute they claim that the manager's trump card was a single sentence, crafted for maximum impact. He delivered it on 3 May to the Madrid board, who, having boasted of having come up with one of the greatest inventions in the history of football, Madrid's *galacticos*, were irritated to the last man:

'I think that Barcelona are the best team in the world in the last 20 or 30 years,' said Mourinho.

Beyond its provocative intent, the statement rang true for a man who always longed to return to the club where he began his technical training and work experience as a psychologist and a propagandist. The Catalan club was, above and beyond even Manchester United, his dream of professional fulfilment.

The board, who had been in large part disappointed in Mourinho for months, called for his instant dismissal. In addition, the club's employees and the players were united in their desire to see him leave. Many of the fans, too, wanted him to go – or at least gazed on the situation with weary indifference. The last league match on 1 June, against Osasuna, revealed painful divisions in the stands of the Bernabéu. *Mourinhistas* and *Antimourinhistas* exchanged whistles, chants and jeers. That afternoon, summing up the three seasons of Mourinho's residence, football was eaten up by the noise.

Pérez tried on his own to save the manager until the very end. On Monday 20 May they met to sign the release agreement. Mourinho, who was not even charged a €1 penalty, was released. For Pérez it felt like a defeat. Madrid had never given so much power and so much money to one coach. For the club, the total cost of the three-year relationship, adding together gross wages, premiums and the payment of his transfer from Inter, amounted to more than €70 million.

In the afternoon, the president announced the termination of Mourinho's contract at a crowded press conference. The players, who followed the televised speech, thought they could see Pérez's true intentions in a furtive confession:

'Maybe, if we'd reached the final of the Champions League, we'd be talking about something else ...'

Pérez never wanted to get rid of Mourinho. In searching for a cause, he attributed his departure to the Dortmund disaster. A disaster that he blamed exclusively on his players.

In his subsequent defence of Mourinho to the members, the president said that what matters at a club like Madrid is not to play according to notions of good taste but to get immediate results. And for that, a tough coach who knows how to lead his flock with a firm hand is required. When asked about the pursuit of a footballing philosophy, an idea that might underpin everything, the response was repeated:

'Our idea is to win.'

In mid-June 2013 Pérez found himself looking for a coach to continue the search for *la décima*. Three weeks after the departure of their former coach, complaints started filtering through from London about insurrections among the Madrid players and other, unspecified events that occurred months or even years ago. These were emitted periodically by Mourinho from Stamford Bridge. It was suggested that he resented almost everyone who had been his subordinate, but especially the two captains, Casillas and Ramos, for having imposed limits on him that the directors had been unable to.

'The selfish players,' said the Chelsea manager, 'who do not care about the club or the fans, are a big problem. Sometimes you come across a couple of players who are not willing to accept a set of rules and that's where problematic relationships start.'

These accusations got right under the Madrid players' skin. Since Mourinho's departure from Spain, thousands of followers started to question their honesty, without really knowing why. Anyone could be subject to suspicion and for any minor detail: Casillas, Ramos, Pepe, Ronaldo, Coentrão, Arbeloa, Khedira, Higuaín, Benzema, Özil, Modrić, Kaká, Varane, Marcelo, Albiol, Callejón, Essien or Alonso; Portuguese, Spanish, Brazilian, Argentinian, French or German – all were doubted, whether to do so was fair or unfair. It was impossible for the average fan not to suspect something if even the president spoke as though these players had done something darkly illegal.

'I just don't see that there was a mutiny,' Pérez stated in one of the many interviews he gave in late May. 'What I do say is that we started this season with a little less hunger, and you could see that in the first four matches, where we dropped eight points. This is the advantage that Barça had over us at the end. This is what produced a very normal reaction from the coach to motivate the players. Because, obviously, we had not started as we should have.'

Exempting the manager from most of the responsibility, assigning him to the role of valiant worker on the day of the great disaster in Dortmund, in the eyes of the president there were no grounds to suspect any form of negligence. Nor did Pérez suggest that Mourinho was, above all else, keen to preserve his reputation, even though this meant Pérez had to suggest in every forum in which he spoke that the players had neglected their duties for reasons that were not clear.

With the passing days, Pérez shared with his manager an unshakeable resentment towards the Madrid squad.

The rumour floated through the air from the offices of the Bernabéu and spread to the dressing room. Over the following months it was talked about by the club staff closest to the president, and circulated by word of mouth among the players and team employees. The recurring gossip was that Pérez, alerted by the coach, had a list of those responsible for the 4–1 defeat in Dortmund. At its head was Casillas, who despite not having played, was considered by Mourinho as someone who was bad for the atmosphere of the dressing room and who even headed a group of the players known to the coach as the 'black sheep' of the squad. Below him on the list were the three forwards who had lined up in attack that fateful night: Özil, Higuaín and Ronaldo.

José Mourinho's most amazing victory in his three years in Madrid was to convince thousands of people that the football was just an accessory. It did not matter that the team's play was unrecognisable and ineffective, it was irrelevant whether the left-back was Marcelo or Coentrão, or that the goalkeeper was Diego López or the best goalkeeper in the history of Spain. Even winning their tenth European Cup stopped being so crucial. Because finally, when the club's administrators arrived at their conclusions, they did not condemn the manager who led the team in the decisive games. He was not even judged for his inability to make his players respect him. For many, what really determined his success was his ability to formulate a message, spread it tirelessly and be convincing. On the street, in certain TV studios, in offices and in the board room, the golden rules of the reality show had repealed the laws of football under a blanket of noise.

CHAPTER 12

BLUE

'He felt the loyalty we feel to unhappiness – the sense that it is where we really belong.'

GRAHAM GREENE, *The Heart of the Matter*

Marcelo, Casillas, Ramos, Pepe, Özil, Ronaldo, Benzema and Arbeloa came into the Sun Life Stadium dressing room, jubilant. As they took off their boots, they repeated again and again in a loud voice the collective conclusion they had come to after being repressed for so long:

'If Florentino had sacked Mourinho in January, Madrid would now have ten European Cups. Let's see if he [Florentino] takes note!'

The humidity of the Miami Gardens atmosphere contributed to the group's catharsis. The players had so anxiously awaited this moment in the days leading up to the game that at the end of the match they felt liberated. Happy. Strong. Finally alone. At last without him. Without his invasive presence. Without his stifling leadership. They had just won with an overwhelming display of attacking football. They felt they had shown the world a truth that been hidden for three years: they were important, they were talented, and Mourinho had inhibited them.

Madrid had just imposed themselves on Mourinho's Chelsea 3–1 in the International Champions Cup Final held on 7 August 2013 in Miami. It was not just a summer friendly. For the players it had been a public display that the team had a great future.

For a few moments they believed that they had indeed reached the end of an era. They thought they had survived a long period of contamination. Most did not realise that the governance of Madrid was still in the hands of Mourinho's greatest ally. Apart from a couple of politically savvy men such as as Arbeloa and Alonso, skilled in handling double-talk, the rest did not pay attention to what was being confirmed in whispers in the club's offices. Florentino Pérez had kept, like treasured relics, certain pieces of advice that his beloved manager had passed to him before they parted, one of which was: 'If you want to build a winning team you should get rid of the "black sheep" and their accomplices.'

A month after the party in Miami, the purge began with the transfer of Higuaín to Napoli. Then Casillas, the captain, went into the reserves, and Özil, the creative genius of the squad, was transferred to Arsenal in exchange for €50 million.

To the perplexity felt by the players on the demotion of Casillas was added the astonishment at the sale of Özil, a player who was considered the most brilliant of the squad, a good team-mate and a fine professional. Well founded or not, rumours started that Carlo Ancelotti, the new coach, was not making all the football decisions because the sale of Özil was technically unjustifiable. Ancelotti, who had given ample proof of his appreciation for Özil in training and friendlies in August, could not have changed his mind so quickly. In the eyes of his players, the Italian had executed a pre-existing master plan, in part designed by Mourinho. One of the most widely repeated comments in the squad during the first week of September 2013 was full of bitterness:

'Before, it was Mendes who picked the team. Now it's Florentino.'

Di María and Coentrão, the two most *Mourinhista* players in the dressing room, found themselves in a paradoxical situation. The club put them up for sell for economic reasons rather than political ones, because neither Ancelotti nor Pérez deemed them necessary. But they found no buyers. Who could afford to pay €30 million for Coentrão? What club would be willing to pay anywhere close to the €40 million it had cost for Di María in 2010? The response from the market was unequivocal: no one. The years of being an assured starter in the world's most legendary team had done nothing to raise their value. Madrid did not receive bids that exceeded even half the cost of the two players that Mourinho had insisted on signing.

If Pérez always suspected the criteria used by Mourinho when shopping in the transfer market, Roman Abramovich had no doubts. The Russian hired Mourinho in the belief that with Hiddink and Guardiola ruled out, there was no one else available able to adapt to the peculiarities of Chelsea. But he opposed, by every means possible, the manager's freedom to construct his own squad. From his experience between 2004 to 2007, Abramovich had reached two conclusions: first, Mourinho was excellent on the training pitch; second, that it was best to restrict his power off it.

There are employees at Chelsea who suggest that Abramovich is wary of Mourinho's charisma and his extraordinary ability to connect with the masses. It was inevitable that fans would see in him a messianic leader, someone who would put the fate of the club ahead of his own interests, when in fact it was Abramovich's heritage that was on the line. It was a marvellous image, but Abramovich knew it was a misleading one. Mourinho was primarily attracted to everything that surrounded the cult of his own personality and behind the cloak of heroism he hid his desire to influence things for his – or his own agent's – good.

Perhaps Madrid's failure in La Liga and the Champions League deprived the two of them the appropriate means of imposing their requirements. In Gestifute they are confident that the coach and his agent would have put the Champions League trophy on the negotiating table with Chelsea had he won it. The truth is that the contract with Abramovich established that decisions on new players would be in the exclusive power of the club. The Russian owner would have the last word. And for this reason Abramovich employed a technical director, Michel Emenalo.

Chelsea's structure is as simple on the outside as it is intricate on the inside. There are doubts about whether Emenalo is a true executive with the power to act in the market or simply an ornamental figure behind whom Abramovich hides. Emenalo's career does not invite the consideration that he might be Chelsea's most important decision maker. When the former Nigerian international joined the club's coaching staff in 2007, his only experience had been taking charge of a female U-12 team in the Tucson Soccer Academy in the United States.

The first thing Mourinho did upon arrival at Chelsea was to manoeuvre for Emenalo's dismissal from the club. The Nigerian offered his resignation. But Abramovich did not accept it.

On 10 June, the same day that Abramovich confirmed the retention of Emenalo, Mourinho was presented at the conference room of Stamford Bridge, his main idea ready for dissemination: the circle of karma had returned him to a state of happiness:

'I'm the happy one. Time flies. It looks like it was a couple of days ago but it was nine years ago. And since then a lot of things happened in my professional life. I have the same nature, I'm the same person, I have the same heart, I have the same kind of emotions related to my passion for football and for my job. But I'm of course a different person. In this moment if I have to describe myself I describe myself as a very happy person.'

Mourinho was at pains to proclaim that he was blessed to have remained unscathed, despite the wear and tear of his life. But there were sharp suspicions that perhaps that was not the case. In the space of a few seconds he had claimed to be the same person and yet also a new man.

Chelsea's meeting with Madrid in Miami had been inconvenient, and he revealed something about himself when giving a self-praising interview to ESPN. He put so much emphasis on how well he had done everything that Fernando Palomo, the interviewer, asked why someone of his importance felt such a need to highlight each achievement.

'Because people forget,' said Mourinho.

Chelsea's decline in investment relative to other seasons was striking, the club spending less than at any time since 2010. They say that Willian (about €35 million) and André Schürrle (€22 million), the two most expensive signings, were made by Emenalo – or whoever is behind him – and that Mourinho's obsession with signing Wayne Rooney never enjoyed the backing of the owner.

Abramovich bristled at the apparent jealousy Mourinho displayed every time he spoke publicly about David Moyes, manager of Manchester United, chosen to fill the position he had always chased.

'Mou speaks to Rooney more than to his wife,' said one agent who worked with Chelsea during the summer.

Mourinho spent many hours in August talking on the phone with Rooney, seducing him and plotting a possible transfer. But Abramovich never wanted anything to do with it. The tension between the owner and the manager came to a head in the third league match of the season when Chelsea and United faced each at Old Trafford. According to one member of the Chelsea staff, Mourinho's line-up was a challenge to the indifference with which Abramovich had responded to his pleas to sign a striker. Chelsea played without a centre-forward until Torres came on in the 60th minute. It was reminiscent of the match that Madrid played in Almería in January 2011, when Mourinho left Benzema on the bench to prove to Pérez that he needed to sign a striker, and that if he didn't he was ready to disregard the one that he currently had. In 2011 Madrid signed Emmanuel Adebayor. In 2013 Chelsea signed Samuel Eto'o.

A Madrid scout discovered Eto'o in Cameroon in 1996. The boy stood out for his athletic physique, despite his lack of years. At the age of 16 he was elastic, fast, strong and capable of accelerating like an adult. Having the ball at his feet seemed to only increase his agility. His zig-zag runs were unpredictable, and he was able to alter direction and yet maintain a lightning stride. In the summer of 1998, when he was promoted to the first team, he was 17 years old. He was still nearly a child but he spoke several African dialects, perfect French, he understood English, and was as fluent in Spanish as a kid from Fuenlabrada. He had an amazing grace and poise. He shared training sessions with players who had just won the Champions League final in Amsterdam against Juventus. It was an overwhelming armoury of attacking talent: Morientes, Raúl, Šuker and Mijatović.

Anyone else would have been overwhelmed by such competition for two places, but Eto'o looked at his rivals with condescension, like a prince observing the evolution of his subjects:

'I train with them and I know I'm as good or better. I'm ready. Why can I not play for Real Madrid?'

Eto'o was tremendous. So competitive, in fact, that he moved to Barcelona and helped them destroy Madrid's hegemony. Ten years later Pep Guardiola had to let him go because he was unable to share the same areas of the pitch with Lionel Messi. The former Barcelona coach lamented his loss for years.

'Eto'o is the best number nine in Europe,' he said.

Attentive enough to dig into the inscrutable corners of the souls of the men he works with, Mourinho has always had a special fondness for the jilted player. He himself was a teenage footballer to whom the gates of professionalism were closed, and he knows that frustration can be transformed into rebellion and struggle. Pride is usually a player's most powerful engine – a player with wounded pride can become a relentless competitor.

Eto'o was anxious to vindicate himself when he joined Inter in 2009. With Mourinho, he found the perfect habitat in which to channel all his rage. He even played at right-back during the successful Champions League campaign in 2010 and forged a relationship with his coach of enduring complicity.

Abramovich was suspicious of a player who, aged 32, would still be charging €13 million net a season. But he gave in and Mourinho finally fulfilled his desire to have alongside him a man whose loyalty was beyond question.

On the day he finally lets the public see his operating manual, in the first article of his code Mourinho will state that no training method, no tactic, no vision nor strategy can ever overcome the power of loyalty.

At Stamford Bridge this complex man was reunited with the devout and united chorus that rang all around the stadium. After years of silence and remorse, he could feel his charisma once again inflame the masses. Back home, the devotion of his own people made him feel powerful, and this emotional recognition allowed him to put to one side the incurable pain of rejection.